New Developments
in the Labor Market

New Developments in the Labor Market:

Toward a New Institutional Paradigm

edited by
Katharine G. Abraham
and Robert B. McKersie

The MIT Press
Cambridge, Massachusetts
London, England

This book was set in Palatino
by DEKR Corporation
and printed and bound
in the United States of America.

Library of Congress Cataloging-in-Publication Data

New developments in the labor market / edited by Katharine G. Abraham and Robert B. McKersie.
   p.   cm.
 Based on papers presented at a conference held at MIT in June of 1987.
 Includes bibliographical references.
 ISBN 0-262-01118-2
 1. Labor market—Congresses.
I. Abraham, Katharine G. II. McKersie, Robert B.
HD5701.3.N5   1990
331.12—dc20   90-5844
                                                                            CIP

Contents

Preface

Understanding the operation of labor markets has been a continuing theme for the work of faculty members within the MIT Industrial Relations Section. Such an emphasis has been especially appropriate given the fact that the section was initially based in the Economics Department when it was established in the late 1930s.

One of the early studies, published in the late 1940s, was jointly authored by George Shultz and Charles Myers. This was before Shultz's name became a household word (he served in many capacities in Washington and most recently as secretary of state). Myers, also an economist, served as director of the section from 1949 to 1980. Their book, entitled *Dynamics of a Labor Market*, which has long been recognized as a classic, investigated the operation of labor markets and wage determination processes.

Recent entries in this ongoing stream of empirical research on labor market developments include studies of youth unemployment, analyses of relationships between internal labor market policies and national employment and training policies, and studies of dual labor market and wage inequality issues.

Work in this area has always had a very strong public policy orientation and has addressed questions of national concern regarding the adequacy of jobs, incomes, and equal employment opportunities for all workers. *Employment Futures*, a book with very important public policy prescriptions, was written recently by Paul Osterman, a member of the section.

Katharine Abraham shaped the concept of this conference when she was a faculty member in the section, and I would like to thank her for her leadership and diligence in creating a forum for the examination and discussion of a cross section of the best studies being conducted within this broad area of labor market research. We have clearly entered a new era, and many of our ways of thinking about the labor market no longer explain what is going on nor do they help prescribe approaches to persistent problems. This theme— the need for a new paradigm—is discussed in the introduction prepared by Abraham.

During the journey we took in creating this cohesive volume, we held a conference at which these papers were presented, discussed, and then subsequently subjected to considerable revision. We would like to thank the authors for their good spirit in attending to the many requests from us for "additional polish." We would also like to thank the many participants at the conference for their close scrutiny of these papers; some of their oral and written comments have been included here.

We would like to express our appreciation especially to the Sloan Foundation and to Albert Rees, then president, for a grant that made it possible to hold the conference and to proceed with publication of these outstanding papers.

Finally, we would like to dedicate this volume to Phyllis Wallace and to recognize and honor her distinguished career. Alice Rivlin has prepared a preface in which she discusses many of the important ideas and contributions of Phyllis Wallace; in so doing, Rivlin reflects on the important changes that have occurred over the past forty years in how we view and grapple with the important themes of employment and economic well-being.

Robert B. McKersie

Phyllis A. Wallace, Scholar/Activist

Alice M. Rivlin

I would like to reflect on what has happened over the approximately four decades of Phyllis Wallace's career. What have we scholar/ activists learned in this remarkable period—from events, from each other, and especially from Phyllis—about how to be more effective in the future?

Phyllis Wallace got her Ph.D. from Yale in 1948. It was the year I started college, the year another Wallace, named Henry, ran for president along with Strom Thurmond, Thomas Dewey, and Harry Truman. Truman won when he thought he'd lost. It was three years after the end of World War II, the third year of the nuclear age, the first year of the Marshall Plan. The Council of Economic Advisors was a brand new organization, just established to carry out the mandate of the Employment Act of 1946. A lot of economists thought the postwar boom was a temporary respite from the threat of secular stagnation. They failed to notice one of the things that would make that prediction wrong: the fact that everyone was having babies. Economists are sometimes slow to pick up on facts.

1948 was a year of hope for many—rebuilding abroad, prosperity at home. Hemlines were down—thought to be a positive economic indicator—television was the new growth industry, colleges were overflowing with returned GIs. But poverty was widespread, not exceptional, especially in the South. Black soldiers came back from defending freedom to segregated schools and colleges, menial jobs, constant humiliation. In Washington, D.C., in 1948 a black citizen could not eat in a restaurant, go to a downtown movie, work or shop in a department store. Women with professional and intellectual aspirations weren't taken very seriously, whatever their race or background.

I don't know exactly what compelled a young black woman named Phyllis Wallace to break through all this prejudice and low expectations for her race and sex or whether she felt like a pioneer, but she certainly was one. For the next four decades she taught and wrote, did research, managed research, served on policy-making groups and boards and committees. In these various ways she applied the skills of a well-trained scholar/activist to some of the most important and intractable problems of our time, especially the problems of alleviating poverty and the damages of racial and sexual discrimination.

So what have we learned in this turbulent period—we scholar/ activists whose careers paralleled or overlapped at least part of Phyllis'? Focusing mainly on poverty and discrimination, let me offer you five general lessons.

Lesson One   The tools of social science are pretty useful for learning about the world and how it works—but one is never through because the world keeps changing.

Actually, it's not easy to put one's hands on analyses of poverty or the economic effects of discrimination written around 1948. Finding such material dating from the 1930s might be easier, but the immediate postwar period did not focus on these issues. Poverty had not been rediscovered as a separate problem. The economics profession was preoccupied with macro issues, especially maintaining full employment. Economists thought that with continued growth and high employment poverty would take care of itself, except for special groups like the aged, who were differentially poor and not tied into the labor market. Racial discrimination was a very big issue but appeared to be a matter of politics and legislation, especially eliminating legalized discrimination in the South.

Sex discrimination just wasn't much of an issue in 1948. Rosie the Riveter was back in the kitchen, and if she was less than delighted to be there, no one paid her much mind. Rosie was white, of course. Her black counterpart never got out of the kitchen—somebody else's kitchen. As Phyllis wrote much later in a nice little book called *Black Women in the Labor Force* (1980), "Black women have been concentrated in the most menial, low-paying, and most unrewarding occupations in the general labor market or have served minority clients in segregated markets as teachers, social workers, nurses, and librarians." At that time, a majority of employed black women were domestic workers, but this wasn't a fact that outraged opinion leaders.

Not until the 1960s did the scholar/activists swing into action on the forefront of the national effort to reduce poverty and increase racial justice. At first the data were inadequate and tools primitive. Lester Thurow in *Poverty and Discrimination*, published in 1969, still relied heavily on poverty estimates that did not even correct for family size, because nothing better was available.

Information about the poor and analysis of those data are infinitely more available and sophisticated in the 1980s—maybe *too* available and sophisticated. But any way you measure it, poverty, after declining in the 1960s, leveled off in the 1970s and increased in the early 1980s.

Moreover, today's poverty is more concentrated among female family heads with children and among blacks and hispanics. These groups are far less easily reached by macroeconomic policy and pose much greater challenges to designers of special programs than do the disabled or the aged. Indeed, we are now in a good position to eliminate aged poverty altogether. All it would take would be an increase in Supplementary Security Income (SSI) and a bigger effort to get people to apply for it. The growing problem of child poverty— especially the pathological combinations of teenage pregnancy, poor education, a drug culture, crime, and general social disorganization— is a much more agonizing one, to which no one I know professes to have good answers. To those searching for answers I commend a fascinating little book called *Pathways to Work* that Phyllis wrote in 1973. It grew out of intensive interaction with small groups of black teenage girls in Harlem and Bedford-Stuy. Some were mothers, some were dropouts, most had little information about jobs and reported bad first experiences in finding them. Most needed help and support they were not getting at home. Phyllis' policy suggestions still sound sensible—and still aren't happening.

Lesson Two Do the most obvious things first (like changing unfair laws and enforcing fair ones), but don't expect that to be the end of the story.

And, by the way, it's hard to be fair to everybody at once and it's impossible to use the legal system for fairness without generating a nontrivial amount of phoniness and an avalanche of paper.

When more objective historians of the twenty-first or twenty-second centuries write about our era—assuming our civilization survives that long—I suspect they will be favorably impressed with our national determination in the 1960s and 1970s to use the legal system to reduce race and sex discrimination and the effects of past discrimination in employment, housing, and education. They will be justified in pointing out, of course, that we waited a long time to do anything about the legacy of slavery, not to mention centuries of mistreating women, and that our national guilty conscience was well deserved. Still, the effort to legislate equal opportunity and enforce it in the courts and to right past wrongs with affirmative action was commendable and at least partially successful.

The legal approach paid off, but we may have run out that string, even reached the point of negative returns. There are costs of aggressive affirmative action. Some genuinely less qualified people get jobs or promotions over more qualified ones, with potential damage to productivity. But I suspect that far more damage is done to the morale of both majority and minority employees by patently sham efforts to consider candidates with no real intention of hiring them or by the appearance of unfairness to white males whose ancestors may have discriminated but who have done no wrong themselves. And economists with a taste for competitiveness do get a bit queasy when society with the best of intentions makes it almost impossible for firms to lay off employees, no matter how unproductive, who can allege some kind of discrimination. We may not have much of a welfare program for the poor, but we certainly have income maintenance for lawyers at nontrivial public and private cost.

Lesson Three   Economic growth is essential, but not sufficient *or* Don't pose false choices between macro and micro.

The experience of the last two decades has taught us all that it is a lot easier to make progress against poverty and discrimination when the economy is growing rapidly, as it was in the 1960s, than when it is stagnating or in a deep recession as in the decade from the early 1970s to the early 1980s. Traditional manpower programs do not create any jobs, they just distribute them slightly differently. Phyllis Wallace has always stressed that a high level of economic activity and a tight labor market were prerequisites to the success of antipoverty and antidiscrimination policy. Her evaluations of traditional manpower-training programs range from modest positive assessments to discouragement. "The main conclusion from these

two studies," she wrote in the mid-1970s, "is that manpower programs did not change black employment patterns. However, these
programs may have produced a cadre of black program managers
who functioned as change agents in the larger society" (1977a, 349).

Lesson Four Economics is useful, but it isn't everything. The really
hard problems are noneconomic.

For what it's worth, my own guess is that most future progress
toward racial and sexual equality will not come out of rewriting or
enforcing the laws or out of better designed government programs,
whether micro or macro. It will come out of better understanding of
how attitudes about sex and race roles are formed in little children,
how they learn self-confidence and self-esteem and coping skills and
risk-taking. We've got a long way to go even in understanding how
intelligent little girls from middle-income families grow up thinking
they can't do math or physics or economics or if they do they can't
speak up in class or risk asking a dumb question just like the boys
do. My hunch is that figuring out how to change these attitudes will
prove a lot more fruitful than legalistic approaches like setting wages
on the basis of comparable worth.

Finally, Lesson Five Progress is slow and discontinuous, but it does
happen if you keep at it.

Looking back over the last forty years of efforts to reduce poverty
and discrimination, one could easily get discouraged. A lot of work
and dedication in and out of government has brought limited success.
Phyllis has written, "The failures of the federal housing programs
have been colossal . . . There is no evidence that Americans are
willing to invest large sums for the purpose of ameliorating residen-
tial segregation . . ." And she went on to point out that, unless we
stop segregation of poor blacks in ghetto neighborhoods, there is not
much hope for equality of opportunity in jobs and education. "The
future stability of American society is inextricably tied to a decrease
in racial segregation" (1977a, 358–59).

On poverty, there has been some progress, some retrogression.
For the aged there has been a clean success and one to be proud of.
Now we have only the residual and highly solvable problem of
poverty among the very old, mostly widows. But for children there
are scary numbers. Millions of children, many of them black and
hispanic, are growing up not only poor, but in female-headed fami-

lies, in neighborhoods with little hope or contact with the rest of the world. In one of her more hopeful moments Phyllis wrote, "Certainly the increased labor force participation of white mothers with small children will elevate the provision of extra-family child care to a national issue."

So there is no room for complacency. Still, few of us would want to go back to 1948. We are not only a more affluent society with much less degrading poverty, we are mostly a more sensitive, caring society, one that would be outraged at many 1948 attitudes toward minorities, the poor, and women, one with more real opportunities. We also know a lot more about our society. We have learned from our failures as well as our successes. This should offer more hope of success in the future.

That all this is true is in some measure due to efforts of the scholar/ activists, of whom Phyllis is a shining example. Her contributions have been manifested not only in her own work, but in her influence on her colleagues and on so many younger scholar/activists.

References

Wallace, Phyllis A. ed. 1976a. *Equal Employment Opportunity and the AT&T Case*. Cambridge, MA: The MIT Press.

Wallace, Phyllis A. 1976b. "Impact of Equal Employment Opportunity Laws," in J. M. Kreps, ed., *Women and the American Economy*. Englewood Cliffs, NJ: Prentice-Hall, 123–145.

Wallace, Phyllis, A. 1977a. "A Decade of Policy Developments in Equal Opportunities in Employment and Housing," in R. H. Haveman, ed., *A Decade of Federal Antipoverty Programs: Achievements, Failures, and Lessons*. New York: Academic Press, 329–359.

Wallace, Phyllis A. 1977b. *Pathways to Work: Unemployment Among Black Teenage Females*. Lexington, MA: Lexington Books.

Wallace, Phyllis A. 1980. *Black Women in the Labor Force*. Cambridge, MA: The MIT Press.

New Developments
in the Labor Market

1 Introduction

Katharine G. Abraham

We are in a period of important changes in the U.S. economy. Diverse forces lie behind these changes: the oil price shocks of the 1970s and early 1980s, the increased uncertainty associated with flexible exchange rates and a more open macroeconomy, technological developments that fundamentally alter the way that work is done, the coming of age of the baby-boom generation, and the entrance of women into the labor force in increasing numbers. In the face of these developments, the labor market paradigm that has given structure to employer/employee relationships since the end of World War II is gradually giving way to a new, though not yet fully articulated, model.

Had the U.S. economy been performing in an exemplary fashion, one might have concluded that the existing labor market paradigm could continue to serve us well. Indeed, in certain respects, the U.S. labor market has been viewed as a model that other countries can learn from. It is true that the U.S. economy has generated an impressive number of new jobs, absorbing between one and two million new workers per year over the past decade. At the same time, by historical standards, productivity growth since the mid-1970s has been slow, and unemployment rates during the 1970s and 1980s have been high. There is also growing concern that the jobs of the future will require a more educated and more adaptable workforce than the current institutional structure is likely to produce. The gap between the earnings of more educated and less educated workers has already widened significantly (see Levy and Michel 1988; Juhn, Murphy, and Pierce 1989). In the absence of strong productivity growth, this has meant that the earnings of many workers have actually fallen in absolute, not just in relative, terms (Levy 1988). Taken together, these facts suggest that the existing labor market model needs to be rethought.

The shape of a successful new labor market paradigm for the United States is at this point still unclear. What is clear is that the new economic environment imposes a difficult set of requirements on any potential candidates. On the one hand, given the growing volatility and uncertainty they face, U.S. employers must be able to adapt more rapidly to changing economic conditions than they have done in the past. On the other hand, society will not be well served if the cost of increased flexibility is reduced commitment on the part of the work force, weakened incentives to invest in human capital, or further widening of the gap between the "haves" and the "have-nots."

The authors of the nine papers collected here include both economists and industrial relations scholars; all share a concern for understanding the evolution of labor market institutions, public policy, and their joint effects in shaping labor market outcomes. Moreover, they share the perspective that policy makers must be concerned with fostering both efficiency and equity in employment, wages, and related labor market outcomes. It is this combination of theoretical and normative perspectives that binds the papers together in a common search for a new labor market paradigm.

Labor Market Structures and Economic Volatility

A central concern of many of this book's chapters is the evolution of the internal labor market structures that mediate employer/employee interactions. Whereas much discussion of the labor market among both academic researchers and policy makers has proceeded as though the labor market were a classical bourse, in fact a great many employees spend the better part of their work lives attached to enterprises where their pay and their job assignments are determined by processes that, at least in the short run, may yield quite different outcomes than would simple obedience to the dictates of the spot market.

In recent years, the study of internal labor markets—the set of administrative rules and procedures governing the pricing and allocation of labor within the enterprise (Doeringer and Piore 1971)—has received renewed attention (see, for example, Lazear 1979, 1981; Osterman 1984, 1988; Kleiner et al. 1987; and Proceedings of the

Goldwater Conference on the New Economics of Personnel 1987). The internal labor market of the typical large U.S. firm exhibits several key features that, taken together, constitute a coherent system. First, within this internal labor market wages are tied to jobs, not individuals, and indeed may bear little relationship to the individual's productivity at any particular point in time. Hiring is concentrated at certain points in the job hierarchy, and for many positions, internal candidates are favored over external ones. Advancement within the internal labor market consists of movement along more or less clearly defined job ladders, with seniority as well as merit playing an important role in determining who gets promoted. Finally, while increases and decreases in product demand do exert an influence on the level of employment within the internal labor market, they do not translate directly into hirings and firings as the simplest economics-textbook model might lead one to expect. Rather, most employers are cautious in hiring and reluctant to fire.

Given these internal labor market structures, individuals could expect to make their careers with a single company, and many did. Hall (1982) reports that, in 1978, more than 50 percent of men aged forty to forty-four were on jobs that, based on previous cohorts' work histories, they could expect to last for twenty years or more. While their work is not directly comparable to Hall's, Abraham and Farber (1987) present evidence that such "career jobs" are common among blue-collar employees as well as among managers and professionals.

Whether or not internal labor markets necessarily develop in the first place because they most efficiently foster attainment of management's objectives (Williamson, Wachter, and Harris 1975), the congruence between the key internal labor market features just outlined and the postwar economic environment is certainly noteworthy. From the end of the second World War through the early 1970s, the American economy enjoyed unprecedentedly steady growth. Though there were certainly downturns in aggregate demand, even the 1958 recession was no more than moderately severe by recent standards. Moreover, the American economy was much less exposed to the sort of intense foreign competition that we take for granted today. In this stable environment, internal labor market structures premised on long-term attachments to a particular firm and on a relatively predictable set of labor requirements made good sense. If an individual expected to be with a particular firm for a long period of time, then how much he or she was paid to perform a particular job was much less important. Advancement along well-trodden paths produced employees with a predictable set of skills who were well equipped to function in the environment for which their training prepared them. Efforts then to avoid layoffs were sensible, insofar as laid-off employees represented a lost investment.

Moreover, while it is certainly true, as emphasized in Paul Osterman and Thomas Kochan's paper in this volume, that not all internal labor markets have functioned in the same way, the extent to which the personnel practices associated with different groups have shared common elements is at least as striking as their heterogeneity. Consider, for example, the practices typically applicable to managerial and professional employees as compared to those applicable to blue-collar employees. The compensation of managerial and professional employees more closely reflects their individual contributions than does the typical blue-collar worker's pay; however, with the exception of a few top executives, there are few whose pay is not constrained by explicit salary guidelines that reflect position held, time in position, and so on. While white-collar job ladders are less rigidly defined than blue-collar job ladders, most managerial and professional employees nonetheless end up advancing along reasonably established paths within a particular department or functional area (Kanter 1984). Seniority is undoubtedly a more important determinant of promotions for the average blue-collar worker than it is for the average manager or professional, but seniority nevertheless appears to play an important role in promotion decisions within many managerial and professional internal labor markets as well (Abraham and Medoff 1985). Finally, blue-collar employees are certainly more vulnerable to permanent layoffs than white-collar employees, but even blue-collar employment appears, at least in the short run, to be adjusted proportionately less than output (see, for example, Fay and Medoff 1985).

As the steady, sustained growth of the 1950s and 1960s has given way to increased economic volatility and slower growth, existing labor market institutions have come under pressure. Whereas internal labor market structures that assure an adequate supply of personnel with a particular sort of experience at a predictable price are congruent with a steady growth environment, structures that enhance the organization's ability to respond to changing conditions offer significant advantages in a more volatile environment. Slower growth rates accentuate the need for flexibility: if overall employment is not rising, the mix of skills present in an organization cannot be altered simply through new hiring, but will require retraining or the replacement of some existing employees with new ones.

While it is too early to tell what the typical work organization will look like ten or twenty years from now, several noteworthy trends that can be interpreted as a response to the more volatile demand conditions just described are apparent. First, there is growing interest in compensation policies that link an individual's pay to either his or her performance or the performance of the work unit. One would not expect workers to find such pay policies acceptable unless they felt that they had some significant influence on the operations of the group to which they were assigned. Participative structures of one sort or another are thus a natural concomitant of performance-based compensation plans.

There is also growing interest in what has been labeled functional and numerical flexibility in labor deployment. The former refers to internal labor market rules that give employers greater freedom to move employees from one job to another within the firm. Well-defined job ladders produce employees who are well qualified for high-level positions in their specialties, but these same employees may be less qualified to assume a different set of responsibilities should the company's orientation change. Providing employees with a variety of experiences may prove to be functional when the company's needs are more difficult to predict in advance.

Numerical flexibility encompasses a wide variety of strategies that permit the firm to more easily adjust the level of labor input to changing conditions, including greater use of temporary employees, contracting out to smaller firms, and more generally, changes in the structure of interrelationships among firms. Implicit in all of this is the question of the appropriate balance between flexibility and security in the design of processes for determining the allocation of labor, a question to which I return below.

While most observers would agree that these changes on the demand side of the labor market have been important, it is interesting that much—even most—of what has been written about the changing nature of work in America has emphasized the changing nature of the American work force. Members of the "baby-boom" generation are widely perceived as being more interested in opportunities for individual development and less interested in nine-to-five jobs with stipulated pensions at retirement than the previous generation. Similarly, many observers have suggested that the growing supply of female workers is responsible for the growth in temporary and part-time employment. Whether the changes in internal labor market structures currently underway represent primarily an accommodation of employers' changing needs or primarily a response to changes in workers' preferences is an important question that, for the most part, is not tackled directly in the papers that follow. Insofar as the arguments presented in these papers are persuasive, however, one must conclude that employers' changing needs are playing a key role in changing the contours of the labor market.

Winners and Losers in the New Economic Environment

A second theme that emerges from the chapters that follow concerns the "winners" and "losers" in recent labor market developments and the influence of public policy on the distribution of labor market opportunities and outcomes. At one level, one can ask whether particular trends or particular policies favor workers at the expense of employers, or vice versa. At another level, questions arise with respect to the effects of these same trends and policies on the allocation of economic well-being across different groups of workers within the labor force.

In today's more volatile economic environment, an important potential conflict exists between the employer's desire for flexibility and the worker's desire for job security. To some extent, as discussed in several of the papers that follow, this apparent conflict may be illusory. For example, better work force training may facilitate freer reallocation of labor across jobs, thereby enhancing both flexibility and security. Similarly, if hours of work or rates of pay can be adjusted in response to changing economic conditions, constraints on an employer's ability to hire and fire may not be especially onerous. Nonetheless, even the most ardent advocates of strengthened worker job rights must concede that, particularly in circumstances requiring significant sectoral realignments, enhanced job protection for workers may well impose significant costs for employers. An important question concerning recent developments, then, is whether a proper balance between flexibility and security has been struck.

In some settings, a new compact governing the employment relationship, borrowed in its essentials from the model offered by the large Japanese firms, appears to be developing. Under the terms of this new compact, workers agree to be flexible in accepting reassignment and taking on new tasks. In return, the firm commits to do everything that it can to preserve continuity of employment for its work force over the long run. From the perspective of the parties to it, this new compact addresses both the employer's need for flexibility and the worker's need for security, albeit with compromises on both sides. A further issue concerns the role played by temporary workers and subcontractors in this sort of arrangement. From a societal perspective, enhanced employment security for the core work force achieved through reduced employment security for a peripheral or buffer work force would not represent a clear net gain.

With respect to the relative economic positions of the various demographic groups making up the U.S. work force, it is well established that women and minorities historically have fared less well than white males. In recent years, both the male/female and the white/nonwhite earnings gap have narrowed. Standard stories regarding the evolution of male/female and black/white earnings differentials, particularly those told by economists, have tended to emphasize the contribution of human-capital characteristics. It is also important to recognize, however, that the way in which work is structured and the way in which employment decisions are made can have an independent influence on the distribution of opportunities and outcomes. To take a familiar example, employers' perceptions of how men's and women's commitment to the labor force are likely to differ may have an important effect on the sorts of career ladders to which men and women have access, and affect their lifetime work histories. The same forces can be assumed to influence the distribution of earnings within broad demographic groups as well.

Federal labor market initiatives affecting the distribution of income have been of two main types: initiatives intended to alter the human-capital characteristics of particular groups of workers, and initiatives intended to alter employers' hiring practices. Several of the chapters included here offer critical assessments of the distributional consequences of actual or potential federal policies, including job security legislation, employment and training programs, and equal employment opportunity regulations.

Plan of the Volume

The in-depth discussion of these themes begins with Sanford Jacoby's historical perspective on the evolution of personnel policies and practices. During the forty-year period from 1930 to 1970, which Jacoby terms the "heyday of organized labor," industrial relations research was focused almost exclusively on the unionized sector of the economy. While this emphasis is certainly understandable given the rapid growth in union membership following passage of the National Labor Relations Act (NLRA) and the prevailing view among academic observers that the nonunion sector would continue to shrink in importance, Jacoby believes that it was seriously misplaced. He notes that, even at its peak in the mid-1950s, the proportion of the work force that was unionized never exceeded forty percent. More important, the NLRA's endorsement of collective bargaining as a matter of public policy notwithstanding, American managers never abandoned their long-established anti-union values. Thus the recent sharp decline in the prevalence of union membership and the corresponding diminution of the unionized sector's role in the economy is, in Jacoby's judgment, more appropriately viewed as a "return to normalcy" than as a surprising new development.

Jacoby bolsters his argument with a careful investigation of policies and practices at three large nonunion companies—Eastman Kodak, Sears Roebuck, and Thompson Products (later TRW)—from the 1930s through the 1960s. He finds evidence that all three companies pursued a wide range of tactics in their efforts to avoid unionization, and characterizes remaining unorganized despite the cost as an "article of faith" among these companies' managers. His examination of the three companies' histories suggests to Jacoby that the nonunion sector was a more active source of new ideas, even during the 1950s and 1960s, than has generally been recognized.

The next three chapters provide important new evidence on the evolution of compensation and work structures. Michael Conte and Jan Svejnar's discussion of worker participation, Katharine Abraham's look at market-mediated work arrangements, and Gary Loveman, Michael Piore, and Werner Sengenberger's chapter on small businesses all focus on a significant recent development that can be identified as a likely response to increasingly uncertain and volatile economic conditions, although in each case other factors have been at work as well.

The growing prevalence of worker participation in decision-making and compensation arrangements under which workers' pay is tied to the fortunes of the firm is the first of these developments. Advocates of such arrangements have claimed that their use can enhance firm performance, while critics have claimed that there are good reasons to expect participative arrangements to have a negative effect on output. Empirical evidence on this important issue has been extremely sparse. An important factor complicating the analysis of the link between participation and firm performance is that participative arrangements tend to occur jointly rather than singly; participation in decision making is often accompanied by financial participation, and vice versa. This means that previous studies that have focused exclusively either on participation in decision making or on some particular form of participation in the firm's financial performance may have produced misleading results.

Michael Conte and Jan Svejnar present the first results from the analysis of a new data set designed to enable identification of the independent effects of various participative arrangements on firm performance. This new data set consists of several years' worth of in-depth information on the internal structure and performance of forty U.S. companies. At each of these companies workers share in the firm's earnings under at least one of three arrangements: participation in a profit-sharing scheme, direct stock ownership, or participation in an employee stock-ownership plan. Interestingly, even though the companies included in the data set were selected exclusively on the basis of whether they employed one of these financial arrangements, it turns out that a third of them also have formal structures for involving nonmanagerial employees in decision making. Conte and Svejnar's empirical results suggest that, as its advocates have claimed, employee participation in the making of management decisions raises productivity. In contrast, they do not find unambiguously positive productivity effects associated with either profit sharing or employee ownership. While this finding should be interpreted cautiously, it suggests that recent legislative efforts designed to encourage financial participation per se may be misguided.

Another recent development that has received considerable attention in the popular and business press is the growing prevalence of a variety of arrangements under which work is performed by "outsiders"—temporary workers, business-service firms, or subcontractors—rather than by a firm's regular work force. Some have argued that the growth in these arrangements has been motivated primarily by employers' desire for greater flexibility in their staffing patterns and that it presages the emergence of a two-tier society in which some individuals hold stable jobs at good salaries while others work irregularly and for lower wages. Alternatively, these developments might be more accurately characterized as simply the natural consequence of the growing complexity of economic life, which arguably has created new niches for firms that provide specialized services to other firms.

In an effort to shed some light on these important issues Katharine Abraham explores employers' motivations for using temporary workers and outside contractors. Abraham finds evidence that the growing use of market-mediated work arrangements is a much more complex phenomenon than much of the popular discussion might suggest. Certain of these arrangements—most notably the use of agency temporaries—do seem to serve the function of buffering the regular work force from fluctuations in demand, and there is evidence that wage and benefits savings are an important factor in employers' decisions to contract out low-skilled work. There is also evidence, however, that the desire to take advantage of outsiders' special expertise is an important factor in many contracting decisions, particularly those involving more highly paid workers.

Gary Loveman, Michael Piore, and Werner Sengenberger consider a similar set of hypotheses concerning the growing share of employment in small economic units that they have documented not only for the United States but also for many other developed economies. The increasing importance of small business might reflect the development of a peripheral sector devoted to producing products for which demand is uncertain or small. Alternatively, it might reflect institutional rigidities that have prevented large firms from responding to changing supply and demand conditions. A third hypothesis is that it reflects technological changes that have reduced economies of scale.

Loveman, Piore, and Sengenberger argue that, in some sense, all of these explanations are at least partially correct. They suggest that the increased uncertainty of the economic environment during the 1970s induced an expansion of the peripheral sector of the economy, which manifested itself in increased small firm employment. This trend was amplified by the availability of substantial numbers of unemployed workers willing to accept employment in the small-firm sector. Once established, however, small firms began to evolve in ways that led to the emergence of a new technological paradigm that the authors term "flexible specialization," a model that Piore has developed at length elsewhere (Piore and Sabel 1984). While some might quarrel with the view that the developed economies are in fact evolving toward the flexible-specialization paradigm, most would view it as an attractive model.

Loveman, Piore, and Sengenberger go on to focus on the relationship between flexible specialization and employment and training policy. A key feature of flexible specialization is the strong linkages that must exist among firms in a region. These linkages include frequent movements of workers from one firm to another. Based on consideration of the German and the Japanese experience with models that come close to the flexible specialization paradigm, Loveman, Piore, and Sengenberger argue for the importance of employment and training structures that combine formal and on-the-job training, and produce skills that are transferable across firms.

The next two chapters address the accommodation of the employer's need for flexibility and the employee's need for job and/or income security within the context of a market economy. This issue is of increasing importance in view of the less predictable economic environment of recent years.

Paul Osterman and Thomas Kochan offer a framework for thinking about employment security. They begin their discussion by contrasting the industrial model of work organization, typical of blue-collar employment in the United States, and the salaried model, typical of managerial and professional employment. The industrial model is characterized by rigid job classifications, promotion on the basis of seniority, and layoffs in inverse-seniority order as needed to adjust the quantity of labor input. The salaried model, in contrast, is characterized by freer reallocation of labor within the enterprise and stronger employment security. Osterman and Kochan note that there has been growing interest in the application of the salaried model to blue-collar employment and discuss current developments in the auto industry in this context. They argue that, at least in the automobile industry, management has been willing to "buy" increased internal flexibility by offering enhanced job security to employees. Osterman and Kochan also recognize, however, that in a volatile economic environment, no firm can guarantee all of its employees a lifetime job. Therefore broader conceptualization of employment security, they argue, must consider not only the stability of employment at particular firms (internal security) but also how easily workers who are displaced from one job are able to secure alternative employment (external security).

From a policy perspective, Osterman and Kochan emphasize the importance of a well-trained work force as a precondition for both internal and external security. Well-trained workers can more readily be reassigned from one task to another within the workplace and, in addition, should experience less difficulty in securing alternate employment if laid off from their jobs. Though somewhat differently motivated, this policy prescription echoes that offered by Loveman, Piore, and Sengenberger. In addition, Osterman and Kochan argue for the institutionalization of efforts to help displaced workers move to new employment, such as job counseling and retraining programs.

Susan Houseman analyzes legal restrictions on an employer's right to lay off workers. It is widely believed that job security regulations, such as those requiring advance notice of layoffs, consultation with employees concerning reductions in the work force, or mandatory severance payments, are a source of inefficiency in the labor market. If job security provisions were efficient, those holding this view reason, one would expect them to be agreed upon by private parties; if they are not, the argument continues, imposing them by fiat can only distort labor market outcomes.

One of Houseman's contributions is the identification of a variety of ways in which job security regulations imposed on private parties by an outside authority may actually enhance labor market efficiency. A legal requirement that employers provide advance notice of layoffs and consult with their workers concerning reductions in force, for example, may help to overcome problems associated with asymmetries in information that would otherwise impede the negotiation of efficient contracts. Mandatory severance payments may serve to internalize the externality associated with the adverse effects of layoffs on the community at large.

If job-security regulations are actually efficiency-enhancing, one might ask why they have been so vociferously opposed by U.S. employers and why European job-security regulations have come under attack from employer groups. Houseman believes that the primary reason for employer opposition is that job security legislation shifts the balance of power in the labor market. Labor market outcomes may be more efficient, but at the same time employees may be made better off and employers made worse off. Were the alleged inefficiency of job security provisions the only consideration motivating opposition to them, Houseman notes, one would not expect either employers or unions to favor them. The fact that only employer groups have opposed these provisions is consistent with the view that the distributional consequences of job security legislation are of primary importance.

Houseman also reviews the development of European job security law. Although this legislation has been subjected to close scrutiny in recent years, the changes made to it have in fact been quite minor. One factor in the relatively widespread acceptance of job security legislation in Europe, even among employers who might prefer to operate without it and who have become more vocal in expressing this view in recent years, is that other institutions in European societies are well adapted to the existence of strong job security regulations. For example, European workers whose hours are reduced are generally eligible to collect partial unemployment benefits. Even though it is difficult for European employers to reduce employment, they are thus more easily able to adjust hours than are U.S. employers. Houseman suggests that careful study of how the European economies have accommodated strong job security provisions may yield useful lessons for U.S. policymakers.

The final three chapters explore changes over time in the labor market position of women and minorities and the role of public policy *vis à vis* the disadvantaged. As noted above, past research on these issues has typically emphasized supply factors, most especially the qualifications of women and minorities relative to those of white males. While the authors of these last three papers would certainly agree that supply factors have an important influence on labor market outcomes, their common point of departure is the recognition that demand factors also contribute in an important way to the distribution of economic outcomes in society.

The chapter by Susan Carter and Peter Philips develops a provocative new hypothesis concerning the stagnation of women's relative earnings over the course of the twentieth century. Earlier research on this subject has emphasized the apparent constancy in working women's relative levels of education and experience over this period. Carter and Philips believe that this cannot be the whole story, however, since women's skills also remained relatively static over the period from the early nineteenth to the early twentieth century, while over that period their relative earnings rose. Carter and Philips attribute the narrowing of the gender gap during the nineteenth century to the decreasing importance of physical strength and the increasing importance of formal education. Had nothing else changed, they would have expected the same factors to have lead to a continued narrowing during the twentieth century. The fact that the gender gap did not continue to narrow leads them to examine the role played by technological and organizational factors as determinants of women's earnings.

During the early years of industrialization, batch production methods were common, capital intensities were low, and each individual worker's output could easily be identified. This meant that payment of piece rates was common and wide variation in the productivity of those employed could be tolerated. Equally important, because individual workers' activities were largely independent, employers could add new groups to the work force without having to worry about how well they would be accepted by current employees. In the later phases of industrialization, however, continuous-process technologies characterized by high capital to labor ratios and team production methods became more prevalent. Under these circumstances payment of piece rates was no longer feasible, and harmonious worker interaction became more important to employers. As a consequence, Carter and Philips argue, employers in continuous-process industries were more likely to pay above-market "efficiency wages" to their workers and also to exclude women, whose addition might be opposed by the existing male work force.

Others have suggested that recent changes in work organization that arguably de-emphasize work force stability may bode well for women's employment and earnings prospects. If Carter and Philips are correct, however, the fact that these new forms of work organization also rely heavily on interaction among members of the work team means that predicting their consequences for women is less straightforward.

Peter Gottschalk also emphasizes the importance of understanding both investments in workers' human capital and employers' hiring policies and practices if we are to understand the position of disadvantaged workers in the labor market.

Gottschalk begins by documenting the narrowing in the earnings gaps between blacks and whites and between women and men from the mid-1960s through the present. While the black/white earnings differential and the male/female earnings differential have shrunk, the inequality of earnings within race/sex groups has risen substantially. This implies that those at the bottom of the earnings distribution are falling behind.

Gottschalk attributes the closing of cross-group wage gaps to convergence in average human-capital characteristics across groups and to federal policies that have successfully altered employers' hiring practices. The increasing inequality of earnings within race/sex groups, however, appears to be less amenable to policy intervention. In spite of a long history of human-capital programs that target disadvantaged workers, Gottschalk argues, we still do not have a good understanding of why these programs so often fail to achieve their stated objectives. Gottschalk speculates that the problem may lie at least in part with employers' scepticism concerning the value of the skills provided by government-sponsored training programs that target disadvantaged workers. If this speculation is correct, one might well conclude that the appropriate policy response would be to serve disadvantaged workers' training needs within the context of a more broadly conceived training and retraining strategy. In this sense, Gottschalk's conclusions resonate with those reached by Osterman and Kochan, and by Loveman, Piore, and Sengenberger.

In the closing chapter Robert M. Solow takes a somewhat broader perspective on labor market policy. He calls the idea that the current unemployment problem reflects structural problems stemming from the poor qualifications of unemployed workers a hardy perennial that resurfaces whenever the unemployment rate goes up. One implication of this view, at least in its more extreme forms, is that expansion of overall demand would do little to reduce the unemployment rate to its previous level. Adherents of this view often advocate the use of employment and training policies to lower the unemployment rate.

In the context of reflecting on the history of employment and training policy in the years since passage of the Manpower Development and Training Act in 1962, Solow takes issue with the position just outlined. He sees employment and training programs as having noteworthy distributional consequences: in at least some cases, they lead to small but measurable improvements in the labor market position of those they serve, though this is largely at the expense of those not served. Employment and training programs do little or nothing, he continues, either to increase the total number of employment opportunities or to reduce the overall unemployment rate. While he agrees that devoting resources to employment and training programs intended to help disadvantaged workers is a good thing, Solow cautions against expecting from such programs what they cannot deliver.

References

Abraham, Katharine G. and Henry S. Farber. 1987. "Job Duration, Seniority, and Earnings," *American Economic Review* 77 (June), 278–297.

Abraham, Katharine G. and James L. Medoff. 1985. "Length of Service and Promotions in Union and Nonunion Work Groups", *Industrial and Labor Relations Review* 38 (April), 408–420.

Doeringer, Peter, and Michael Piore. 1971. *Internal Labor Markets and Manpower Analysis*. Lexington, Massachusetts: Lexington Books.

Fay, Jon A., and James L. Medoff. 1985. "Labor and Output Over the Business Cycle," *American Economic Review* 75 (September), 638–655.

Hall, Robert. 1982. "The Importance of Lifetime Jobs in the U.S. Economy," *American Economic Review* 72 (September), 716–724.

Juhn, Chinhui, Kevin M. Murphy, and Brooks Pierce. 1989. "Wage Inequality and the Rise in Returns to Skill," Chicago: University of Chicago Department of Economics Working Paper.

Kanter, Rosabeth Moss. 1984. "Variations in Managerial Career Structures in High-Technology Firms: The Impact of Organizational Characteristics on Internal Labor Market Patterns," in Paul Osterman, ed., *Internal Labor Markets*. Cambridge, Massachusetts: MIT Press, 109–132.

Kleiner, Morris M., Richard Block, Myron Roomkin, and Sidney Salsbury. 1987. *Human Resources and the Performance of the Firm*. Madison, Wisconsin: Industrial Relations Research Association.

Lazear, Edward. 1979. "Why Is There Mandatory Retirement?" *Journal of Political Economy* 87 (December), 1261–1284.

Lazear, Edward. 1981. "Agency, Earnings Profiles, Productivity and Hours Restriction," *American Economic Review* 71 (September), 606–620.

Levy, Frank. 1988. *Dollars and Dreams*. New York: W.W. Norton.

Levy, Frank, and Richard Michel. 1988. *Individual Earnings by Sex, Education, and Age: Recent U.S. Trends*. Washington, D.C.: Joint Economic Committee of the U.S. Congress.

Osterman, Paul, ed. 1984. *Internal Labor Markets*. Cambridge, Massachusetts: MIT Press.

Osterman, Paul. 1988. *Employment Futures: Reorganization, Dislocation and Public Policy.* New York: Oxford University Press.

Piore, Michael, and Charles Sabel. 1984. *The Second Industrial Divide.* New York: Basic Books.

Proceedings of the Goldwater Conference on the New Economics of Personnel. 1987. Tempe, Arizona, April 10 and 11, 1986. *Journal of Labor Economics* 5 (October).

Williamson, Oliver, Michael Wachter, and Jeffrey Harris. 1975. "Understanding the Employment Relation," *Bell Journal of Economics* 6 (Spring), 250–280.

2

Norms and Cycles: The Dynamics of Nonunion Industrial Relations in the United States, 1897–1987

Sanford M. Jacoby

This chapter develops a historical framework for analyzing the human resource policies and practices of nonunion companies in the United States. An examination of union growth patterns shows that over the past one hundred years, those patterns have moved in regular cycles that correspond to long-wave economic activity. The upswing of a cycle is associated with a high degree of employer innovation to contain unionization; during a downswing, the most successful innovations from the preceding period are consolidated into a coherent model of nonunion industrial relations. Although the specific characteristics of the models vary, each model is composed of elements that reflect enduring employer norms related to union avoidance. This chapter also presents some historical data on the development of nonunion personnel practices. A fair amount is known about the activities of nonunion firms before the 1930s and since the 1960s, but less is known about the intervening years that spanned the heyday of organized labor. A detailed look at the personnel policies of several major nonunion companies during those critical years shows that it was a time when employers were developing the nonunion model that has now become prevalent in U.S. industry. A postscript to the chapter attempts to explain the persistence of employer hostility to unions in the United States as compared to other nations.

The UCLA Academic Senate and the UCLA Institute of Industrial Relations provided financial support for this research. The author is grateful to Walter Fogel, Walter Galenson, and Daniel Nelson for helpful comments.

Blind Spots

Throughout the post-World War II period, industrial relations researchers tended to ignore U.S. industry's nonunion sector. They focused their research instead on the employment and labor relations practices of unionized companies. During the last few years, however, a number of industrial relations scholars have begun to pay attention to developments within the nonunion sector (Verma 1983; Foulkes 1980; Kochan, Katz, and McKersie 1986), as have scholars in several other disciplines. Economists (Freeman and Medoff 1984) and sociologists (Fenwick and Olson 1986) are examining nonunion compensation and personnel practices, while in the field of labor law, collective bargaining is being supplanted by topics of concern beyond the organized sector, such as employment discrimination and termination (Holloway and Leech 1985).

Because social scientists have a strong interest in public policy, they are attracted to new and emerging issues. Hence, the recent shift in academic concerns can be traced to the sharp contraction in private-sector union membership that began in the 1980s. Likewise, the previous generation of industrial relations researchers exhibited a scholarly blind spot when it came to the study of nonunion firms. During the years that generation was in graduate school—roughly from 1935 to 1960—the spotlight was on the union sector, where a new industrial relations system was being forged that in turn raised important issues for public policy. As a result, young scholars in those years were preoccupied with the study of union organization and collective bargaining, particularly as practiced in the mass production industries organized during the 1930s and 1940s. There was also a normative aspect to the postwar industrial relations scholars' paradigm: a belief that nonunion firms did not merit serious scrutiny because they were considered socially retrograde in light of public policies encouraging collective bargaining. Granted, it was harder to obtain information on nonunion firms than on the highly public, and publicized, union sector; this may have deterred research efforts. But whatever the explanation, that generation of scholars downplayed the significance of events in the nonunion sector by attributing nonunion practices to reactive, imitative "spillover" and "threat" effects, and gave too much importance and weight to developments in the union sector. This is not to deny that spillovers occurred, that the union sector was the source of much innovation in personnel policies, or that managers in nonunion settings often looked over their shoulders at developments in organized firms. Indeed, many personnel practices in nonunion firms were adopted for the express purpose of avoiding unionization, as is still the case today. Nevertheless, academia and the mass media did slight the nonunion sector, thereby creating the erroneous impression that unionism had greater appeal, dynamism, and acceptability than was actually the case. Bear in mind that the density of private-sector union membership (the percentage of private-sector nonagricultural workers belonging to unions) barely reached two-fifths of the labor force even during wartime; grew for only twenty-five years, from 1933 to 1958; and subsequently failed to sustain that level, dropping from 35 percent in 1958 to 16 percent in 1985. We therefore need to rethink our conception of labor relations in the United States and put the years between 1930 and the present in proper historical perspective.

If we take a broad view of, say, the last hundred years, the *leitmotiv* of U.S. industrial relations is not the growth of organized labor but, instead, management's persistent and often stubborn resistance to unions. Among the many traditions in labor relations, this one has shown the greatest continuity. Although management's attitudes have evolved over the years—becoming more solicitous toward employees and more sophisticated in its techniques than before—its philosophical appraisal of unions and of the contributions they might make to the workplace have, with some notable exceptions, exhibited surprisingly little change. Following Fox's (1974) terminology, this philosophy can be dubbed unitarianism: managers emphasize the common objectives and values that unite the employer and the employees, while viewing unions as the propagators of illegitimate and unnecessary conflict. A contrasting philosophy is pluralism, which portrays the workplace as a coalition of groups with divergent interests and aspirations. Here unionism has a role to play as a pressure group challenging managerial rule and engaging in joint rule-making on behalf of the employees. Whereas pluralism was the dominant philosophy of the postwar generation of industrial relations scholars, something for which they have been thoroughly condemned in recent radical critiques (Stone 1981), it can hardly be said to have had wide acceptance in managerial circles, even during the period of reputed pluralist hegemony, that is, from the 1940s through the 1960s. Instead, as a few observers warned during those years (Barkin 1950; Brown and Myers 1957) and as recent historical research has shown (Harris 1982), most managers, including those within the heavily unionized, core manufacturing firms, had an overwhelmingly conservative opinion of unions and adopted a seemingly flexible stance merely as a tactical strategy. Were a more nuanced and extensive appraisal to be made of postwar pluralism, something that cannot be undertaken here, it would find pluralism to have been a prescriptive norm urged upon U.S. managers by government officials and industrial relations scholars (as in the case studies published by the National Planning Association; see Golden and Parker 1955), not a widely accepted tenet of managerial belief.

In light of all this, it is a mistake to say that "the dominant industrial relations system of the 1930 to 1960 period was collective bargaining and job-control unionism" (Kochan, Katz, and McKersie 1986, 264). First, this characterization overlooks or slights both the innovations in personnel practices and the anti-collective-bargaining activity of nonunion firms, not only in their own plants but in their public relations and lobbying efforts as well. That is, it simply reinforces the erroneous impression created by postwar industrial relations researchers that little of interest was happening outside of the union sector. Second, and worse, the statement leads to a conjunctural analysis of the post-1960 growth of the nonunion sector, in which the development of an alternative nonunion model is seen as something new and unprecedented, the result of factors that came into play during the 1960s and 1970s. It would be more accurate to portray events in recent decades as a shift back to what has been the baseline for industrial relations in the United States for the last century. The years between 1930 and 1960 were actually an aberrant period in which two models—the union and the nonunion—contested each other, with the nonunion model eventually reasserting its traditional dominance in the years since 1970. Moreover, as several writers have recently noted (Jacoby 1983; Dubofsky 1985), there are striking parallels between the 1980s and the 1920s, the latter being another decade that witnessed competition between the models, followed by a "return to normalcy," to use the conservative phrase of that day. This cycling of industrial relations philosophies and practices bears closer scrutiny.

Cycles in Industrial Relations

If one examines historical data on private-sector union density, two facts stand out. First, union growth and decline alternate in long waves of years (trends or moving averages) in addition to continual annual fluctuations. Second, over the past century, the number of years in which union density declined is greater than the number of years in which it grew: 56 percent of the years between 1897 and 1985 were spent in union decline.[1]

Some of the observed variation in union membership density can be explained by the conventional economic factors used in longitudinal models of union growth (Stepina and Fiorito 1986; Fiorito and Greer 1982). The models do a reasonable job of tracking annual movements, but are less helpful in explaining the major turning points shown in figure 2.1. This has forced modelers to introduce social and political variables that are thought to have some effect on union growth. The procedure, although it leads to fairly good explanatory results, is typically performed on an ad hoc basis, usually without any well-developed theory to guide the choice of variables. Moreover, although the models have been separately applied to data from different nations (Pencavel 1971), this begs the obvious and still unanswered question of what causes cross-national variations in unionization levels, or more specifically, why unionization levels are so much lower in the United States than in other countries with similar industrial relations systems.

The swinging pendulum of long-wave theory provides one way of explaining the chunky movements shown in figure 2.1. Ever since Kondratieff, economists have studied long-term cycles in economic activity. Although the evidence on long swings is not entirely convincing (Rosenberg and Frischtak 1984), it does paint a tantalizingly plausible picture. Researchers have found, for example, that prices in the United States exhibit regular, long swings from inflation to deflation, with a full cycle (peak to peak) lasting roughly 50 years. Previous peaks were in 1873 and 1920; the troughs in 1896 and 1933. In addition to the price cycle, economists have found that industrial production moves in long waves, with the most recent peak occurring in 1973. Since then, aggregate growth and productivity have slowed considerably. At least until the 1920s, the price cycle and the production cycle moved in concert, and it is possible that they are once again becoming synchronous (Van Duijn 1983). Although aggregate prices moved upward during the 1970s, much of the increase was due to the OPEC oil price shocks; and in the last few years, some wages (for example, those in the union sector) and many commodity prices (for example, oil and metals) have been falling. A number of

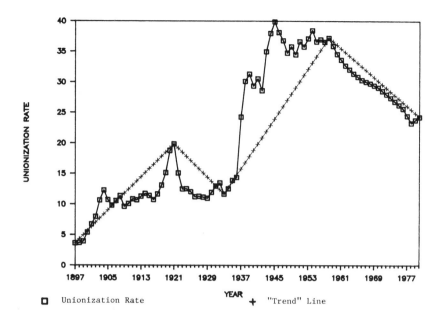

Figure 2.1

Private-sector union density, 1897–1980

Notes: Union density is the percentage of nonagricultural, private sector employees belonging to unions. The numerator excludes Canadian members, public-sector members, and agricultural members of unions. Figures on government and agricultural employment were extrapolated for the years 1897–1899. The annual data for 1897–1958 include members of directly affiliated local unions whereas the biennial data for 1960–1980 do not include them.

The "trend" line is not based on a statistical fit but simply connects the major turning points (1897, 1921, 1933, 1958) shown in the table.

Sources: U.S. Department of Commerce, Bureau of the Census, *Historical Statistics of the United States: Colonial Times to 1970,* part 1, Washington, D.C.: GPO, 1975, 126, 137, 177-178. Stanley Lebergott, *Manpower in Economic Growth.* New York: McGraw-Hill, 1964, 512, 522. U.S. Bureau of Labor Statistics, *Handbook of Labor Statistics,* Bulletin no. 2070, December 1980, 402-409. Courtney D. Gifford, ed., *Directory of U.S. Labor Organizations.* Washington, D.C.: Bureau of National Affairs, 1982–ed., 1, 55, 63, and 1986–ed., 67; Leo Troy and Neil Sheflin, *Union Sourcebook: Membership, Structure, Finance, Directory.* West Orange: IRDIS, 1985, A-1.

explanations for these long waves have been proffered, including innovation clusters (Schumpeter 1939), interactions between economic and demographic factors (Easterlin 1968), and social structures of accumulation (Gordon, Edwards, and Reich 1982), in which institutions that foster capital accumulation at the beginning of a long wave later become troublesome barriers to the continuation of the economic growth process.

These swings have obvious relevance to union growth, especially since they approximately match the turning points shown in the table. First, economic theory suggests that during upswings—inflationary periods accompanied by rapid growth and relatively tight labor markets—workers seek union representation to protect real wage levels, causing a rise in union membership. Because these are auspicious times for successful strikes, unionized workers are able to increase their relative pay, spurring additional interest in unionism. Labor's bargaining power during the upswing makes it difficult for unionized employers to rid themselves of unions. But with the onset of the downswing, prices and growth rates start to decline and labor markets slacken. These conditions provide employers an opportunity to dislodge the unions. Although some firms are able to achieve this, others—those that are heavily unionized or geographically immobile—find union elimination to be an infeasible (though still desirable) objective, forcing them instead to seek wage relief, productivity improvements, and more cooperative labor relations. Slippage in the relative wages and working conditions of organized workers make unions less attractive to the unorganized, causing further reductions in union membership. Second, long-wave movements are also associated with changes in the industrial structure of the economy. During upswings, new industries emerge while older industries are carried along by the economy's buoyancy; during downswings, the older industries contract and sometimes disappear entirely. Simply by virtue of their age (meaning that unions have had more time to organize them), those older industries tend to be more heavily unionized. Hence their shrinkage provides another explanation for the link between long swings and union growth.

In addition to these economic links, there are social and political factors to consider. Paralleling long swings in economic activity have been shifts in social attitudes and social policy. During the upswings of 1896–1920 (the Progressive era) and 1933–73 (the New Deal era, broadly defined), public attitudes toward social reform and toward interest groups like organized labor were generally favorable; the reverse was true of economic downswings, such as the 1920s and the years since 1973. These shifts in social attitudes have played important roles in the union growth process: first, by allowing labor and its allies to foster policies favorable to unions (for example, the Wagner Act); and second, by influencing the calculus of private decisions, making it socially acceptable to join or support unions during upswings and equally acceptable to shun or undermine them during downswings.

But the matter is more complex than that. Although social and political attitudes change during a long swing—moving from conservative to liberal and back again—it would be fallacious to assume that all elements in a nation's sociopolitical structure shift in a uniform fashion. Rather, there exist what might be called social constants, immutable factors that persist over time, giving national social systems a distinctive character and setting the social and political boundaries for the long swings. In the United States, these social constants would include the absence of feudal traditions, a heterogeneous working class, and, of interest here, an employing class that has always been hostile to organized labor, regardless of specific economic conditions.

True, American managers have economic reasons for avoiding unions. Unions impose actual or potential strike costs on unionized firms and, as a result, those firms are forced to pay wage premia. Given that most industries are only partially unionized, wage premia hurt firm profits and market share. How much they hurt will depend on whether unions can raise productivity and reduce unit labor costs in unionized firms, an issue presently under debate by economists. But management hostility to organized labor typically transcends these economic considerations. Opposition to unions, as expressed in unitarian managerial philosophies, derives from a set of *beliefs*— in the virtues of individualism, in the employer's freedom to control his property without interference from either government or unions (Berthoff 1964), and in the economic harm caused by unions—rather than from a careful weighing of the actual costs and benefits of unionism. Although there are historical instances of employers welcoming unions for economic reasons, either as a stabilizing force in highly competitive industries like apparel or construction, or as a prop to oligopolistic pricing practices in industries like steel, these are exceptional cases. Even in steel, Myron C. Taylor of U.S. Steel failed in the late 1930s to convince other steelmakers like Tom Girdler (Republic), Ernest Weir (National), and Eugene Grace (Bethlehem) that the virtues of price stabilization outweighed the vice of unionism (Ulman 1958).

However, *after* a firm is organized, economic considerations will shape management's decisions about the appropriate industrial relations strategy to pursue. At best, firms will tolerate the union because the cost of dislodging it is too high, but at the same time they will try to weaken or circumvent it, and then to eliminate it whenever that is possible, typically during a downswing (unless, as mentioned, dislodging costs do not fall enough during the downswing to make this a feasible strategy, as with some heavily unionized or immobile firms; see Kochan, Katz, and McKersie 1986). In other words, economic factors influence the feasibility and timing of hostile management actions, but are not the sole or even the most important determinant of management's hostile attitudes and beliefs.[2]

This continuing hostility to unions has had two important consequences. First, along with the other social constants referred to, management's strong opposition to organized labor accounts for the comparatively low basal levels of unionization found in the United States, an issue discussed later in this chapter. Second, it plays an important role in the union growth cycle, setting an upward limit on unionization levels during upswings and hastening their erosion during downswings. In other words, management actions—not simply product and labor market swings, worker preferences, and union resources—are an important determinant of union-density trends. This can be seen most clearly in the union-avoidance policies pursued over the course of a long-wave cycle.

Upswings in the economy have been marked by societal ferment and shifting social norms, in addition to union growth. As a result, employers fearful of unionization during the upswings have to scrap some of their industrial relations policies from the preceding downswing or bring them into line with the period's new social and economic realities. They also have to devise and experiment with new policies and techniques intended to gain tactical advantages over unions and to ensure continued employee loyalty. These innovations may be entirely the work of managers and their consultants (such as the wage incentive plans of the decade of the 1900s), but they also often involve preemptive imitations of recent union gains, both economic and noneconomic. During upswings "threat effects" are common, and personnel practices spill over from the union to the nonunion sector. Because of their firefighting approach to preventing unionization, most companies are unable to put together a coherent ensemble of effective personnel policies, although a few pioneering firms do. Nevertheless, during the upswing there is considerable diffusion of a variety of personnel innovations—not all of them effective—because even the most expensive or outlandish technique may be perceived as profitable in light of the "clear and present danger" posed by unions.

During an economic downswing, employers refine their strategies: the most successful union-containment policies of the preceding period are retained, while the less effective ones are shed. What had been experimental and innovative during the upswing (such as systematic personnel management, which first appeared in the 1910s) now becomes standard operating procedure in many nonunion companies. As successful personnel innovations from the earlier period are consolidated, there emerges an identifiable nonunion model of industrial relations. Managers now are better able to put together a coherent system because less of their energy is spent on tactical labor relations problems and because more conservative social and political conditions exist that allow the pursuit of policies that previously had been difficult to implement. (For example, the American Plan was launched after, rather than during, the first World War because public and governmental support for unions waned after the war; for the same reason, employers today can be more forthright about their opposition to unions than was the case thirty years ago.) Companies that are perceived to be on the leading edge in applying the nonunion industrial relations model are widely imitated and receive publicity from what has become a sympathetic, pro-business press. But those companies are not necessarily the true pioneers. Instead, they are simply the firms that are experiencing relatively high growth and profitability during the downswing. The popular impression is that these high growth and profit rates are the result of innovative personnel policies, but the causal relationship may also run in the opposite direction or not exist at all.

Two critical issues during the downswing period are the extent to which the nonunion model is diffused throughout industry, and the resources that firms devote to it. These will affect the degree of unionization during the next upswing. Diffusion rates and funding levels will depend on management's perception of the present and future probability of unionization as well as the cost to the firm should it occur. Although unionization is less likely during the downswing, its cost may actually increase because unions tend to have more bargaining power than organizing power during these periods (look, for example, at union-nonunion wage differentials during the early 1930s or today). But regardless of these considerations, managers will have memories of the previous upswing and may act to prevent a recurrence of union-organizing successes.

Some cynics would argue that the ability to remain nonunion over the course of a long economic cycle has less to do with the firm's personnel policies than with its financial position. After all, it is argued, look at what happened in the 1930s to the supposedly innovative nonunion companies of the 1920s; a similar fate will likely befall today's high technology firms when hard times come, as they always do. To this I would respond, yes, financial resources are often necessary to support an innovative personnel program, but resources alone are no guarantee that a firm will adopt such a program and remain nonunion. In other words, money matters, but it is not all that matters. A well-heeled firm can be organized if it has backward personnel policies (including those on compensation), and a cash-strapped firm can avoid organization if, when hard times come, it can draw on a fund of employee trust and loyalty built up during better years. Of course, at some point that fund may exhaust itself, which was one of the problems faced by progressive firms during the 1930s.

Norms of Opposition

Another source of historical continuity can be found in the policies that managements have relied upon to insulate their firms from unionism. Going back to the turn of the century, one can identify five basic norms around which nonunion personnel policies have clustered. They are:

1. *paternalism*, the gamut of employee welfare programs and non-wage compensation plans designed to build employees' identification with and loyalty to the firm;

2. *participation*, offering employees structured channels to influence organizational policies and practices;

3. *union substitution*, providing wage levels and fair rules of workplace allocation (hiring, promotion, dismissal) that match those garnered by unionized employees;

4. *coercion*, using force, threats, or sanctions to deter workers from organizing or joining unions; and

5. *labor law*, resorting to legal action or legislative lobbying to discourage the forming and maintenance of unions (court injunctions, yellow-dog contracts, and legislation like the Taft-Hartley act would be included here).

Each of these norms can be analyzed using Hirschman's (1970) model of organizational adjustment. Firms strive to prevent employee exit in the form of quits and of membership in a union, both of which are viewed as exit into a competing organization.[3] Preventing exit to a union is achieved through participation, or voice, channels that give employees an alternative to the union influence mechanism, and through personnel policies that substitute for the benefits that a union could provide employees. To build employee loyalty, which increases the probability that when the chips are down an employee will choose not to exit to a union, managers rely on paternalistic welfare programs. Participation also builds employee loyalty, since workers tend to be more loyal to organizations they are able to influence. Through coercion, by job loss or other threats, management can increase the cost of choosing exit. Like coercion, using the law to hem in organized labor can raise the cost of exit by making it more difficult to create and maintain unions. For example, the use of yellow-dog contracts before 1932 left unions financially liable when they successfully recruited new members, while Taft-Hartley's allowances for employer free speech raised the cost to unions of conducting organizing campaigns and winning elections.

As time goes by, some of the specific policies associated with these norms are discarded and replaced because their effectiveness is vitiated by long-wave shifts in the economy, in the composition of the labor force, and in social attitudes (as reflected, in part, by legal constraints). Other policies, however, remain consistent in form as a result of unchanging cultural and ideological proclivities on the part of workers and managers (for example, such welfare programs as company athletics; see Fones-Wolf 1986). Institutional inertia and rigidity also play a role, giving rise to a correlation between the age of an organization and its use of certain human resource policies

(Stinchcombe 1965). This combination of change and inertia produces a kind of geological structure of human resource policies within organizations. At any point in time, one finds strata of policies associated with a particular norm; each stratum represents an older policy carried over from an earlier period. Together with social constants and the persistence of norms, this geological structure gives a distinctively "American" stamp to our industrial relations system as it moves through time.

A Look at the Cycles

Let us now examine the content of the norms in each of the cycles shown in figure 2.1. Although only a brief sketch is possible here, it will help to flesh out the arguments presented above. The place to start is with the 1897–1921 upswing, a time of social unrest and social reform that produced significant gains in union membership, particularly at the cycle's start (1897–1904) and finish (1916–20). Those gains fueled numerous and significant personnel policy innovations at a large number of firms. Toward the end of the upswing, a handful of progressive companies like Dennison Manufacturing and Leeds & Northrup managed to meld those innovations into a coherent system of nonunion industrial relations—a system that later served as a model for other firms.

The initial managerial response to the upsurge in unionism was paternalistic programs ranging from thrift clubs, compulsory religious observances, and citizenship instruction to company housing, outings, and contests (Brandes 1976; Jacoby 1985).[4] Many, though by no means all, of the programs were intended to prevent unionization, either by holding out hefty benefits that could be withdrawn after a strike or by psychologically immunizing the employees against unionist nostrums by making workers more sedulous, patriotic, and loyal. Next, employers began to provide participative alternatives to unions, starting with the Filene Cooperative Association, founded in 1903, and followed over the next twenty years by a variety of shop committees and employee representation plans. Not all of those plans were motivated by anti-union animus, but many were, particularly those adopted during and immediately after the first World War (Nelson 1982). Third, employers instituted a range of "unionesque" personnel policies, chiefly rules and procedures governing movement within the firm's internal labor market. These provided a measure of equity and security to the work force and were administered by the new personnel departments that companies had established during the war (Jacoby 1985). Finally, when these positive incentives failed to deter unionism, employers turned to more coercive policies (dismissals, blacklisting, and other threats) or to legalistic measures like court injunctions and lawsuits alleging restraint of trade.

The downswing of 1922–33 began with a shift to coercive policies in the form of an employers' open-shop offensive known as the American Plan (Wakstein 1964), which, along with a brief but sharp depression, depleted the ranks of organized labor. Yet as the threat of unionization receded, employers did not abandon the various employee incentives engendered in welfare programs, participation, and unionesque personnel policies. Instead, following the example set by pioneering firms like Dennison, they synthesized the most successful policies associated with the five norms into a nonunion model of industrial relations. This model received attention from the press, from foreign visitors, and from employer organizations like the Special Conference Committee and the American Management Association (Balderston 1935; Bernstein 1960).[5] But unlike in the preceding upswing, when personnel innovations did not depend in any obvious way on the nature of the firm or industry, such as its technical sophistication or profitability, the nonunion model now prevailed in the dynamic new industries that had high and stable profit levels—electrical machinery, scientific instruments, chemicals, public utilities—and was less common in the older or declining industries such as machinery, steel, textiles, and meatpacking (Jacoby 1985). Moreover, because the nation as a whole was more politically conservative during this period than in the earlier upswing, employers had an easier time obtaining public support for their anti-union position. For example, more labor injunctions were issued during the 1920s than during the previous two decades combined (Witte 1932).

Despite these prophylactic measures, the downswing period closed with a sudden reversal of labor's misfortunes. The next cycle, which lasted from 1934 to 1958, was a time of major growth for U.S. unions. They gained not only new members but also newfound public approval and political influence of an unprecedented degree. For these reasons, I refer to this cycle as "the great upswing." Indeed, the upswing was so strong that during the first decade of the succeeding downswing, which began in 1959, the labor movement was able to maintain much of its public standing and political power.

Too, although union density declined during the 1960s, it did so very gradually, due in part to the stimulative effects of the Viet Nam war. The war also helped to stave off economic stagnation until the early 1970s, when the contraction phase of the long-wave cycle began, with its attendant change in industrial structure (Killingsworth 1978). Thus, the 1960s were a pendent period that can be viewed either as the tail end of the great upswing or as the beginning of the downswing that we are still experiencing. In any event, to better understand the current downswing, the long-wave model of industrial relations suggests that one needs a clear picture of how employers addressed the critical problems that they faced during the preceding upswing. Thus, the remainder of this paper analyzes in detail the 1934–58 cycle (the "great upswing") and the emergence of a new nonunion model during that period.

A Closer Look at the "Great Upswing"

The onset of the great upswing came as a surprise to those managers who thought they had resolved the problem of union avoidance during the 1920s. Managers of newly unionized companies suffered an "unparalled loss of self-esteem and community standing" (Nelson 1986), while those in companies that had succeeded in staving off unionization struggled to find an effective formula for maintaining their nonunion status. A bellicose minority of the newly unionized firms intensified their application of the earlier nonunion model, hoping that it would shake loose what they mistakenly believed to be the tenuous hold that unionism had taken on their employees. These "belligerents," as Harris (1982) termed them, launched new employee representation plans or breathed new life into plans that had become dormant; they strengthened their personnel departments and added unionesque rules and internal labor market procedures; they devoted more resources to their quasi-pecuniary welfare programs; and, in particular, they tried to coerce their employees to stay out of unions through a range of what were now unlawful labor practices. Other firms—in fact, the vast majority—did many of these same things, although they eventually gave up on coercion in favor of building a *modus vivendi* with their new bargaining partners. Among these were companies like General Motors, General Electric, and U.S. Steel, whose managers accepted unionization as an inevitable, if unpleasant, new fact of life and strove to make the situation as much to their benefit as possible. It was these companies that received the most attention from academic observers, few of whom, however, realized the weakness of the companies' commitment to collective bargaining. Indeed, by the mid-1940s, managements in these companies had regained some of their self-confidence and began to take more aggressive steps to contain union inroads. Their effort to pass the Taft-Hartley bill was one manifestation of this turnabout; others were their gradual relocation of plants to southern states and their implementation of a new set of personnel policies intended to weaken the popularity of unionism. General Electric, for example, was commonly depicted as a firm that had accepted unionism, but in the early 1950s it began to move its plants south and adopted Boulwarism as an approach to undermining its existing unions (Northrup 1964). In designing that approach, GE managers, like those at other unionized firms, looked to the nonunion sector for inspiration as well as concrete ideas.

Avoiding unionization during those early years might be ascribed to luck: the result of a close vote against the union or of a company's location in areas or industries in which unions were weak. Oftentimes, however, more than luck was involved. I have been conducting historical case studies of three large companies that were (and are) largely or entirely nonunion: Eastman Kodak, Sears Roebuck, and Thompson Products (later TRW). My research shows that these companies shared a number of characteristics that helped them resist organization during the great upswing. First, their managements were deeply committed to avoiding outside unions; company unions might be tolerated or even encouraged, but any other kind of union was an anathema. Although this sentiment was widespread among American managers in general, what distinguished these companies from their competitors was their persistent willingness to devote sizable resources to union-avoidance efforts. Second, over the years the three companies retained strong personnel departments backed by the companies' top executives, who consistently paid close attention to corporate employee relations programs and, again, devoted resources to them. Both Sears and Kodak, for example, took special pains to maintain their personnel programs during the early 1930s, that is, when unionism was in decline and other firms at the time were cutting back in this area and weakening the authority of their personnel departments, actions that came to be resented by employees who felt that their employers had reneged on the implicit contract inherent in the nonunion model of the 1920s (Brody 1980). Finally, throughout the years of the great upswing, the companies were highly innovative and willing to experiment with new policies to preserve their nonunion status.

The three companies differed greatly in size, technology, and other key characteristics. The vast majority of Kodak's 30,000 employees (as of 1940) was employed in Rochester, New York, where the company manufactured cameras, photographic film, and related products. Whereas Kodak was a technology-based organization with some highly skilled employees, Sears was almost exclusively a retailer, with an enormous work force (over 100,000 in 1941) employed in stores and mail-order plants across the nation. Thompson Products, the smallest of the three companies (16,000 employees in 1946), manufactured automotive and aircraft parts, with the bulk of its largely blue-collar work force employed at several plants in the Cleveland area.[6]

It is instructive that despite these differences the three companies pursued very similar strategies for maintaining employee loyalty and deterring unions throughout the period in question. All were strongly paternalistic and encouraged their employees to think of themselves as "members of the family" (TRW Papers, box 39). This norm was pursued to the greatest extent by Eastman Kodak, which was an exemplar of the cradle-to-grave approach of corporate welfarism. Even before the great upswing, Kodak provided its "clan" (a company term) with a profit-sharing plan, retirement annuities, medical and dental programs, paid vacations, athletic facilities, free legal advice, emergency loans, and other benefits (Webber 1924; Folsom 1929). Not only were those programs continued during the 1930s, but they were expanded and made more generous at regular intervals. Kodak was among the rare companies in the United States to provide unemployment benefits during the depths of the Great Depression, and in later years its benefit levels were among the highest of any employer in the nation—union or nonunion (Plummer 1939; Paul 1984).

Another early leader in the corporate welfare movement was Sears. As at Kodak, the scope and generosity of its welfare programs made Sears a bellwether in this area both before and during the great upswing. Its lucrative profit-sharing plan, unlike those at most other firms, remained intact throughout the Great Depression (*Business Week* 1932; Emmet and Jeuck 1950). Top management believed that these benefits were "tangible evidence to the organization of management's concern for the welfare of its employees [and] effective as symbols chiefly because they are substantial, and because, as such, they demonstrate the sincerity and weightiness of management's concern." In particular, the profit-sharing plan was thought to symbolize to employees that "they and the company are one, that there is no important conflict of interest between those who own and those who work, that they are in effect 'working for themselves'" (Worthy 1949, 17).

Although Thompson Products offered its employees paid vacations and insurance programs, the company's relatively small size precluded the same elaborate system of welfare benefits as at Kodak and Sears. A pension plan, for example, had to wait until 1944. Nevertheless, the firm used its small size to great advantage; its top managers made regular appearances on the factory floor and expressed a personal interest in each employee. The company had a supervisor of employee services who visited the homes of sick employees and helped employees with various personal problems. In addition, Thompson sponsored an Old Guard Club, a recreational association with a dozen different sports leagues, a company orchestra, family nights and bingo games at the company's plants, boat rides, clambakes, and field days (TRW Papers, box 133; Seybold 1946).

Another strategy of all three firms was to provide the same range of employment policies and safeguards as could be found in unionized firms. They each set wages and fringe benefits at levels that equalled or bettered those obtained by comparable unionized workers. In addition, they matched union standards for labor allocation procedures. Hiring, promotions, and separations were carried out according to standard rules enforced by strong personnel departments that had the respect of the line organization.[7] A seeming deviation from union practice was the relatively lesser weight assigned to seniority as a promotion and layoff criterion. Yet the differences here were smaller than management pronouncements suggested. While the personnel manager at Thompson Products publicly attacked unions for "making merit count for nothing," his firm adhered strictly to seniority in making layoffs and, as in many unionized firms, allowed seniority to govern when worker ability was judged equal (Livingstone 1946, 14; TRW Papers, box 39).

Employment security, a subject of great importance to all American workers over those years, was given a high priority at each company. Sears and Kodak maintained open-door policies for handling employee complaints about discipline and dismissal, policies backed up with guarantees of fair treatment, or what Kodak called its "code of industrial relations" (Cochrane 1956). Kodak was among the nation's first companies to stabilize production and eliminate seasonal fluctuations in employment, while Sears became well-known for its innovative constant-income plan (Folsom 1939; Van Vlissengen 1939). Enhancing employment security at all three firms were promotion policies that consistently favored incumbent employees over outsiders. Moreover, lower- and higher-level managers were typically "home grown."

The three firms closely scrutinized developments in the union sector. During the 1940s and 1950s, the personnel manager at Thompson's largest plant regularly compiled reports on wage trends, seniority rules, and bargaining issues in the union sector; these were used as guidelines in setting the firm's own employment practices (TRW Papers, boxes 110,113). At Sears, the head of personnel administration, Clarence B. Caldwell, sent a memo to the company's president in which he argued that, in light of several organizing drives then under way at Sears stores, the company "should certainly continue to look at all policies with the question: are they likely to keep out the union?" (Caldwell 1952, 29). Some observers have interpreted those imitation or "threat effects" as an effort by nonunion managements to share in the productivity gains induced by the shock of unionization, but I have found little evidence to support that view. Instead, the close tracking and matching of union sector policies were in keeping with the firms' long-established method of ensuring that they remained unorganized. The continuing irony in that method, however, was that it best served the purpose of thwarting unionism by introducing the same reforms the unions were seeking at the time. Thus, although top executives at the three firms were not particularly enamored of the unions' rigid approach to job security and other matters, they were willing to meet the challenge more than halfway in order to preserve their nonunion status.

Providing mechanisms for employee participation was an area where the three companies diverged from one another. Sears, for example, set up an advisory council in 1939 to oversee its profit-sharing plan. Employee representatives from the various geographic and functional divisions of the company were elected each year to serve on the council, which made recommendations about running the plan. The representatives had little real power and the election rules were unilaterally promulgated by management. Yet the company gave a great deal of publicity to the council, claiming that it "symbolizes the democratic spirit of the organization" and was an example of "industrial democracy in action" (*Sears News-Graphic* 1956). In addition, in 1938 Sears launched what was known as the "Big Board," or the "Sears Forum," an annual meeting, usually held in Chicago, at which employees heard reports from management about the company's performance and its plans for the coming year. Employees were allowed to submit questions, and these sometimes were mildly critical or controversial.

But what made Sears unique in this area was its employee attitude testing program, initiated in 1939 (Jacoby 1986). One of the earliest and most sophisticated industrial applications of behavioral science to workplace problems, this program served as a model for many other companies. Although it had a research component that made important contributions to a number of academic disciplines, it was primarily developed as part of the company's ongoing effort to forestall unionization. To gauge employee morale, Sears regularly surveyed employees at various units, using both questionnaires and nondirective interviewing. The process allowed employees to speak their minds about their problems, while at the same time providing management with data that identified "potential trouble spots" that could lead employees to join unions. Indeed, recent research done by the company shows a high correlation between a unit's survey score and subsequent unionization attempts (Hamner and Smith 1978). The survey was a considerably more sophisticated strategy for avoiding unions than, say, a corporate welfare program, which did not require a high level of technical proficiency to administer. Reliable surveying depended crucially on specialized assistance from outside professionals familiar with the latest findings in the behavioral and social sciences. Among other things, this assistance—and the program's ties to avowedly neutral researchers and universities—conferred scientific legitimacy on the program.

Thompson Products adopted a different strategy for employee participation: company unionism. Although many of the employee representation plans started in the 1930s had proved to be Trojan horses for managements—because they were later captured by outside unions—a few companies were able to pilot their plans around those unions as well as the Wagner Act and the National Labor Relations Board (NLRB). Like DuPont and Weirton Steel, Thompson Products was one such company. All the available evidence suggests that Thompson's company unions were initiated and subtly controlled by management, particularly in their early years (Shore 1966). Nevertheless, despite repeated organizing drives at its Cleveland plants in the 1930s and 1940s, and again during the 1960s, Thompson's independent union proved resistant to challenge by popular outside unions such as the United Automobile Workers (UAW).

The key to management's success at Thompson was its ability to convince employees that their interests were better served by company unions than by "outside unions that preach hate [and are] not at all concerned with trying to build a better business so that there will be more to divide" (Livingstone 1946). To win the employees' hearts and minds, the company relied on an elaborate employee communications program. Thompson trained its foremen in human relations and industrial psychology, telling them that workers wanted a boss who was "easy to talk to," "appreciative," and "sympathetic." Foremen also received training in basic economics and related subjects so that the employees would "not be receptive to 'crack-pot' theories of economics, on which labor agitators thrive." "Drive home sound economic thought now," they were instructed, and "don't miss an opportunity to make friends with employees" (Livingstone 1946, 21; Baritz 1960, 189). To increase its presence on the shop floor, the company hired from its blue-collar ranks dozens of "personnel supervisors," who were to be always available to help workers with their personal problems and work-related grievances. Twice during a shift, the supervisors made a circuit of the employees in their assigned area, and occasionally they were joined by the president and other executives who strolled with them around the shop, stopping to talk to the workers (Livingstone 1942; TRW Papers, box 29). As the company acknowledged, one advantage of having these supervisors was that "their close contacts with employees [allowed them] to report on trends of thought developing in the organization," that is, on any proclivities toward outside unions that employees might be harboring (Seybold 1946, 80). Finally, the company held a series of lavish dinners at a local hotel each year so that workers had the opportunity to socialize with their supervisors and to hear speeches by the company's top officers.

During a union-organizing campaign, Thompson's communications program shifted into high gear. First, the company hastened to respond to union organizing and other threatening developments by printing brochures and leaflets that were handed out to employees or posted on bulletin boards around the plant. For example, when the company heard one Saturday that a recent election had been set aside by the NLRB, the news was immediately posted on all bulletin boards. On Monday, when union organizers were handing out flyers hailing the ruling, "the Thompson people shrugged it off as 'old stuff'" (*Factory Management & Maintenance* 1946, 109). Second, the company was exceedingly blunt and direct in responding to union publicity. It distributed a newsletter titled "Let's Have the Truth!" to all employees at work and occasionally also mailed it to their homes. The publication contained point-by-point rebuttals of union charges and claims, as well as choice invectives accusing UAW leaders of being communists, drunkards, criminals, and enemy aliens. Foremen were sent advance copies of these publications and were expected to discuss them in their work groups. Third, Thompson relied on a variety of media to get its point of view across, including pamphlets, booklets, flyers, letters, reports, and "captive audience" speeches by Frederick C. Crawford, the company president.

The NLRB censured Thompson Products on several occasions for having overstepped the boundaries of the Wagner Act, which forbade employers from taking an active role in union campaigns and elections. The board criticized the company for having "engaged in energetic election campaigning rather than in mere opinion expressing," and added that the company's communications "passed from the realm of the free competition of ideas envisaged by the First Amendment into that of coercion" (NLRB 1946). But instead of quietly complying with these orders, Thompson Products fought the NLRB at every opportunity. The free speech issue was a point of vulnerability for the board during the 1940s, and the company received sympathetic rulings from circuit courts that were critical of the board. Moreover, through his position as an officer of the National Association of Manufacturers (NAM), Crawford led a political attack on the Wagner Act that paved the way for the Taft-Hartley amendments of 1947. In 1943, when he was president of the NAM, Crawford had established an alliance between the NAM and the U.S. Chamber of Commerce that resulted in the development of an employers' legislative program for labor law reform. Among other things, the program sought a relaxation of the Wagner Act's restrictions on company conduct during union organizing campaigns. In 1946 and again in 1947, Ray Livingstone, Thompson's vice president for personnel management, appeared in Washington to testify in favor of this program, which ultimately was enacted as the Taft-Hartley amendments to the Wagner Act (Shore 1966; TRW Papers, boxes 28, 29).

Although some have characterized the NAM's attempt to amend the Wagner Act as the work of an unrepresentative group of conservative employers from small- and medium-sized companies like Thompson Products (for example, Cleveland 1948), in fact the effort had the backing of a cross-section of the nation's employers (Gable 1950; Harris 1982). Moreover, the companies that supported the NAM's lobbying efforts included several large, nonunion companies, notably Eastman Kodak and Sears Roebuck. T.J. Hargrave, president of Kodak, served on the NAM's industrial relations program committee, the body that fashioned the legislative and lobbying strategies (Gable 1950), while Sears made its influence felt through Clarence Caldwell's position as head of the employee relations committee of the American Retail Federation (Caldwell 1950). General Robert E. Wood, chairman of Sears, was a key supporter of several conservative organizations concerned with labor law reform, including the National Economic Council and American Action (which also tried to draft Senator Taft as the Republican candidate for president in 1948; see Wood 1948; Worthy 1984).

Rather than being a new development, this lobbying and legislative activity was in keeping with earlier attempts by nonunion employers to use the political system as a method for deterring unionism. Previously, however, those efforts had been focused on the courts; now, because of the Wagner Act and the greater lobbying and electoral activity of the unions themselves (for example, the CIO's political action committees), employers redirected their activity toward seating favorable legislators sympathetic to their cause and toward securing legislation like the Taft-Hartley Act. Since the passage of the act, there has been substantial disagreement over the advantages conferred upon management by the act's right-to-work provisions (Ellwood and Fine 1983; Farber 1985); but there is little doubt that the act's free speech and unit determination amendments have significantly weakened union organizing power and encouraged a more aggressive employer posture along the lines that Thompson Products charted during the 1930s and 1940s (Dickens 1983; Shister 1958; Klein and Wanger 1985).

Finally, when positive inducements did not deter their employees from seeking to organize unions, the three companies were still willing to resort to illegal forms of coercion. A prime example of this was Sears and its labor relations manager Nathan Shefferman.[8] The Shefferman story is fascinating in and of itself, but its historical significance derives from Shefferman's having been a harbinger of today's "management consultants"—hired hands who aid companies in defeating union-organizing drives. Although his early activities at Sears are not well documented, the McClellan committee hearings in the U.S. Senate and other sources provide a glimpse at the soon-to-become-ubiquitous techniques Shefferman used in the late 1940s and 1950s to defeat union-organizing campaigns at Sears (NLRB 1954; Shefferman 1961; U.S. Congress 1957). These included creating "vote-no committees," made up of loyal employees who received coaching and funds from Shefferman; surveying employee attitudes in the midst of a campaign, in part to identify pro-union workers, who were subsequently transferred to other stores; establishing "rotating committees" to elicit employee complaints; and bringing in the Teamsters union to mount diversionary campaigns. (Shefferman had cultivated a friendship with Dave Beck, the Teamsters' president, for whom he made numerous purchases at discount from Sears.)

Although Sears later repudiated Shefferman and his tactics, the fact that the company employed him for over twenty years suggests that top executives believed his services were quite valuable indeed. The irony in all this is that Sears was the sort of organization one would least expect to need the likes of Shefferman; it treated its employees well, put a high value on sound personnel management, and kept itself attuned to employee grievances (Bell 1958). The explanation for the company's actions lies in its single-minded antipathy to unions. Remaining unorganized, whatever the cost, was an article of faith among managers at Sears, from General Wood on down, and much the same could be said about managers at Kodak and Thompson Products. Although their opposition to unions had an economic basis and was couched in those terms, it was ultimately driven by deeper and less calculated motives.

A New Nonunion Model

Each of the three companies developed its own solution to the problems posed by the surge of unionism during the great upswing. Of the three, Sears came closest to synthesizing the most successful elements into a coherent ensemble, although it lacked Kodak's communitarian approach to employee welfare and Thompson's extensive communications network. Of course, during the 1940s and 1950s there were several other influential and innovative nonunion companies—including DuPont, Eli Lilly, IBM, and Northrop—that pursued policies similar to those at Kodak, Sears, and Thompson. The activities of all these firms became known to the wider management community through articles in the business press and through the information network provided by organizations like the NAM, the Conference Board, and the American Management Association. Smaller companies and even some unionized firms experimented with the various programs and policies initiated by the nonunion pioneers, adopting some and rejecting others (for example, company unionism). As a result, by the 1960s—when a new downswing was underway—there gradually emerged out of the experiences of these companies a new nonunion model that was a blend of the most successful union-avoidance strategies that had been devised during the preceding upswing.

The model's basic feature was an organizational commitment to a strong personnel department, one that influenced important corporate decisions and that received considerable resources and support from top management. Other features included a panoply of employee welfare programs associated with sophisticated (often pecuniary) paternalism; various unionesque personnel policies and procedures, with an emphasis on employment security; extensive reliance on employee communications techniques developed by a new cadre of behavioral scientists; political activities to secure favorable labor laws; and, when all else failed, quasi-legal or illegal forms of employee coercion. Some of these features were carried over from the earlier nonunion models; others were first developed during the great upswing. But all of them were consistent with the norms of the twentieth-century American approach to keeping unions out.

As in previous downswings, many of the firms that in recent years have been touted as exemplars of the "new" nonunion approach are not true pioneers, but instead tend to be companies located in dynamic, profitable industries in the service and high technology sectors. Thus, neither Sears nor Kodak is currently seen as a leader. The exception here is Thompson Products: since its merger with Ramo-Wooldridge in 1958 and its transformation into TRW, the company has come to be viewed as a prime example of the new nonunion model (see, for example, Kochan and Verma 1985), although TRW's current reputation is largely the result of changes in its practices since its merger.

Whether today's crop of model nonunion firms will manage to stay unorganized during a future upswing—should that ever occur—will strongly depend on the resources they devote to their existing personnel programs. Clearly, the present economic climate and the receding threat posed by unions have eased the pressures to maintain these programs and to adopt new ones. But nevertheless, continued diffusion and innovation depend not only on the actual likelihood of unionization but also on how firms perceive the cost of unionization. Most managers in the United States continue to view those costs as high, in part because of the signficiant union-nonunion compensation differential that still exists, and in part because of the persistence of a set of values—with deep historical roots—that gives great weight to union avoidance. In the remainder of this paper, I will briefly examine the origins of those values in a comparative perspective.

Postscript: American Exceptionalism

It is a well-known fact that unionization rates in the United States are lower than those in other advanced industrial nations. Explanations for this exceptionalism typically adduce a variety of factors that may account for the American worker's relatively weak interest in unionism: the absence of feudalism in the United States, early mass enfranchisement, working-class heterogeneity and resultant cleavages among workers, fluid class boundaries, high rates of social mobility, the frontier pressure valve, and the dominant value system that stresses individualism and personal achievement (Perlman 1928; Commons 1932; Hartz 1955; Laslett and Lipset 1974; Davis 1986). Ever since Sombart's 1906 essay, "Why Is There No Socialism in the United States?" these factors have also been used to explain another kind of exceptionalism—the failure of radical or socialist ideologies to sink deep roots in the American working class and produce left-wing political parties linked to organized labor.

A problem with much of this literature is that it gives too much emphasis to the labor side of the picture. As this paper has attempted to show, employer activities are an important determinant of the relatively low unionization rates found in the United States. In fact, the term exceptionalism could just as easily be applied to American employers as to American labor; their hostility toward unions has always been more extreme than that of employers in other nations. Fifty years ago Lewis Lorwin, a noted labor economist, wrote that "employers in no other country . . . have so persistently, so vigorously, at such costs, and with such conviction of serving a cause opposed and fought trade unions as the American employing class" (Lorwin 1933, 355). Lest it be thought that things have changed since then, bear in mind that Hugh Clegg, a careful student of comparative industrial relations, recently concluded that "employer hostility to trade unionism in the United States is more vocal and virulent than in Europe" (1976, 22). Given this hostility, it is hardly surprising that the United States has experienced more frequent and more bloody labor violence than any other industrial nation (Taft and Ross 1969; Gitelman 1973). Although it is certainly the case that employers in other nations would, other things being equal, prefer to do without collective bargaining, they have been prodded by a variety of social, economic, and political influences toward a grudging or calculated acceptance of unionism, something that has never happened in the United States. Thus, the point is not that American employers are innately more hostile to unions than other employers, but rather that they have been less constrained in expressing their hostility.

Why is this? A place to start is with the existence of feudal traditions and the relatively slow growth of industrial capitalism in continental Europe, factors that also figure in explanations of labor exceptionalism (Hartz 1955). One legacy of European feudalism was the existence of strong governments prior to the emergence of industrial capitalism. As for slow growth, although European employers were far from powerless, they had to contend for political power with various groups opposed to industrial development and threatened by the emergence of economic concentration, including small merchants, farmers, and, in some cases, a landed gentry. Because of the countervailing political power exercised by nonbusiness groups, European employers were unable to take control of the state apparatus that could have been used to eliminate trade union opposition. As a result, in nations like France and Sweden, unions were able to form political alliances and achieve political influence that resulted in state power being used to compel employers to eschew violence and recognize unions. In France, for example, despite strong employer opposition to unions, the government on numerous occasions forced French employers to recognize them. In Sweden, the government encouraged employers to avoid violence and to negotiate with the unions during the critical labor confrontation of 1905 (Friedman 1985; Schiller 1975; Shalev and Korpi 1980).

Another legacy of feudalism was the support given by the European working classes to socialist political causes. In the literature on labor exceptionalism, it is assumed that the same factors that prompted European workers to vote for the left also drew them into unions, and that political and industrial mobilization were mutually reinforcing. But that explanation omits any mention of the role played by employers, and so fails to tell us why employers in Europe were relatively tolerant of organized labor. After all, without that tolerance unions undoubtedly would have been much weaker. A more subtle explanation along these lines has been provided by Ulman (1985), who stresses the relationship between working-class radicalism and employer attitudes. In Germany, the Netherlands, and Scandinavia, employers were often willing to grant recognition to unions because they perceived the threat from the socialist left to be more serious than the threat posed by collective bargaining. Channeling working-class discontent into trade union activity was therefore viewed by employers as a way of displacing conflict to a more manageable and less threatening arena. It was thus that European employers came to a calculative acceptance of trade unionism.

The situation in the United States before passage of the Wagner act was in sharp contrast to the European case. Here, at least in the North, no segment of the political elite was opposed to the industrial form of capitalist development. Consequently, U.S. industrialists wielded a degree of political power that was unmatched by their European counterparts, and they were never compelled by the state (which was much weaker than in Europe) to recognize unions. In their fight against organized labor, employers could count on assistance from the courts, local police, state militias, and even federal troops.[9] Moreover, U.S. firms were often large, multi-unit operations with sizable financial resources. The combination of political and economic power made it exceedingly difficult for unions or radical groups like the Knights of Labor to win pitched battles against industrial managements. In fact, the American Federation of Labor (AFL) rejected the Knights' radical political aspirations in favor of collective bargaining partly because Samuel Gompers and other AFL leaders appreciated the futility of a political contest with U.S. capital. This strategic decision was one important reason why a mass working-class party never posed much of a threat in this country. As a result, employers did not have to make a Hobson's choice between socialism and collective bargaining, as did their European counterparts.

Another difference between Europe and the United States was the existence in this country of a dominant value system that emphasized individual achievement, success, and property rights. This, too, has been offered as an explanation for labor exceptionalism (Lipset 1961), but it is important to realize that these values also provided employers a way to justify their resistance to unions in terms that were shared by merchants, farmers, and other groups which, in the European case, would have been reluctant to support employer attacks on organized labor (Edwards 1981). This made it easier for employers to sway the judiciary and to rationalize the use of state power against unions. Even in Canada, which in most other respects closely resembled the economic and social characteristics of the United States, the existence of a different set of national values—one that placed less emphasis on individualism—created a legal environment more hospitable to unions and a managerial stance less antagonistic toward them (Hofstede 1984; Lipset 1986).

But what about Great Britain, a country also similar in many respects to the United States? Here, at least in the late eighteenth and early nineteenth centuries, employers were often hostile to unions, pushing for the Combination Acts in the 1790s and engaging in lockouts such as those that were prevalent in the 1850s. Yet by the beginning of the present century, British employers had become tolerant of unions to a much greater extent than their U.S. counterparts. In the steel industry, for example, at the same time as Andrew Carnegie was hiring Pinkertons to drive the steelworkers' union out of Homestead, British employers were establishing several conciliation and arbitration mechanisms to deal peaceably with their unions (Holt 1977). As always, Great Britain is a special case because of the relatively early date in world history that industrialization and unions had emerged on the scene. By the end of the nineteenth century, when mass production industries began to sprout up around the world, British unions had already fought and won key battles with

British employers. Because unions were firmly entrenched in the working classes, British employers in the new mass production industries were forced to accommodate to them. At the same time, however, U.S. steelmakers and other industrialists could look over at their British counterparts and vow never to allow the same thing to occur here.

From an employer's perspective, if Britain was a case of first-mover disadvantages, Japan served as an example of the virtues of being last. In a celebrated essay on late development, Ronald Dore (1973) argued that because Japan was a latecomer on the world industrial scene, its employers could see the handwriting on the wall: they knew that unionism was inevitable in Japan, and so, beginning in the 1910s, they took steps to ensure that unions would develop in a fashion that employers could live with. Japanese employers introduced a permanent employment system and other personnel innovations intended to ensure that workers would develop a high degree of loyalty to and identification with the individual enterprise. During the interwar period, they encouraged the development of enterprise unions as the preferred substitute for more independent and adversarial forms of unionism; and during the postwar years they succeeded in defusing a movement toward militant unionism (Shirai 1983; Moore 1983). Because Japanese employers were largely successful in preventing the emergence of adversarialism as practiced in the United States, they were much more willing to recognize and support unions than were their U.S. counterparts.

These factors help to explain the origins of employer exceptionalism in the United States. But why did hostility to unions continue after passage of the Wagner Act, which compelled employer recognition of unions if a majority of the employees desired collective bargaining? First, there was the persistence among U.S. employers of anti-union values, which had become part of managerial culture and tradition in the United States. Second, a radical alternative to collective bargaining never again received mass support after the defeat of the Knights of Labor, thus removing the Hobson's choice faced by European employers. Third, low union densities in the United States in themselves helped to perpetuate employer hostility: few industries were completely organized, and so nonunion firms had an additional incentive to remain unorganized to preserve their relative labor cost advantage. The Wagner Act, because it encouraged single-firm rather than multiemployer bargaining, reinforced this logic by making it difficult for unions to establish industrywide bargaining. In Europe, however, those issues were moot because of the existence of either de facto industrywide bargaining or de jure wage standardization, the latter resulting from laws requiring contract extension. Although partial organization reduced the *organizing* power of U.S. unions, some scholars have argued that, paradoxically, it raised their *bargaining* power by allowing strikes to pose a greater threat to a firm's market share (Ulman 1985). This point is arguable, however, since unionized employers easily can and do relocate their operations to the nonunion hinterland. In any event, the fact that the union sector has been plagued by mutual threats—of market-share loss and of relocation—has done little to promote either cooperative labor relations or employer friendliness toward unions.

Considerable research remains to be done on the topics discussed here. U.S. industrial relations are now in a state of flux and the shape of the future is extremely difficult to discern. It is my belief that historical and comparative research, although not the most popular or well-funded methodologies of modern social science, nevertheless can help us to better understand our present situation. In particular, comparative research on managerial strategies in industrial relations, which once was a thriving endeavor (for example, Bendix 1956; Kerr et al. 1960), should be revived and closely examined to develop richer and more plausible explanations of recent employer activities in the United States as they differ from those in other countries. Comparative analysis, like historical research, can also be used to examine the interplay between universal, "rational" factors (such as economic behavior) and the historically and nationally specific institutions that shape employer actions. Historical research is especially helpful in understanding how change comes about in labor-management relations and in analyzing the long-run dynamics of an industrial relations system, as I have attempted to do in this paper. Admittedly, I have painted a picture of American industrial relations using a very broad brush, but that is because I have sought to highlight central tendencies and long-term trends rather than the range of employer responses to unionism or the short-run movements contained within a long wave. Finally, note that although a common fallacy of historical analysis is the presumption of continuity, the record of labor-management relations in the United States affirms the adage that "history never repeats itself, but sometimes it rhymes."

Notes

1. It would be illuminating to carry the analysis back before 1897, but poor and confusing data on those years make that task a difficult one. Between 1891 and 1896, total AFL membership held steady at about 250,000. Data on the years before 1891 pose the conceptual problem of how to count members of the Knights of Labor, which, although it had 700,000 members at its peak, included farmers and other independently employed persons (Wolman 1924, 32).

2. There is little doubt that the post-1970 widening of the union/nonunion wage differential created an incentive for the adoption of more intensive union avoidance strategies by partially unionized and nonunion firms. But it is important to keep in mind that other factors mattered too, such as long-wave increases in labor market slack and in political conservatism, both of which affected the feasibility of union avoidance, as did the emergence of a new nonunion model of industrial relations. Finally, note that wage dispersion would have been less of a problem for unionized employers in the 1980s had the preceding two decades not seen the emergence of a sizeable non-union sector in most industries. In light of all this, a plausible counterfactual hypothesis is that union avoidance by unionized firms would have increased in the late 1970s and early 1980s even if there had been no change in union/nonunion wage dispersion.

3. This terminology is a bit confusing, since membership in a union is usually viewed as a form of voice that is an alternative to exit from the firm (Freeman and Medoff 1984). Here, however, unions and firms are seen as organizations that compete for worker loyalties, although it is possible—as research in the early 1950s showed—for a worker to have dual loyalties (Stagner 1954).

4. Although some companies had instituted welfare programs like company towns (for example, the Pullman Palace Car Company at Pullman, Illinois) and profit sharing (for example, the Procter & Gamble plan) before 1897, these were isolated and sporadic efforts.

5. The winnowing process by which employers shed the less successful aspects of each norm was most obvious in the case of welfare programs. Once many employees had expressed resentment over employer paternalism, firms shifted their resources away from highly paternalistic "uplift" activities like Bible classes and home visiting toward quasi-pecuniary programs such as profit sharing, stock ownership, group insurance, pensions, and paid vacations.

6. Of the three companies, Kodak was the least unionized: none of its facilities was organized during the entire great upswing period. Sears bargained with unions at a few of its stores on the Pacific coast, and some of its drivers and warehouse employees were organized. But unionized employees accounted for fewer than 5 percent of total company employment in

1950, far less than the industry average (Jacoby 1986). With the exception of one Detroit plant organized by the UAW in 1942, all of Thompson's plants were represented by independent or company unions.

7. Although Sears was more decentralized and allowed its local managers greater discretion than either Kodak or Thompson, basic personnel policies at Sears were set by the parent organization. Local personnel managers rarely deviated from those policies, in part because the parent organization controlled managerial promotions (Caldwell 1940).

8. Shefferman was labor relations manager for Sears from 1935 to 1948. In 1948 his position was eliminated, but he continued to work with Sears on retainer until his activities were exposed by the McClellan Committee in 1957.

9. Said Lorwin (1933, 355), "In no other Western country have employers been so much aided in their opposition to unions by the civil authorities, the armed forces of the government, and the courts."

References

Balderston, C. Canby. 1935. *Executive Guidance of Industrial Relations.* Philadelphia: University of Pennsylvania Press.

Baritz, Loren. 1960. *Servants of Power: The Use of Social Science in Industrial Relations.* Middletown, Connecticut: Wesleyan University Press.

Barkin, Solomon. 1950. "A Trade Unionist Appraises Management Personnel Philosophy," *Harvard Business Review* 28 (September), 59–64.

Bell, Daniel. 1958. "Nate Shefferman, Union Buster," *Fortune* 57 (February), 120–121*ff.*

Bendix, Reinhard. 1956. *Work and Authority in Industry.* New York: Wiley.

Bernstein, Irving. 1960. *The Lean Years: A History of the American Worker, 1920–1933.* Boston: Houghton-Mifflin.

Berthoff, Rowland. 1964. "The 'Freedom to Control' in American Business History," in David Pinkney and Theodore Ropp, eds., *A Festschrift for Frederick B. Artz.* Durham: Duke University Press, 112–156.

Brandes, Stuart D. 1976. *American Welfare Capitalism, 1880–1940.* Chicago: University of Chicago Press.

Brody, David. 1980. "The Rise and Decline of Welfare Capitalism," in David Brody, ed., *Workers in Industrial America.* New York: Oxford University Press, 48–81.

Brown, Douglass V., and Myers, Charles A. 1957. "The Changing Industrial Relations Philosophy of American Management," *Proceedings of the Ninth Annual Meeting of the Industrial Relations Research Association*, 84–99.

Business Week. 1932. "Sears Roebuck Profit-Sharing Meets the Test of Depression," March 23, 14.

Caldwell, Clarence B. 1940. "Formulation and Measurement of Personnel Policies." Address delivered to the Second Annual Personnel Conference of the Pacific Northwest Personnel Association, Portland, October 10.

Caldwell, Clarence B. 1950. *Report of the Committee on Employment Relations.* Washington, D.C.: American Retail Federation.

Caldwell, Clarence B. 1952. Memorandum to F.B. McConnell, February 26. Evanston, Illinois: Worthy Papers.

Clegg, Hugh A. 1976. *Trade Unionism Under Collective Bargaining.* Oxford: Basil Blackwell.

Cleveland, Alfred S. 1948. "NAM: Spokesman for Industry?" *Harvard Business Review,* 26 (May), 353–371.

Cochrane, Craig P. 1956. "Kodak's 'Open Door' Policy," pamphlet, Kodak file. Ithaca, N.Y.: Cornell University Labor-Management Documentation Center.

Commons, John R. 1932. "Labor Movements," in Edwin Seligman, ed., *Encyclopaedia of the Social Sciences,* vol. 8. New York: Macmillan, 682–696.

Davis, Mike. 1986. *Prisoners of the American Dream.* London: Verso.

Dickens, William. 1983. "The Effect of Company Campaigns on Certification Elections," *Industrial and Labor Relations Review* 36 (July), 360–375.

Dore, Ronald. 1973. *British Factory—Japanese Factory: The Origins of National Diversity in Industrial Relations.* Berkeley: University of California Press.

Dubofsky, Melvyn. 1985. "Industrial Relations: Comparing the 1980s with the 1920s," *Proceedings of the Thirty-Eighth Annual Meeting of the Industrial Relations Research Association,* 227–236.

Easterlin, Richard A. 1968. *Population, Labor Force and Long Swings in Economic Growth: The American Experience.* New York: Columbia University Press.

Edwards, P.K. 1981. *Strikes in the United States, 1881–1984.* Oxford: Basil Blackwell.

Ellwood, David, and Fine, Glenn. 1983. "Effects of Right-to-Work Laws on Union Organizing." Cambridge, Massachusetts: NBER Working Paper No. 116.

Emmet, Boris, and Jeuck, John E. 1950. *Catalogues and Counters: A History of Sears Roebuck and Company.* Chicago: University of Chicago Press.

Factory Management and Maintenance. 1946. "Two-Way Information Flow Pays Off," 104 (May), 108–112.

Farber, Henry S. 1985. "The Extent of Unionization in the United States," in Thomas A. Kochan, ed., *Challenges and Choices Facing American Labor.* Cambridge, Massachusetts: MIT Press, 15–43.

Fenwick, Rudy, and Olson, Jon. 1986. "Support for Worker Participation: Attitudes Among Union and Nonunion Workers," *American Sociological Review* 51 (August), 505–522.

Fiorito, Jack, and Greer, Charles R. 1982. "Determinants of U.S. Unionism: Past Research and Future Needs," *Industrial Relations* 21 (Winter), 1–32.

Folsom, Marion B. 1929. "Kodak Retirement Annuity, Life Insurance, and Disability Benefit Plan." New York: American Management Association General Management Series No. 108.

Folsom, Marion B. 1939. "Stabilization of Employment and Income," *Management Record* 1 (February), 17–24.

Fones-Wolf, Elizabeth. 1986. "Industrial Recreation, the Second World War, and the Revival of Welfare Capitalism," *Business History Review* 60 (Summer), 232–257.

Foulkes, Fred K. 1980. *Personnel Policies in Large Nonunion Companies.* Englewood Cliffs: Prentice-Hall.

Fox, Alan. 1974. *Beyond Contract: Work, Power, and Trust Relations,* London: Faber.

Freeman, Richard, and Medoff, James. 1984. *What Do Unions Do?* New York: Basic Books.

Friedman, Gerald C. 1985. "Politics and Unions: Government, Ideology, and the Labor Movement in the United States and France, 1880–1914." Doctoral dissertation, Harvard University.

Gable, Richard W. 1950. "A Political Analysis of an Employers' Association: The National Association of Manufacturers." Doctoral dissertation, University of Chicago.

Gitelman, H.M. 1973. "Perspectives on American Industrial Violence," *Business History Review* 47 (Spring), 1–23.

Golden, Clinton S., and Parker, Virginia D., eds. 1955. *Causes of Industrial Peace Under Collective Bargaining.* New York: Harper.

Gordon, David M., Edwards, Richard C., and Reich, Michael. 1982. *Segmented Work, Divided Workers.* Cambridge, England: Cambridge University Press.

Hamner, W. Clay, and Smith, Frank J. 1978. "Work Attitudes as Predictors of Unionization Activity," *Journal of Applied Psychology,* 63 (1978), 415–421.

Harris, Howell John. 1982. *The Right to Manage: Industrial Relations Policies of American Business in the 1940s.* Madison: University of Wisconsin Press.

Hartz, Louis. 1955. *The Liberal Tradition in America.* New York: Harcourt.

Hirschman, Albert O. 1970. *Exit, Voice, and Loyalty.* Cambridge, Massachusetts: Harvard University Press.

Hofstede, Geert. 1984. *Culture's Consequences: International Differences in Work-Related Values.* Beverly Hills: Sage Press.

Holloway, William, and Leech, Michael J. 1985. *Employment Termination: Rights and Remedies.* Washington: BNA Press.

Holt, James. 1977. "Trade Unionism in the British and U.S. Steel Industries, 1880–1914," *Labor History* 18 (Winter), 5–35.

Jacoby, Sanford M. 1983. "Union-Management Cooperation in the United States: Lessons from the 1920s," *Industrial and Labor Relations Review* 37 (October), 18–33.

Jacoby, Sanford M. 1985. *Employing Bureaucracy: Managers, Unions, and the Transformation of Work in American Industry, 1900–1945.* New York: Columbia University Press.

Jacoby, Sanford M. 1986. "Employee Attitude Testing at Sears Roebuck and Company, 1938–1960," *Business History Review* 60 (Winter), 602–632.

Kerr, Clark, Dunlop, John T., Harbison, Frederick, and Myers, Charles A. 1960. *Industrialism and Industrial Man: The Problems of Labor and Management in Economic Growth.* Cambridge, Massachusetts: Harvard University Press.

Killingsworth, Charles. 1978. "The Fall and Rise of the Idea of Structural Unemployment," *Proceedings of the Thirty-First Annual Meeting of the Industrial Relations Research Association,* 1–13.

Klein, Janice, and Wanger, E. David. 1985. "The Legal Setting for the Emergence of the Union Avoidance Strategy," in Thomas Kochan, ed., *Challenges and Choices Facing American Labor.* Cambridge, Massachusetts: MIT Press, 75–88.

Kochan, Thomas A., and Verma, Anil. 1985. "The Growth and Nature of the Nonunion Sector Within a Firm," in Thomas Kochan, ed., *Challenges and Choices Facing American Labor.* Cambridge, Massachusetts: MIT Press, 89–118.

Kochan, Thomas A., Katz, Harry, and McKersie, Robert B. 1986. *The Transformation of American Industrial Relations.* New York: Basic Books.

Laslett, John H.M., and Lipset, Seymour Martin, eds. 1974. *Failure of a Dream? Essays in the History of American Socialism.* Garden City: Doubleday.

Lipset, Seymour Martin. 1961. "Trade Unions and Social Structure," *Industrial Relations* 1 (October), 75–89.

Lipset, Seymour Martin. 1986. "North American Labor Movements: A Comparative Perspective," in Seymour Martin Lipset, ed., *Unions in Transition: Entering the Second Century.* San Francisco: Institute for Contemporary Studies, 287–322.

Livingstone, Raymond S. 1946. "Can There Be Peace with Unionism?," pamphlet. Cleveland: Thompson Products Company.

Livingstone, Raymond S. 1942. "Settling Disputes Without Interrupting Production," *Management Record* 4 (December), 385–391.

Lorwin, Lewis. 1933. *The American Federation of Labor.* Washington: Brookings Institution.

Moore, Joe. 1983. *Japanese Workers and the Struggle for Power, 1945–1947.* Madison: University of Wisconsin Press.

National Labor Relations Board, Eighth Region. 1946. "Report on Objections," Case No. 8-R-1989, Thompson Products Company, June 3.

National Labor Relations Board, First Region. 1954. "Trial Examiners Report," Case No. 1-CA-1402, Sears Roebuck and Company, January 27.

Nelson, Daniel. 1982. "The Company Union Movement, 1900–1937: A Reexamination," *Business History Review* 56 (Autumn), 335–357.

Nelson, Daniel. 1986. "A History of the Rubber Workers." Akron, Ohio: University of Akron Department of History Working Paper.

Northrup, Herbert. 1964. *Boulwarism.* Ann Arbor: University of Michigan Press.

Paul, Karen. 1984. "Fading Images at Eastman Kodak," *Business and Society Review* 48 (Winter), 54—59.

Pencavel, John H. 1971. "The Demand for Union Services: An Exercise," *Industrial and Labor Relations Review* 24 (January), 180–190.

Perlman, Selig. 1928. *A Theory of the Labor Movement.* New York: Macmillan.

Plummer, Leigh S. 1939. *Getting Along with Labor: Practical Personnel Programs.* New York: Harper.

Rosenberg, Nathan, and Frischtak, Claudio. 1984. "Technological Innovation and Long Waves," *Cambridge Journal of Economics* 8 (March), 7–24.

Schiller, Berndt. 1975. "Years of Crisis, 1906–1914," in Steven Koblik, ed., *Sweden's Development from Poverty to Affluence, 1750–1970.* Minneapolis: University of Minnesota Press.

Schumpeter, Joseph A. 1939. *Business Cycles,* vols. 1 and 2. New York: McGraw-Hill.

Sears News-Graphic. 1956. "The Sears Forum," April 12, 12–13.

Seybold, Geneva. 1946. "Organization of Personnel Administration." New York: National Industrial Conference Board Studies in Personnel Policy No. 73.

Shefferman, Nathan W. 1961. *The Man in the Middle.* Garden City: Doubleday.

Shalev, Michael, and Korpi, Walter. 1980. "Working Class Mobilization and American Exceptionalism," *Economic and Industrial Democracy* 1 (February), 31–61.

Shirai, Taishiro. 1983. "A Theory of Enterprise Unionism," in Taishiro Shirai, ed., *Contemporary Industrial Relations in Japan*. Madison: University of Wisconsin Press.

Shister, Joseph. 1958. "The Impact of the Taft-Hartley Act on Union Strength and Collective Bargaining," *Industrial and Labor Relations Review* 11 (April), 339–351.

Shore, Harvey. 1966. "A Historical Analysis of Thompson Products' Successful Program to Discourage Employee Acceptance of Outside Unions, 1934–1947." Doctoral dissertation, Harvard University.

Sombart, Werner. 1906. *Why Is There No Socialism in the United States?* White Plains: International Arts and Sciences Press (1976 reprint).

Stagner, Ross. 1954. "Dual Allegiance to Union and Management: A Symposium," *Personnel Psychology* 7 (Spring), 41–80.

Stepina, Lee P., and Fiorito, Jack. 1986. "Toward a Comprehensive Theory of Union Growth and Decline," *Industrial Relations* 3 (Fall), 248–264.

Stinchcombe, Arthur L. 1965. "Social Structure and Organizations," in James G. March, ed., *Handbook of Organizations*. Chicago: Rand-McNally.

Stone, Katherine, 1981. "The Postwar Paradigm in American Labor Law," *Yale Law Journal* 90 (June), 1509–1580.

Taft, Philip, and Ross, Philip. 1969. "American Labor Violence: Its Causes, Character, and Outcomes," in H.D. Graham and Ted Robert Gurr, eds., *Violence in America: Historical and Comparative Perspectives*, vol 1. Washington, D.C.: U.S. Government Printing Office, 221–301.

TRW Papers. Western Reserve Historical Society, Cleveland.

Ulman, Lloyd. 1958. "The Union and Wages in Basic Steel," *American Economic Review* 48 (June), 408–475.

Ulman, Lloyd. 1985. "Some International Crosscurrents in Labor Relations," in Eric Flamholtz, ed., *The Future Directions of Employee Relations*. Los Angeles: UCLA Institute of Industrial Relations, 42–110.

U.S. Congress. 1957. *Hearings Before the Senate Select Committee on Improper Activities in the Labor or Management Field,* part 14. Washington, D.C.

Van Duijn, Jacob J. 1983. *The Long Wave in Economic Life*. London: George Allen and Unwin.

Van Vlissengen, Arthur. 1939. "Fifty-Two Paychecks a Year," *Factory Management and Maintenance* 97 (January), 56–57.

Verma, Anil. 1983. "Union and Nonunion Industrial Relations Systems at the Plant Level." Doctoral dissertation, MIT.

Wakstein, Allen M. 1964. "The Origins of the Open-Shop Movement, 1919–1920," *Journal of American History* 51 (December), 460–475.

Webber, John E. 1924. "Making Kodaks and Contentment," *American Industries* 25 (November), 27–30.

Witte, Edwin E. 1932. *The Government in Labor Disputes.* New York: McGraw-Hill.

Wolman, Leo. 1924. *The Growth of American Trade Unions, 1880–1923.* New York: National Bureau of Economic Research.

Wood, Robert E. 1948. Letter to Lamar Fleming, Jr., June 17. West Branch, Iowa: Hoover Presidential Library, Robert E. Wood Papers.

Worthy, James C. 1949. "Factors Contributing to High Morale Among Sears Employees," unpublished report. Chicago: Sears Archives.

Worthy, James C. 1984. *Shaping an American Institution: Robert E. Wood and Sears Roebuck.* Urbana: University of Illinois Press.

Discussion

James Medoff (Harvard) commented that employers can affect the probability that their work forces will become unionized both directly through their choice of plant-level policies and indirectly through their influence on labor law and its administration, and their influence on public opinion. He was disappointed that the paper neglected the role of public opinion, since he believes that the deteriorating public image of unions has contributed to the decline in the percentage of the work force that is organized in the United States. Arguing that employers' plant-level policies are a key determinant of public attitudes toward unionism, Bennett Harrison (MIT) questioned the usefulness of attempting to disentangle their independent influences. Paul Osterman (MIT) noted that there is a serious simultaneity problem with interpreting data on public approval of unions and the percent of the work force that is organized. Medoff also would have liked a clearer assessment of the relative importance of sophisticated employer policies—the paternalism, participation, and union substitution activities identified by Jacoby—versus playing hardball—the use of force and legal action—in employers' anti-union strategies.

Harry Katz (Cornell) drew attention to the tension in the paper between what he termed the short-wave explanation and the historical explanation of the evolution of employers' anti-union strategies. Employers' practices toward unions might be different today than in the past because the economic environment they face is different;

alternatively, they might be different because employers have learned from previous experience. Medoff commented that union/nonunion wage differentials have been large in recent years; one would have expected this to strengthen employers' opposition to unionization. Robert McKersie (MIT) cited employer surveys showing that employers perceive productivity to be lower in union than in nonunion plants. This perception may have reinforced the effects of high union wages on employer antipathy toward unions.

Other participants directed their comments toward what lessons the historical experience contains for the future. Tom Kochan (MIT) suggested that researchers and trade unionists alike need to understand the advantages offered by nonunion operation. Peter Doeringer (Boston University) noted that unions historically have succeeded where management is less savvy and less worker-oriented. Given nonunion employers' growing sophistication with respect to their personnel practices, he expressed pessimism that traditional unions would enjoy any major resurgence in the years ahead. Rather, he expected unions to appeal to workers primarily in settings where employers have made mistakes or in settings, such as the building trades, where employers do not play an important role in structuring workers' careers. Doeringer went on to suggest that employers interested in keeping traditional unions out ought to be interested in company unions, since it is often easier to implement human resource policies when some type of labor organization is present.

3

The Effects of Worker Participation in Management, Profits, and Ownership of Assets on Enterprise Performance

Michael A. Conte and Jan Svejnar

In recent years, there has been increased interest on the part of managers, policy makers, and researchers in organizations that provide financial and decision-making participation to employees. This interest reflects a number of broader trends in the U.S. economy: changes in capital and labor markets, a newly emerging view on corporate ownership and governance, and federal and state tax incentives targeted to promote employee ownership.

Arguably the most significant recent trend in capital markets has been the replacement of equity ownership with debt. At least 5 percent of the outstanding value of corporate equity has disappeared each year since 1983 as a result of such transactions. Until 1988, employee stock ownership plans (ESOPs) neither affected nor were much affected by this trend; ESOPs were largely a phenomenon of closely held companies, and only about 16 percent of ESOPs formed prior to 1984 were financed by debt. Prior to 1987, public companies had borrowed less than $1 billion to finance their ESOPs. But this has changed radically in the two years since then. Total new ESOP debt was about $3 billion in 1988, and over $4 billion was borrowed by or for public company ESOPs in the first quarter of 1989 alone.[1]

The leveraged buyouts and going-private transactions accompanying these capital market changes have had an important effect on managerial compensation systems. In a study of all public company buyouts from 1979 through 1985 with a purchase price of at least $50

This is a revised version of a paper presented at a conference on "New Developments in Labor Markets and Human Resource Policies," Massachusetts Institute of Technology, June 11–12, 1987. The authors gratefully acknowledge the financial support of the U. S. Department of Labor (Grant No. 21-36-80-21) and the National Science Foundation (Grant No. SES 8420801), and wish to thank Robert E. Moore and Steven J. Arbour for valuable computational assistance.

million, Kaplan (1989) reports that the compensation of the typical business unit manager after a leveraged buyout is almost twenty times more sensitive to performance than that of the typical public company manager. While the transition from relatively risk-free forms of compensation to compensation systems that are tied to corporate performance is not as dramatic for nonmanagers, it does appear to be occurring. The prevalence of wage givebacks and stock-for-wages agreements earlier in the decade introduced an element of flexibility into nonmanagerial compensation. The trend is seen clearly in retirement benefits. Calculations by Kruse (1989) show that the percent of employees covered by defined benefit pension plans, in which the employer bears the risk of stock performance, fell from 34.5 percent in 1980 to 29.2 percent in 1986. Defined contribution plans (principally ESOPs, deferred profit sharing plans, and 401K plans), in which employees bear the risk of stock performance, have simultaneously grown in proportion. Based on an analysis of plan filings, Kruse found that deferred profit-sharing plans covered "12.8 percent of the private wage and salary workforce in 1980 and 17.9 percent in 1986," while ESOPs covered 6.3 percent in 1980 and 12.8 percent in 1986. Conte (1989) recently found that employees in public ESOP companies receive about 12 percent of compensation from participation in the plan, versus about 6 percent for employees in public profit-sharing companies and only about 3 percent for employees in public companies with defined benefit pension plans. Hence, the lifetime wealth of nonmanagers in public companies has become substantially more tied to the performance of their employer.

Meanwhile, the broad underpinnings of corporate ownership and governance are being challenged. According to Jensen (1989), "The publicly held corporation . . . has outlived its usefulness in many sectors of the economy and is being eclipsed." The game of trading stocks on open markets, which many would argue is a zero-sum game, is being replaced by the positive-sum game of holding them "patiently" in various types of trusts, including ESOPs. The argument for encouraging this transition via tax assistance relies strongly on the potential for improving the nature of the game and, as a result, realizing increases in real productivity.

Reflecting a willingness to gamble on these potential improvements, policy makers have provided considerable assistance to the formation of ESOPs and other forms of employee ownership. Between 1974 and 1986, sixteen federal laws providing or modifying tax incentives for ESOPs and for producer cooperatives were passed, and another federal law that established a cooperative bank was passed in 1980. Meanwhile, nineteen states have passed legislation to encourage employee ownership (Rosen and Whyte 1985).

In spite of these developments, there exists little published information on the ways that employee-owned and participatory firms are organized, let alone formal modeling of or empirical evidence on the most important relationships. In consequence, little is known about the effects of ownership, profit sharing, or increased participation in decision making on firm performance, or about whether the effects themselves vary according to the type and size of firm under consideration or the form of participation (financial versus decision making). Although many advocates stress the welfare aspects of worker participation in justifying supportive intervention, the question of how participation affects operational efficiency is clearly a crucial, and as yet unresolved, one.

In the following section, we present the main hypotheses about the productivity effects of financial and substantive participation that have been advanced and discuss their applicability. The limited writings to date do outline two distinct and competing hypotheses, one indicating that participative firms will be less technically efficient (i.e., less productive) than conventionally operated firms, and the other indicating that they will be more technically efficient. One of the main reasons for the lack of a unified theoretical development to date is the diversity of organizational forms in which workers may participate in capital ownership and decision making. We discuss these alternative organizational forms with special emphasis on the resulting difficulties in estimating productivity effects and drawing general conclusions. We have devoted a section to our approach to gathering a data set uniquely suited to analyzing the independent influences of employee participation in ownership, profits, and decision making within the firm, as well as the econometric framework we have used for deriving quantitative estimates of the magnitude of these influences. We have also presented the results from our ongoing research on these data and, together with some conclusions, have indicated our plans for future analyses.

Theoretical Approaches and Hypotheses

The existing theoretical work on the effects of worker participation is not based on rigorous economic theory; the general themes, however, are clear, and lead to testable hypotheses with important policy implications. The most highly formalized approach is that of Jensen and Meckling (1976, 1979), who see worker participation as always having deleterious effects on firm performance. Jensen and Meckling's analysis is based on the theory of contractual agency relationships. Their reasoning starts from the assumption that the set of contracts specifying the disposition of costs and rewards in large part determines the behavior of agents in the firm. It is then reasonable to specify formally the nature of these intra-firm contractual relations as an element in the production function:

This can be summarized more formally by representing the production function of the firm as $Q = F_\Theta (L,K,M,\phi,T)$, where Q is the quantity of output; L, K, and M are, respectively, the labor, capital, and material inputs; T is a vector describing the state of knowledge and physical technology relevant to production; ϕ is a generalized index describing the range of choice of "organizational forms," or internal rules of the game available to the firm given Θ; and Θ is a vector of parameters or characteristics describing the relevant aspects of the contracting and property rights system within which the firm exists.[2]

This observation would command little disagreement in the literature, as much of the work to date has in fact adopted a production function framework. The contribution of Jensen and Meckling's work lies in supplying a rationale for negative values of the coefficients on the worker participation variables in ϕ. They do so by analyzing the dual, or cost, function, and identifying three types of agency costs: monitoring expenditures by the principal(s); bonding expenditures by the agent(s); and a residual loss. According to the following arguments, each of these costs is increased by participative arrangements within the firm.

In a modern corporation, the objective of owners is taken to be wealth maximization, whereas the objective of managers is assumed to be their own utility maximization. The first implication of this division of ownership and control is that, in the absence of monitoring, managers will disregard the interests of the owners and utilize the firm's assets to further their own goals. In the extreme case, this involves driving the firm to bankruptcy. Hence monitoring, which is costly, is nonetheless necessary. Monitoring costs are assumed to increase with the number of agents, and this implies that a broad dispersion of decision-making rights is costly. Yet it is precisely this broad distribution of decision-making rights that defines the participatory firm (i.e., a firm in which workers participate in decision making).

The second argument is that participative firms will have higher bonding costs because they have more "managers." Bonding costs are essentially the costs of ensuring that managers will not engage in malfeasance or anti-contractual activities.

The first two arguments are, hence, arguments against worker participation in management. The third one militates against worker participation in profits and in ownership of assets. It asserts that the residual loss will be greater in participatory than in nonparticipatory firms. The argument is based on the premise that the greater the number of persons with contractual rights to share in residual gains, the smaller will be the incentive for each to undertake the effort and stress associated with reaping these gains and the worse the economic performance of the firm. On the basis of these three arguments, Jensen and Meckling conclude that the effect of participative arrangements on output will be unambiguously negative.

Adopting a remarkably similar framework, other authors, including Thomas and Logan (1982), Vanek (1970), Horvat (1982), and Cable and Fitzroy (1980a,1980b), demur from Jensen and Meckling's conclusions. Cable and Fitzroy (1980b) predict that employees in participatory firms will display "a positive collusion to maximize joint wealth," implying that the residual loss will actually be smaller in participative than in traditional firms due to a greater identification by members of the firm with commonly held goals. In part this argument rests upon extra-economic motivations, such as solidarity (emphasized in Vanek 1970), but part of it is strictly economic, as profit sharing and stock ownership bring the traditionally disparate goals of workers, managers, and capital owners closer together. This "alignment" of objectives is important because it decreases monitoring costs in the presence of asymmetric information (see, for example, Bradley and Gelb 1981).

This argument is based on the premise that every member of a firm, whether officially designated as a manager or not, actually engages in decision making about some aspect of firm performance. Correct decisions in these matters require information that is held primarily by employees. Further, employees have specific knowledge about the behavior of fellow workers that is unavailable to official managers. This knowledge, if communicated, can increase managerial control over the workplace, and it can simultaneously decrease the cost of monitoring workers. The phenomenon of increased managerial control in firms in which managers cede certain aspects of authority to employees has been noted and subjected to measurement in the social-psychology literature (Tannenbaum 1974).

The economics literature has stressed that, in nonparticipatory firms, workers have incentives to provide only minimum acceptable effort and disclose little, if any, information leading to improvements in productivity. It has also documented the lowering of monitoring costs in participative environments such as the Mondragon cooperatives in Spain (Bradley and Gelb 1981) and the U.S. producer cooperatives (Greenberg 1980).

The arguments in favor of worker participation hence predict that all three forms of participation (i.e., participation in ownership, profits, and decision making) will lead to superior economic performance of the firm. The benefits are expected to come primarily from lower monitoring costs and a smaller residual loss.

The idea of bonding costs has usually been ignored by those favoring worker participation, although Vanek (1970) and others have noted that the success of participation depends upon the ability of the firm to disseminate and process information. This has, in turn, generated the related hypotheses that participation will be more successful, and hence more frequently observed, in smaller than in larger firms, and that, in large participatory firms, there should typically be individual participatory schemes organized within smaller units (i.e., divisions or workshops) rather than a single scheme for the firm as a whole. A related observation by Dreze (1983) is that workers' risk aversion and limited wealth will prevent the rise of significant worker ownership in capital-intensive industries. Optimal risk sharing and capital market operations would hence make worker-owned bakeries more likely than worker-owned tankers.

The predictions about where one is likely to find participatory firms are interesting, and they certainly merit empirical investigation. To our knowledge, the only study in this area is Conte and Svejnar's (1989) study of the determinants of ESOP adoption in sixty-four U.S. firms. The principal findings of that study were that, for public firms that adopted their ESOPs prior to 1987, adoption was likely to occur in firms that were not unionized and that had a lower than average rate of return on equity prior to adoption. Firms that adopted ESOPs tended to be in industries characterized by relatively small average firm sizes, but also to be larger than the average firms in these industries.

Returning to the above theoretical arguments about the likely economic effects of worker participation in ownership, profits, and decision making, one must conclude that this is an empirical issue. However, the approach to empirical verification is complex. For example, several theoretical models of labor adjustment in labor-managed firms imply that, if workers maximize expected utility, labor will be optimally treated as a quasi-fixed factor, with wages rather than employment varying with market conditions (see, for example, Steinherr and Thisse 1979; Bonin 1984; and Spinnewyn and Svejnar 1986). This implies that the measured value of both labor productivity and total factor productivity in highly participative firms will be lower in recessionary periods than at other times, and may be temporarily lower than that of their "capitalist twins" even if their technical production functions are identical. Hence, estimates of the impact of participation on technical productivity may be sensitive to business cycle conditions at the time the underlying data are collected. The data for this study were collected in 1980 and 1981, which was a recessionary period. Therefore, any bias would be against finding positive productivity effects for participation.

A second important issue is self-selection, both at the level of the firm and at the level of the employee. Only a small percentage of ESOP and profit-sharing companies in the U.S. were begun with these institutions in place, and, hence, the presence of these plans may be endogenously determined, leading to possible estimation bias. Clearly, the finding reported above that ESOP adoption has tended to occur in firms with low earnings underscores the importance of the endogeneity issue. Endogeneity is a concern at the employee level as well for companies with direct employee ownership, though not for ESOP companies, since all (nonunion) employees typically are covered by the ESOP plan.

Self-selection at the level of the firm is related to a third important issue, namely, the life cycle of participative firms. Life-cycle effects are of special concern in those participative firms wherein employees participate in ownership. Ben-Ner (1984), Miyazaki (1984), and others have discussed this issue, and Estrin and Jones (1986) have been able to detect life-cycle effects for cooperatives in certain industries in France. The issue is of particular importance in the United States, where many ESOP companies have become participative as a result of the failure of a previously existing conventional firm, and subsequently abandoned employee ownership when the firm was restored to profitability. Moreover, it is extensively documented (see, for example, Berman 1967; and Bradley and Gelb 1983) that the incentives to sell highly successful cooperative firms, and/or to sell workers' shareholdings in successful ESOP firms, have often led to the dissolution of successful participation schemes. Controlling for life-cycle patterns, especially those affecting the adoption of participative agreements, is clearly necessary to obtain unbiased econometric estimates of the productivity effects of these arrangements.

Fourth, most of the studies of the performance effects of employee ownership in the United States have adopted profitability as the performance criterion. A number of interesting results have been reported (see Conte and Tannenbaum 1978; and Tannenbaum, Cook, and Lohmann 1984); there are however, numerous problems with using profits to measure the impact of participation. The principal problem is that increased profits may reflect factors other than increases in efficiency. Especially in the United States, reorganization as an employee-owned company can have substantial tax consequences.[3] Moreover, even apart from tax effects, reorganization as an employee-owned company may be accompanied by higher levels of required debt service and requirements to repurchase the stock of retiring employees, both of which serve as a drain on liquidity. The effects of these and other features of employee stock ownership plans on the accounting profit statement are not straightforward; they do serve, however, to diminish the usefulness of either before-tax or after-tax net income as an indicator of efficiency in the firm's operations. As a result, a new group of studies have concentrated on the underlying production function relationships in participative firms (see, for example, Jones and Svejnar 1985; Defourney, Estrin, and Jones 1985; and Estrin, Jones, and Svejnar 1987). That is the approach followed here as well.

Structural Features of Participative Firms

Worker participation can take the form of profit sharing, of individual or collective claims to assets of the firm, or of a sharing in decision-making rights. With the possible exception of profit sharing, each of these elements tends to be adopted in combination with one or both of the others.

Profit sharing is perhaps the simplest form of participation. There is no information that we are aware of indicating the extent of other participatory elements in U.S. profit-sharing companies; we expected, however, that profit sharing would be infrequently accompanied by nonmanagerial participation in decision making. Surprisingly, in our sample of eleven nonemployee-owned, profit-sharing firms, four, or 36 percent, indicated the presence of an active program of employee involvement in decision making. While our sample is obviously too small to generalize from, this supports our argument for a multifaceted approach to data gathering.

Employee-owned firms naturally incorporate both profit and loss sharing in the form of appreciation and depreciation in share values. Hence, employee-owned firms always have at least an element of profit sharing. In addition, many employee-owned companies have explicit cash profit-sharing programs and/or contribute shares of company stock to employee accounts on the basis of net income. This is true of fourteen, or almost one-half, of the thirty-one companies in our sample that have either an ESOP or direct nonmanagerial employee ownership.

Companies with ESOPs exhibit large firm-to-firm variation in arrangements for participation in decision making. Publicly traded ESOPs are required by law to issue voting stock to employee-owners, although plan participants may never actually get to vote their shares. This is because many plans require full vesting before the participant can vote and in some plans all of the shares in the ESOP are voted in a block by trustees. Privately owned ESOP companies are not required to have voting shares,[4] although about 15 percent do (Ivancic and Rosen 1986). Interestingly, the voting of shares is not necessarily indicative of a high level of participation in decision making in the company. One reason is that there are extremely few ESOP companies in which employees own a majority of the shares. Another reason is that employee voting rights are not typically accompanied by special access to company information or special representation on the company's board of directors. Hence, employees as shareholders have about as much say in company decisions as nonemployee, nonmajority shareholders. Especially in closely held private companies, this may not be much of a say.

On the other hand, at a small number of ESOP companies employees have substantial decision-making rights. These are mainly companies in which the ESOP was adopted to avert a bankruptcy or closure and usually are 100 percent employee owned. Even in these cases, however, it is not unheard of for employees to have little say in management decisions. This points to the malleability of the ESOP as an instrument of worker participation. ESOP companies exhibit a wide variety of institutional arrangements for profit sharing, risk taking, and decision making.

Equally broad are the institutional arrangements in place at producer cooperatives (PCs). Among U.S. PCs, for example, the dominant form is the individual ownership PC, wherein each member purchases one or more shares at the going rate (shares in some plywood cooperatives have sold for as much as $60,000). At these PCs, the original Rochdale principle of "one man, one vote" typically remains a strong influence. Even in cases where a member may own more than one share, he or she usually has only one vote. Additionally, in virtually all of the U.S. PCs, income—including the year-end surplus—is distributed on a per-hour-worked basis.

The European PCs are quite different from their U.S. counterparts in the institutions that govern internal, or collective, ownership. In France, a minimum of 15 percent of the annual surplus must be reinvested in the firm (Estrin, Jones, and Svejnar 1987). Although no such external requirements are imposed upon Italian and British cooperatives, at these enterprises there is generally a high level of company saving that is never paid out to shareholders. Hence, many of the European cooperatives are largely internally owned, in this sense being a hybrid between for-profit and not-for-profit firms. This phenomenon is virtually absent in the U.S. cooperatives, except for a small number of recently formed PCs that have adopted the by-laws of the Industrial Cooperative Association.

In spite of the differences in their capital structure, PCs worldwide are highly similar in their distribution of decision-making rights. In general, the one person, one vote rule is followed and no control rights of any type are ceded to outsiders, not even in those cases where outsiders are permitted to own shares. In addition, although PCs exhibit a broad variety of formal and informal control structures, all entail representation from all groups of workers. As a result, the PCs as a group are the most democratic of all types of participatory firms.

As a general summary statement, one can say that ESOP and profit-sharing companies have a fairly standardized financial structure, but exhibit broad disparities *inter alia* in the way that worker participation in decision making is structured, while the reverse is true of producer cooperatives.

Several studies have been performed comparing the performance of specific groups of participative firms with that of conventional companies (for example, Berman 1967; Bellas 1972; and Thomas and Logan 1982). While such studies are instructive, it is apparent from the brief discussion just concluded that there is great variation in the institutional framework of participative firms. This makes it difficult to generalize about the underlying structural relationships on the basis of data from only one type of firm, and underscores the advisability of a multiple regression framework, which allows for statistical control of covarying types of participation. In the following section, we discuss our data set, which includes information from all three basic types of participatory firms, and our methodology for assessing the productivity impact of each of the three basic elements of participation: profit sharing, employee ownership, and participation in decision making. In acknowledgment of the growing empirical literature on the effects of trade unions on productivity, we have estimated this effect as well.

Data and Methodology

The data we analyze were collected from forty U.S. companies that agreed to supply a broad variety of operating information and that also permitted us to administer questionnaires to a stratified random sample of thirty to fifty employees. The sample of forty companies resulted from a wide-ranging effort to sample four populations: (1) profit-sharing companies, (2) companies with employee stock ownership plans, (3) producer cooperatives in the plywood industry, and (4) companies with programs for employee participation, but with no employee ownership or profit sharing. For each type of firm, we compiled extensive lists of possible contacts from publicly available sources and selected randomly from these lists. Responses from companies in the fourth group were so limited that we abandoned our attempt to include representatives of this group in our sample. However, thirteen firms in the first three groups proved to have participatory schemes, and we are, therefore, able to estimate the effects of employee participation on productivity from our data. Since nine of the forty firms have a positive degree of unionization, we examine its impact as well.

It is difficult to judge the representativeness of the firms in our sample in relation to the populations from which they were drawn. Hence, we do not attempt to generalize excessively from our sample. Our goal is, rather, to estimate the impact of each of the three basic forms of participation in the context of one mixed sample and draw preliminary conclusions.

For each firm in the sample, we collected time-series data on operations including employment, fixed investment, electricity and fuels usage, sales, purchased materials, beginning and ending inventories, and industry (SIC) codes. We also collected time-series information on the value of employee share ownership, both direct ownership and ownership through an employee stock ownership trust (ESOT), and on the total equity value of the firm, from which we were able to construct measures of the percentage of company assets owned by nonmanagerial employees. Finally, we collected non-time-series data on the formal structures of participative decision making and the amount of profit-sharing bonuses, as well as assessing employee perceptions about the extent of their influence on decision making within the company via the employee surveys. In this analysis, we do not utilize the data on extent of profit sharing, nor do we utilize the employee perceptions data. Rather, we estimate only the effect of having profit sharing in the compensation scheme, and the effect of the presence of a formal program for employee participation in decision making.

From these data, we constructed three main operating variables: Q = value added, L = total hours worked, and F = value of electricity and fuels used. Since capital measures are questionable and since we were unable to construct an adequate direct measure of capital for more than a few of the firms, we follow that branch of the production function literature that uses the variable F as a proxy for capital services used.

In addition to Q, L, and F, we have constructed several organizational variables that we use to assess the productivity impact of the various institutional (participatory) schemes. These variables are:

%ESOT = percentage of company stock owned by nonmanagerial employees indirectly through an ESOT;

%DIROWN = percentage of company stock owned directly by nonmanagerial employees;

PROFITSHARING = a dummy variable coded 1.0 when the firm offers profit sharing to nonmanagerial employees, and 0.0 otherwise;

PARTICIPATION = a dummy variable coded 1.0 when the firm has an employee participation plan, and 0.0 otherwise;

%UNION = percentage of the firm's labor force that is covered by a collective bargaining contract;

BANKRUPT = a dummy variable coded 1.0 if the reason for starting employee ownership was the bankruptcy of the firm, and 0.0 otherwise; and

NONEMPLOYEE OWNED = a dummy variable coded 1.0 if the firm has no nonmanagerial employee ownership, and 0.0 otherwise.

All of these variables are available in at least two consecutive years for all but four of the sample firms, and for as many as eight consecutive years for fourteen firms.

Key features of the background information just described are presented in tables 3.1 and 3.2. Table 3.1 shows the basic participation characteristics of each firm in the sample, while table 3.2 provides summary measures for the sample as a whole. As can be seen from these two tables, the sample displays substantial variation in all the relevant variables. Perhaps the most interesting aspect of this information is that only fifteen of the forty firms have only one of the characteristics of interest, whereas seven of the firms have three of the four characteristics. Recall that, in targeting firms for inclusion in the study, we developed independent lists of companies with ESOPs, direct ownership, and profit sharing. Hence the inclusion of numerous firms with more than one participative characteristic reflects the pattern in which they naturally occur, although we do not claim that the distribution of characteristics in our sample accurately reflects their joint distribution in the economy.

It is also of particular interest that fourteen of the twenty-one ESOP firms in our sample do not have employee participation in decision making. This is not an unexpected finding, as the majority of privately owned firms nationwide do not provide for pass-through voting of employees' stock in the ESOT. It is of some policy relevance, however, as both the U.S. Department of Labor and the Internal Revenue Service have argued that employees who own shares in an ESOT should be provided the same decision-making rights as other

Table 3.1
Characteristics of firms in the sample

Firm no.	ESOT plan with non-managerial shareholdings	Profit-sharing plan	Direct ownership by non-managers	Employee participation plan	ESOT adopted due to threat of bankruptcy
1		Y	Y		
2		Y	Y	Y	
3			Y	Y	
4	Y	Y			
5	Y		Y		
6		Y			
7	Y	Y		Y	
8			Y		
9		Y	Y	Y	
10	Y	Y			
11		Y		Y	
12	Y				
13		Y			
14	Y				
15	Y				
16	Y	Y			
17	Y	Y			
18	Y		Y	Y	
19		Y			
20	Y				
21		Y		Y	
22	Y		Y	Y	
23	Y				
24		Y			
25	Y		Y		Y
26	Y				
27	Y	Y			
28	Y			Y	
29	Y				
30					
31					
32			Y		Y
33		Y	Y	Y	
34	Y		Y	Y	
35	Y	Y			
36		Y			
37		Y			
38		Y		Y	
39		Y		Y	
40	Y				
Number	21	21	12	13	2
Percent	53%	53%	30%	33%	5%

Table 3.2
Summary of the continuous variables

	Mean	Standard deviation
%ESOT[a]	0.27	0.28
%DIROWN[a]	0.48	0.45
%UNION[a]	0.69	0.31
Value added (Q)[b]	$9,056,000	$14,622,000
Work hours (L)	444,000	593,000
Utility cost (F)[b]	$227,000	$384,000

Notes:
a. The means and standard deviations are over the sample of relevant firms, i.e., firms that have the characteristic. For example, of firms in the sample *that have an ESOT*, nonmanagerial personnel own an average of 27 percent of the firm through the ESOT (in addition to any direct holdings that they might have).
b. Data are in constant (1972) dollars.

shareholders in the company. Evidence that ESOPs without employee decision-making rights provide the same productivity benefits as those with employee decision-making rights would lend support to the opposing view. Our data set is uniquely suited to address this policy issue.

Table 3.1 shows further that twenty-one of the companies in our sample have profit-sharing plans, twelve have some degree of direct ownership by nonmanagerial employees, and thirteen have a plan for employee participation in decision making. Finally, it shows that only two of the twenty-one ESOP companies adopted their plan to save the company from bankruptcy. This low incidence is roughly consistent with national norms, even though ESOPs adopted for this reason have attracted the most public attention.

Table 3.2 shows that the mean percentage of nonmanagerial ownership through the ESOT (for the companies in the sample that have an ESOP) is 27 percent. This is considerably higher than the national average, and reflects the fact that the lists we worked from in targeting companies for inclusion in the analysis contained the most well-known ESOP companies, which tend to be those with a relatively large percentage of assets in the ESOP.[5] Hence, our conclusions may not correctly characterize the impact of having a small ESOP.

The average direct ownership in our sample (for companies that had any direct ownership by nonmanagers) is 48 percent. This reflects the fact that five of the twelve direct-ownership companies in our sample are producer cooperatives, with greater than 95 percent of shares directly owned by employees. Among the remaining companies in the sample with direct ownership, the amounts involved were quite small. This accounts for the high standard deviation (.45) of the %DIROWN variable.

For the nine unionized firms in the sample, the average percentage of employees covered by a union contract is 69 percent. The average 1972-dollar denominated value added is $9,056,000, while the average number of work hours is 444,000 (equivalent to about 225 full-time employees), and the average 1972-dollar fuel cost is $227,000.

The specification that we have used to estimate the productivity effects of the various institutional schemes is an augmented Cobb-Douglas production function:

$$\ln Q = \alpha_0 + \alpha_1 \ln L + \alpha_2 \ln F + \beta Z + \epsilon, \tag{1}$$

where Z is a column vector of the various participatory variables (%ESOT, . . . , NONEMPLOYEE OWNED), and β is the corresponding row vector of coefficients. The specification in equation (1) treats the effect of the Z variables as disembodied, and it is the simplest specification that can be used for our purposes. The specification is also the most parsimonious among the various models that have been used in the literature, and it has found empirical support in other contexts (see, for example, Jones and Svejnar 1985).

Our strategy has been to estimate equation (1), first by ordinary least squares (OLS) and then by instrumental variables (IV). The OLS method has the advantage that its parameter estimates are relatively robust to specification error, but it may suffer from inconsistency in the presence of endogenous regressors. The IV procedure is consistent but, depending on the availability of instruments, it may be less efficient.

Empirical Results

An important aspect of our study is that we estimate jointly the effects of various forms of participation and of unionization. Other existing studies have focused exclusively on either the participatory variables or the effect of unionization. As such, they may have suffered from omitted variable bias and led to misleading policy conclusions. In order to assess the seriousness of this problem, we present in table 3.3 parameter estimates for two versions of equation (1), one with the unionization variable included (reported in the first column), and one with it omitted (reported in the second column).

In these OLS equations, the coefficient on NONEMPLOYEE OWNED is -0.25 or -0.22, depending on the specification, and is statistically significant. This indicates that having some employee ownership has a positive impact on productivity. However, this positive employee ownership impact is diminished by 0.61 to 0.69 percent for every added percent of nonmanagerial employee ownership through an ESOT and is diminished by 0.48 to 0.52 percent for every added percent of nonmanagerial direct ownership. There are at least two plausible interpretations of these results. First, it is possible that the impact of employee ownership is nonlinear, with small amounts having a positive effect, but with the total effect becoming less positive, and finally negative, as the percentage of nonmanagerial employee ownership becomes greater. An alternative possibility is that the OLS results reflect the endogeneity of the %ESOT and %DIROWN variables. It may be, for example, that the presence of ESOTs with a high percentage of the firm's total assets is a consequence rather than a cause of inferior productive performance. Firms that have high percentages of nonmanagerial employee ownership may be systematically different from firms with smaller amounts in other ways as well (for example, in their industrial concentration). We have partially accounted for possible endogeneity by including the variable BANKRUPT in the estimating equations. This enables us to control for the fact that some employee ownership schemes have started as a result of bankruptcy and are, therefore, highly correlated with poor prior performance. The coefficient on the BANKRUPT variable is, indeed, significantly negative, thus suggesting that employee-owned enterprises that were created from bankrupt firms continue (at least for a while) to display inferior total-factor productivity. We also reestimated the equations using instrumental variables techniques; these results are discussed below. There are, of course, other ways to tackle the endogeneity issue. We plan to explore alternative approaches in future research.

The effect of profit sharing is positive, but statistically insignificant, when the %UNION variable is included, but becomes significant

Table 3.3
OLS estimates of the augmented Cobb-Douglas production function
dependent variable = ln(value added)

	Including unionization variable	Without unionization variable
ln$L$	0.44	0.44
	(0.065)	(0.06)
ln$F$	0.32	0.31
	(0.05)	(0.05)
%ESOT	−0.69	−0.52
	(0.29)	(0.19)
%DIROWN	−0.61	−0.48
	(0.15)	(0.12)
PROFITSHARING	0.12	0.15
	(0.11)	(0.08)
PARTICIPATION	0.14	0.08
	(0.08)	(0.08)
%UNION	0.44	—
	(0.14)	
BANKRUPT	−1.2	−1.3
	(0.29	(0.28)
NONEMPLOYEE OWNED	−0.25	−0.22
	(0.10)	(0.09)
Time	0.13	0.13
	(0.02)	(0.02)
Intercept	5.8	6.0
	(0.43)	(0.41)
Number	155	177
R^2	0.86	0.85

Note: Values in parentheses are standard errors.

when %UNION is dropped. The lack of a profit-sharing effect in what is evidently the better specification is a bit surprising, given that the variable has been found to have a significant positive coefficient in other Western countries (see, e.g., Estrin, Jones, and Svejnar 1987). The results in table 3.3 indicate that the positive measured effect of profit sharing in other studies may reflect omitted variable bias.

The coefficient on employee participation in management is positive and nearly significant at the 5 percent level when %UNION is included, but becomes clearly insignificant when %UNION is dropped from the regression.

Unionization appears to have a large and significant positive effect on productive efficiency; the union parameter suggests that a 1 percent increase in union coverage increases total factor productivity by 0.44 percent. This finding is consistent with other recent evidence on the productivity impact of unions (Freeman and Medoff 1984) and, in conjunction with the sensitivity of other parameter estimates to inclusion of the %UNION variable, indicates that it is important to control for the degree of unionization in estimating the impact of other features.

As we mentioned earlier, the problem of endogeneity of regressors may be a serious one, in that firms decide not only on the level of inputs but also on the nature of the various participation schemes. In view of these problems, we have also estimated equation (1) by instrumental variables. All regressors, except for BANKRUPT, NONEMPLOYEE OWNED, and Time, were treated as endogenous. The instruments used were two-digit SIC dummies interacted with time, producer prices, BANKRUPT, and NONEMPLOYEE OWNED. The IV estimates are presented in table 3.4.

There are two important differences between the IV and OLS results. First, the profit-sharing effect changes its sign, although it is not significant in either specification. Second, two of the ownership variables (NONEMPLOYEE OWNED and %ESOT) become insignificant, although %DIROWN retains its negative sign and a high degree of statistical significance. This supports the view that prior estimates of the effects of profit sharing suffer from estimation bias due to omitted variables and/or endogeneity. It is also clear that endogeneity is an important issue in estimating the productivity impact of employee ownership.

Table 3.4
IV estimates of the augmented Cobb-Douglas production function
dependent variable = ln(value added)

	Including unionization variable	Without unionization variable
ln$L$	0.23 (0.10)	0.21 (0.11)
ln$F$	0.49 (0.09)	0.52 (0.09)
%ESOT	−0.56 (0.36)	−0.57 (0.37)
%DIROWN	−0.71 (0.21)	−0.85 (0.20)
PROFITSHARING	0.06 (0.19)	0.26 (0.17)
PARTICIPATION	0.27 (0.13)	0.22 (0.13)
%UNION	0.36 (0.17)	—
BANKRUPT	−1.3 (0.32)	−1.5 (0.32)
NONEMPLOYEE OWNED	−0.22 (0.15)	−0.20 (0.15)
Time	0.09 (0.03)	0.08 (0.03)
Intercept	6.8 (0.70)	6.8 (0.72)
Number	155	177
R^2	0.77	0.75

Note: Values in parentheses are standard errors.

Participation in management retains its significance in the specification that includes the %UNION variable and it remains the only participation variable whose effect we find to be unambiguously positive, ranging from 8 to 27 percent. The BANKRUPT variable also retains its significance in the IV regression, confirming that conditions leading to bankruptcy have lasting effects on the productivity of a firm's operation. However, the remaining significance of the %DIROWN variable may result from the fact that it was not possible to control for the industry distribution of the producer cooperatives in the sample in this analysis. Prior studies of these firms (Berman 1967; Bellas 1972) have shown them to be substantially more productive than nonemployee-owned firms *in their industry*. This paper's finding is also in contrast to recent results in Estrin, Jones, and Svejnar (1987) on the productivity impact of individual share ownership in European cooperatives.

Preliminary Conclusions and Plans for Future Research

Our empirical findings contribute to the growing body of literature on the effects of employee ownership, profit sharing, participation in decision making, and trade unionism on productive efficiency. Our results to date yield several conclusions: (1) firms that offer workers participation in management tend *ceteris paribus* to be more productive; (2) taking the endogeneity of regressors into account, one cannot reject the hypothesis that productive performance is unrelated to the degree of indirect (ESOP) employee ownership; (3) the impact of direct ownership on productivity is significantly negative; (4) in contrast with previous findings, the presence of profit sharing does not appear to affect productivity; and, (5) our results support previous findings on the positive efficiency impact of unionization. Some previous studies have found that the positive union effect disappears when using instrumental variables, but this does not occur in our analysis.

The positive effect of participation in management gives important support to the proponents of such schemes. This is especially so since existing studies have found the effect to be consistently nonnegative but at times insignificant (see, for example, Estrin, Jones, and Svejnar 1987; and Levine and Tyson 1989). It is unclear, however, whether this result can or should be translated into policy recommendations. There are two reasons for caution. First, the results we report are for a limited sample and need to be replicated with a larger, scientifically selected, sample. Second, it is unclear that there is any feasible policy initiative that would encourage participative decision making as we measured it (i.e., the existence of formal institutions within firms for involving employers in company decisions) without simultaneously compromising generally accepted property rights. It has been suggested that ESOP tax deductions be afforded only to ESOP companies that pass through voting rights or that have other representation mechanisms for employees. It is not clear, however, that employee representation necessarily leads to the adoption of significant participative institutions. To mandate or effectively subsidize such institutions directly would be difficult if not impossible.

Our results do not provide support for an extension of incentives for employee ownership or for profit sharing. However, as with participative decision making, previous studies have always found the effect of these plans to be non-negative, if sometimes insignificant. The results here do not contradict this pattern, allowing for the possibility of positive findings concerning these arrangements' impact in a larger sample.

Notes

1. The cited statistics are from U.S. General Accounting Office (1985) and from National Center for Employee Ownership (1989).

2. Jensen and Meckling (1979, 470–471).

3. See, for example, Lowenstein (1985) for an analysis of the tax consequences of the Dan River employee stock ownership plan.

4. Employee-shareholders in privately-held companies, however, must be entitled to vote their shares on issues that require more than a majority vote, such as liquidation, sale, or relocation.

5. At the time that we targeted companies for inclusion in the study, there were no lists available of companies with ESOPs. A recent GAO report indicates that compiling a representative, much less a complete, list from official government sources would have been difficult and prone to many errors. We relied on a broad search of the business periodical and academic literature to compile our list.

References

Bellas, C.J. 1972. *Industrial Democracy and the Worker-Owned Firm: A Study of Twenty-One Plywood Companies in the Pacific Northwest.* New York: Praeger.

Ben-Ner, A. 1984. "On the Stability of the Cooperative Type of Organization," *Journal of Comparative Economics* 8 (September), 247–260.

Berman, Katrina V. 1967. *Worker-Owned Plywood Companies: An Economic Analysis.* St. Louis: Washington State University Press.

Bonin, John P. 1984. "Membership and Employment in an Egalitarian Cooperative," *Economica* 51 (August), 295–305.

Bradley, Keith, and Gelb, Alan. 1981. "Motivation and Control in the Mondragon Experiment," *British Journal of Industrial Relations* 19 (July), 211–231.

Bradley, Keith, and Gelb, Alan. 1983. *Worker Capitalism: The New Industrial Relations.* Cambridge, Massachusetts: MIT Press.

Cable, J., and Fitzroy, F. 1980a. "Cooperation and Productivity: Some Evidence from West German Experience," *Economic Analysis and Workers' Management* 14, 163–180.

Cable, J., and Fitzroy, F. 1980b. "Production Efficiency, Incentives, and Employee Participation: Some Preliminary Results for West Germany," *Kyklos* 33, 100–121.

Conte, Michael A. 1989. "Employee Stock Ownership Plans in Public Companies," *Journal of Employee Ownership Law and Finance* 1 (Fall), 89–137.

Conte, Michael, and Tannenbaum, Arnold S. 1978. "Employee-Owned Companies: Is the Difference Measurable?," *Monthly Labor Review* 101 (July), 23–28.

Conte, Michael, and Svejnar, Jan. 1989. "Employee Stock Ownership, Profit Sharing, and Enterprise Performance." Pittsburgh: University of Pittsburgh Department of Economics Working Paper.

Defourney, Jacques, Estrin, Saul, and Jones, Derek C. 1985. "The Effects of Workers' Participation on Enterprise Performance," *International Journal of Industrial Organization* 3 (June), 197–217.

Dreze, Jacques. 1983. "Labor Management and Labor Contracts: A General Equilibrium Approach," Irvo Jahnsson Lectures.

Estrin, Saul, Jones, Derek C., and Svejnar, Jan. 1987. "The Productivity Effects of Worker Participation: Producer Cooperatives in Western Economies," *Journal of Comparative Economics* 11 (March), 40–61.

Estrin, Saul, and Jones, Derek C. 1986. "The Determinants of Workers' Participation and Productivity in Producer Cooperatives." Clinton, New York: Hamilton College Department of Economics Working Paper.

Freeman, Richard B., and Medoff, James L. 1984. *What Do Unions Do?* New York: Basic Books.

Greenberg, E.S. 1980. "Participation in Industrial Decision Making and Work Satisfaction," *Social Science Quarterly* 60 (March), 551–569.

Horvat, B. 1982. *The Political Economy of Socialism.* Armonk, NY: Sharpe.

Ivancic, Cathy, and Rosen, Corey. 1986. "Voting and Participation in Employee Ownership Firms." Oakland, California: National Center for Employee Ownership Working Paper.

Jensen, Michael C. 1989. "Eclipse of the Public Corporation," *Harvard Business Review* 67 (September/October), 61–74.

Jensen, Michael C., and Meckling, William H. 1976. "Theory of the Firm: Managerial Behavior, Agency Costs, and the Ownership Structure," *Journal of Financial Economics* 3 (September), 305–360.

Jensen, Michael C., and Meckling, William H. 1979. "Rights and Production Functions: An Application to Labor-Managed Firms and Codetermination," *Journal of Business* 52 (October), 469–506.

Jones, Derek C., and Svejnar, Jan. 1985. "Participation, Profit Sharing, Worker Ownership, and Efficiency in Italian Producer Cooperatives," *Economica* 52 (November), 449–465.

Kaplan, Steven. 1989. "The Effects of Management Buyouts on Operating Performance and Value," *Journal of Financial Economics*, 24 (October), 217–254.

Kruse, Douglas. 1989. "Profit Sharing in the 1980s: Disguised Wages or a Fundamentally Different Form of Compensation?," New Brunswick: Rutgers University Institute of Management and Labor Relations Working Paper.

Levine, David, and Tyson, Laura D'Andrea. 1989. "Participation, Productivity, and the Firm's Environment," in Alan Blinder, ed., *Paying for Productivity*, Washington: Brookings Institution, 183–243.

Lowenstein, Louis. 1985. "Management Buyouts," *Columbia Law Review* 85 (May), 730–784.

Miyazaki, Hajime. 1984. "On Success and Dissolution of the Labor-Managed Firm in the Capitalist Economy," *Journal of Political Economy* 92 (October), 909–931.

National Center for Employee Ownership. 1989. *The Employee Ownership Report* (March/April), Oakland, California.

Rosen, Corey, and Whyte, William Foote. 1985. "Encouraging Employee Ownership: The Role of Government," in *Employee Ownership: A Legislative Guide.* Oakland, California: National Center for Employee Ownership, 2–28.

Spinnewyn, Frans, and Svejnar, Jan. 1986. "Optimal Membership, Employment, and Income Distribution in Unionized, Participatory, and Labor-Managed Firms." Pittsburgh: University of Pittsburgh Department of Economics Working Paper.

Steinherr, A., and Thisse, J.F. 1979. "Is There a Negatively Sloped Supply Curve in the Labor-Managed Firm?," *Economic Analysis and Workers' Management* 13, 23–33.

Tannenbaum, Arnold S. 1974. *Hierarchy in Organizations: An International Comparison.* San Francisco: Jossey-Bass.

Tannenbaum, Arnold, Cook, Harold, and Lohmann, Jack. 1984. "The Relationship of Employee Ownership to the Technological Adaptiveness and Performance of Companies." Ann Arbor: University of Michigan Survey Research Center Working Paper.

Thomas, Henk, and Logan, Chris. 1982. *Mondragon: An Economic Analysis.* London: George Allen and Unwin.

U.S. General Accounting Office. 1985. *Initial Results of a Survey on Employee Stock Ownership Plans and Information on Related Economic Trends.* Washington, D.C.: U.S. Government Printing Office.

Vanek, Jaroslav. 1970. *The General Theory of Labor-Managed Market Economics.* Ithaca: Cornell University Press.

Discussion

Woody Powell (University of Arizona) commented that the effects of participative arrangements on organizational outcomes may well depend upon other firm characteristics. For example, the benefits associated with participative arrangements may be stronger in small firms or in firms utilizing technologies that impose a high degree of interdependence on the work force. Harry Katz (Cornell) was struck by the fact that participative arrangements tend to occur jointly rather than singly and noted that there may be important interactions among them. Thus, he reasoned, it would make more sense to think about the effects of different packages of participative arrangements, or more generally, the effects of different human resource systems, rather than trying to analyze the independent effects of particular policies taken one by one.

Al Rees (Princeton) was concerned that skill-level differences across different types of firms could account for the productivity differences documented in the paper. He would have preferred the use of a skill-adjusted labor input measure in place of the authors' unadjusted hours of work measure. Henry Farber (MIT) was troubled that, although the sample includes firms with a variety of participative arrangements, it includes no nonparticipative firms. Comparison of participative firms with nonparticipative firms might yield different results. Data on nonparticipative firms also would permit the authors to model why some firms have participative arrangements and others do not. Conte and Svenjar responded to Rees and Farber that these are issues they plan to address in future work.

4

Restructuring the Employment Relationship: The Growth of Market-Mediated Work Arrangements

Katharine G. Abraham

The development of internal labor markets has played a central role in industrial relations theory and research over the past three decades. Within an internal labor market, the compensation and allocation of labor are governed by administrative rules and procedures, rather than determined in direct response to market forces. Insulation from immediate market pressures has some significant potential advantages. For one thing, administrative decision making economizes on market transactions costs. Many internal labor markets are characterized by the presence of career ladders that encourage long-term employment relationships. Such relationships permit the development of firm- or industry-specific skills that workers who change employers frequently do not acquire, thereby enhancing work force productivity. In addition, they make it possible to structure compensation over the work life in ways that strengthen employees' incentives for good performance. Finally, if workers have a preference for stable employment, an employer who can offer stability may be able to pay a lower wage than otherwise would be necessary.[1]

While the advantages just enumerated are surely significant in many settings, this does not mean that it will *always* be efficient to have work performed within the organization rather than contracted for on the open market. Over much of the twentieth century, the

This paper was originally prepared for the "New Developments in Labor Markets and Human Resource Policies" conference held at MIT's Endicott House, June 11–12, 1987. The research on which it is based was conducted while I was a research associate at the Brookings Institution. Ronald Ehrenberg, Susan Houseman, Frank Levy, Paul Osterman, participants in a seminar at the Bureau of Labor Statistics, and participants in the Endicott House conference gave me helpful comments on earlier drafts. I am grateful to Kelly Eastman for research assistance. The views expressed here are my own, and should not be attributed to the trustees, officers, or staff members of the Brookings Institution.

long trend has been toward stronger attachments of workers to their firms and more highly developed internal labor markets (Jacoby 1985; Carter 1988). But there is growing evidence that this trend has slowed and that the pendulum may have begun to swing in the opposite direction. During the past few years, considerable interest has been focused on the growing use of a variety of alternative work arrangements that have in common the substitution of market-mediated transactions for direct employment relationships. These include temporary employment, production subcontracting, and contracting out for a variety of business support services.

Much of the recent discussion has focused on the potential cost savings enjoyed by employers who make use of a flexible work force that can be paid only for work actually performed. Cost savings associated with lower hourly wages and less generous benefits packages for those working under flexible staffing arrangements are also frequently mentioned.[2] Technological factors, in particular economies of scale in the provision of specialized services, have received much less attention. One of this paper's main objectives is to sort out, albeit in a rough way, the relative contributions of the desire for flexibility in staffing levels, the ability to reduce per-hour labor costs, and economies of scale in the provision of specialized services to employers' use of market-mediated work arrangements. I also consider whether changes in the strength of any or all of these motivations can plausibly account for the growing prevalence of these work arrangements over the past decade.

Trends in Market-Mediated Work Arrangements

Data on the various sorts of market-mediated work arrangements that organizations rely upon are unfortunately rather limited. The Bureau of Labor Statistics' (BLS) monthly payroll survey provides good information on the level of employment in different industries and the Bureau of the Census (BOC) produces somewhat more disaggregated data for the service sector at five-year intervals, when the Census of Service Industries is conducted. Inferences concerning the growth of market-mediated work arrangements can be made using these sources of information, but must rely on the categorization of firms in particular industries as providers of market-mediated services.

Gaps in the official statistics are most critical if one is interested in identifying short-term or casual hiring onto organizations' own payrolls, or the contracting out of work other than business support services. The employer survey that I carried out jointly with the Bureau of National Affairs (BNA) collected information on these activities.

Data on employment in the business service sector (SIC 73) from the BLS's monthly payroll survey are summarized in table 4.1. As shown in the table, the business service sector includes temporary-help agencies as well as firms providing a broad array of specialized services ranging from computer programming and data processing to building cleaning and maintenance. Over the 1972 to 1986 period, when total nonagricultural employment grew at an annual rate of 2.2 percent, business service employment as a whole grew at an annual rate of 7.3 percent, more than three times as fast, and its share of total employment increased from 2.4 to 4.8 percent.

Payroll survey data on temporary-help industry employment are not available prior to 1982, but temporary-help firms are the largest component of the personnel supply services classification, and personnel supply services grew at an annual rate of 11.5 percent over the 1972 to 1986 period. The temporary-help industry grew almost 20 percent per year between 1982 and 1986, and by 1986 employed 807,000 people. Nonsupervisory employment in the temporary-help sector corresponds more closely to the number of people actually working as agency temporaries; according to unpublished BLS estimates, by 1986 that totalled 787,000 people. To put this into some perspective, in 1986 there were 283,200 employees in the steel industry (SIC 331), 684,400 employees engaged in manufacturing computers and semiconductors (SIC 3578 plus SIC 5674), and 833,000 employees in the automobile industry (SIC 371). It should be noted that nonsupervisory employees in the temporary-help industry average somewhat fewer hours per week than the typical nonsupervisory worker (30.2 versus 34.8 hours in 1986).

A second source of information on employment in the business service sector is the Census of Service Industries. Data from this census are reported in table 4.2. The most recent available data from this source are for 1982. The BLS and BOC data are not wholly comparable, but yield a consistent picture of the pattern of business service employment growth.[3] The most interesting feature of the BOC data is that they are broken out for somewhat finer industry

Table 4.1
Growth in the use of temporary help and outside contracting; current employment statistics survey

	Employment (in thousands)			Annual growth (percent)		
	1972	1982	1986	1972–1982	1982–1986	1972–1986
Business services (73)	1,790	3,286	4,781	6.3	9.8	7.3
Advertising (731)	122	161	202	2.8	5.8	3.7
Credit reporting and collection (732)	76	75	98	-0.1	6.9	1.8
Mailing, reproduction, and stenographic (733)	82	135	195	5.1	9.6	6.4
Services to buildings (734)	336	524	681	4.5	6.8	5.2
Personnel supply (736)	221	555	1,017	9.6	16.3	11.5
Temporary help (7362)	—	401	807	—	19.1	—
Computer and data processing services (737)	107	365	591	13.1	12.8	13.0
Programming and software (7372)	—	112	216	—	17.8	—
Data processing (7374)	—	199	278	—	8.7	—
Miscellaneous business services (735, 739)	846	1,465	1,997	5.6	8.1	6.3
Management and public relations (7392)	—	366	550	—	10.7	—
Detective and protective services (7393)	—	349	445	—	6.3	—
Total nonagricultural payroll employment	73,675	89,566	99,610	2.0	2.7	2.2

Note: The data reported for 1972 and 1982 came from U.S. Department of Labor (1985) and the 1986 data from U.S. Department of Labor (1987).

Table 4.2
Growth in the use of temporary help and outside contracting: census of service industries

	Employment (in thousands)			Annual growth (percent)
	1972	1977	1982	1972–1982
Business services (73)	1,759	2,297	3,152	6.0
Advertising (731)	111	119	146	2.8
Credit reporting and collection (732)	63	64	61	–0.3
Mailing, reproduction, and stenographic (733)	92	106	142	4.4
Services to buildings (734)	333	426	540	5.0
Personnel supply (736)	267	432	609	8.6
Office temporary help (pt. 7362)	120	203	253	7.7
Nonoffice temporary help (pt. 7362)	59	128	217	13.9
Computer and data processing services (737)	127	204	354	10.8
Programming and software (7372)	38	51	127	12.8
Data processing (7374)	79	136	183	8.8
Miscellaneous business services (735, 739)	765	946	1,301	5.5
Management and public relations (7392)	143	209	353	9.5
Detective and protective services (7393)	212	280	340	4.8

Note: The data reported in this table came from U.S. Department of Commerce (1975, 1980, 1984).

categories than the BLS data. They confirm that there has been especially rapid growth in temporary-help employment since 1972 and, in addition, reveal that nonoffice temporary-help employment has grown much more rapidly than office temporary-help employment. Agencies specializing in nonoffice temporaries accounted for only a third of total temporary-help service employment in 1972, but for more than 45 percent of the total by 1982. This shift in the composition of the temporary-help sector is consistent with considerable anecdotal evidence that firms have broadened the scope of their reliance on temporary workers in recent years (*New York Times* 1984; Boston Globe 1987).

The official statistics, then, suggest that employers' use of the market-mediated work arrangements associated with business service employment, including the use of agency temporaries, has increased substantially over the past fifteen years. These data, however, do not preclude the possibility that this growth represents the substitution of some types of market-mediated work arrangements for others, rather than a change in the overall importance of market-mediated work arrangements. For example, employers might now use agency temporaries to perform tasks that previously would have been performed by short-term hires.

The survey I conducted in collaboration with the BNA provides some additional information on organizations' use of various market-mediated work arrangements, including not only the use of agency temporaries and contracting out to business service firms, but also short-term hiring onto organizations' own payrolls and other sorts of contracting out. This survey was mailed during May 1986 to 799 human resource executives at private firms. We received 442 usable replies. At large firms, the answers generally applied to a particular facility or division rather than to the entire firm; at small firms, the answers generally applied to the entire firm, though it can be assumed that many of these firms conduct all of their operations at a single site. The unit of observation in the survey sample thus corresponds more closely to an establishment concept than to a firm concept. While the survey sample covered a broad spectrum of industries, the distribution of replies is strongly skewed toward manufacturing, finance, insurance, real estate, and health care, and away from trade and services other than health care. In addition, firms with fewer than fifty employees were not represented in the survey sample. There is some evidence that the survey respondents' practices are not too far out of line with those of other employers, but appropriate caution should be used in generalizing from the survey results. Abraham (1988) provides a more detailed description of this survey; a copy of the survey questionnaire can be found in Bureau of National Affairs (1986).

The first three sections of the survey questionnaire were devoted to questions about the use of agency temporaries, short-term hires, and on-call workers. Respondents were given definitions of these terms, which are reproduced here in appendix 4.A. For over 90 percent of the 442 organizations represented in the survey, some use of at least one of these categories of workers was reported. On average, agency temporaries added about 0.6 percent to the hours worked by the regular work force over the course of 1985. This number is consistent with the estimated share of agency temporaries in hours worked derived from BLS payroll survey data. Short-term hires and on-call workers added about 0.8 percent to the hours worked by survey respondents' regular work forces during 1985.[4] If these proportions are similar to those in other firms, a reasonable guess would be that the total use of all types of temporary workers is slightly more than twice as large as the use of agency temporaries alone. Given the unofficial BLS estimate that employment of agency temporaries averaged over three-quarters of a million people during 1986, this would imply that the aggregate employment of all types of temporary workers combined averaged something over 1.5 million people during the same period.

The fourth section of the survey questionnaire contained questions pertaining to activities contracted out by the responding organization, differentiating between contract work contributing directly to the organization's output and contract support services. (Definitions of contracting activities given to respondents are reproduced in appendix 4.A.) Some 46 percent of responding organizations reported at least some contracting out of production/service operations (subcontracting) during 1985, though this most commonly accounted for less than 5 percent of total production. The survey data also imply that 57 percent of responding organizations contracted out for at least one sort of administrative/business support service.[5] Unfortunately, the answers to the survey questions cannot be translated into estimates of the volume of work done under such arrangements.

The fifth section of the survey questionnaire is the most relevant for assessing changes over time in organizations' use of various

Table 4.3
Growth in the use of temporary help and outside contractors: Bureau of National Affairs survey

| | Percent of firms reporting use in 1985 compared to use in 1980, relative to regular employment | | | |
	Greater	Less	About the same, not applicable	Don't know, no answer
Agency temporaries	40	15	40	5
Short-term hires	25	12	54	10
On-call workers	15	4	69	11
Administrative/business support contracts	13	6	67	14
Production subcontracting	13	6	66	16

Note: All reported percentages are based on 441 replies to the Bureau of National Affairs survey, described in the text.

market-mediated work arrangements. The answers to the questions on this subject are summarized in table 4.3. Respondents were asked whether their use of each market-mediated work arrangement during calendar year 1985 was greater, about the same, or less than their use in 1980, relative to the size of their regular work forces. For each of the arrangements, the modal answer was that there had been no change in the arrangement's importance. Nonetheless, there were consistently two to three times as many respondents reporting that their use of the arrangement in question had grown between 1980 and 1985 as reporting that it had declined. These answers suggest that the growth in temporary-help agency employment in recent years is not attributable to declines in other functionally equivalent work arrangements and, indeed, that there has been across-the-board growth in the use of market-mediated work arrangements.

Reasons for the Use of Market-Mediated Work Arrangements

Why do organizations rely on temporary workers or contract work out to other organizations, rather than having work performed by regular employees in-house? At least three separate motivations for reliance on the sort of market-mediated work arrangements I am

interested in are likely to be important. First, the use of such arrangements may enhance the organization's ability to adjust both the
quantity and the skill mix of labor input to changing circumstances
while buffering the regular work force from fluctuations in demand.
Second, where internal labor market constraints are operative, turning a particular task over to an outside individual or organization
may be the only way to take advantage of low market wage rates.
These first two motivations have their origins in limitations on
employers' freedom of action within the internal labor market. For
this reason, they are particularly interesting from an industrial relations perspective. Finally, a decision to contract out may not reflect
labor market conditions at all, but rather an increased demand for
specialized services that many firms cannot produce economically in-
house. I discuss these motivations in turn, then in the next section
of the paper consider available evidence on their relevance.

Increased Flexibility in Staffing Levels and Mix

While internal labor market structures have some significant advantages, they also raise the costs associated with adjusting the size of
the regular work force. Given the expectation that employment relationships will be long lasting, it makes sense for employers to be
selective in their hiring and to provide appropriate training for those
they do hire. Firing an employee then results in the loss of a significant investment. Even temporary layoffs may be expensive, since
some temporarily laid-off workers may accept other employment
rather than wait to be recalled. Moreover, in situations where
employees have come to expect stability in their working relationships, firings and layoffs may adversely affect employee morale. All
of this suggests that, absent some other means of absorbing fluctuations in demand, there are likely to be situations in which regular
employees are kept on the payroll through slack periods. Assigning
some tasks to temporary workers or other outsiders during periods
of peak demand may make it possible for employers to hire a smaller
regular work force and to keep that work force more fully utilized
during periods of lower demand. This strategy will offer many
employers the potential for significant cost savings even if supplemental staffers earn higher hourly wages and/or are less productive
than regular employees.

Perhaps equally important, the use of temporary workers or other outsiders to buffer regular employees from fluctuations in demand may make it possible for a firm to establish a stronger relationship with its regular work force than would otherwise be possible. For example, if fluctuations in demand can be absorbed by supplementals, it may be feasible to invest in specialized training for regular workers that would otherwise be too risky. Regular workers who know they have a secure future with the firm may also be more willing to accept reassignment, to put in extra effort during busy periods, and so on.

Organizations' decisions concerning the use of temporary workers and/or outside contractors can be modeled formally, but the most important conclusions to emerge from this sort of modeling are intuitively straightforward. First, increases in the variability or uncertainty of demand for the organization's products or services will lead to increased reliance on flexible staffing arrangements, in the sense that the expected ratio of temporary to permanent employment rises. Second, increases in either the costs of hiring or the costs of firing regular employees will raise the extent of reliance on supplementals. Third, reliance on supplementals will be greater the higher regular employees' wages are compared to supplementals' wages. Finally, within any organization, reliance on supplementals will be greater in positions requiring less firm-specific skill.[6]

All of this does assume that firms and workers view regular employment relationships as worth investing in and thus worth preserving. Not all regular jobs fall into this category. In some situations, firms may choose to segment their internal labor markets, making considerable investments in and offering attractive career paths to some groups of regular workers, but providing little training and little incentive to remain with the firm to other groups of regular workers. The latter groups could then serve the buffer role just outlined for temporaries or outside contractors. The major problem with any segmented internal labor market strategy is that it may be difficult to maintain clear boundaries between different groups of workers within a single internal labor market. Using workers hired for an explicitly temporary term or bringing in outside contractors to fill the buffer role avoids the potential adverse consequences of laying off less valued regular employees.

Increased Wage Flexibility

The preceding discussion implicitly assumes that regular employees can perform any given volume of work at less expense to the firm than a series of temporaries or an outside contractor. This may not always be true. For example, a unionized firm's wages may be set by contract at above-market levels. In this situation, the firm may be able to cut the costs of certain activities if it can have work done by outsiders. A similar argument can be made concerning firms that pay high wages for "efficiency wage" reasons. Efficiency wage models suggest that some employers may pay their employees above-market wages because they hope that the fear of losing a good job will encourage those employees to work harder than they otherwise would (see Yellen 1984; Katz 1986). This strategy is especially likely to be appealing when monitoring employees' day-to-day performance would be costly. Paying above-market wages may also be a sensible strategy if it reduces the firm's turnover rate (again, see Yellen 1984; Katz 1986). Paying high wages may be a sensible way of reducing supervision costs or turnover costs among the firm's "core" work force, but there is little obvious return to paying high wages to the cleaning staff or others performing less central tasks. This suggests that high-wage firms may find it attractive to contract out at least some low-skill activities. In addition, increases in the wage gap between high-wage and low-wage firms should increase high-wage firms' potential gains from contracting out and thus should lead to increased use of work arrangements under which tasks are performed for high-wage firms by outsiders.

This conclusion does assume that the firm does not have the option of pursuing a differentiated compensation strategy, paying core workers well and paying other workers only market wages. In the union sector, the firm does not have the freedom to set relative wages for different jobs in this fashion. But even in the nonunion sector, workers' ideas about internal equity may well be such that, if some workers are highly paid, all must be highly paid. Available evidence is consistent with this view. In separate analyses of Area Wage Survey data, both Blau (1977) and Groshen (1986) find significant establishment wage differentials that are consistent across occupations. That is, establishments that pay high wages to workers in some occupations tend to pay high wages to workers in all other occupations as well.

Ideas about what is "equitable" are, of course, in part determined by past practice. This implies that a new firm may have more freedom to set relative wages than a firm that has been in business for some time. But a firm that wishes to alter long-standing wage differentials is likely to encounter significant employee resistance. Employers may have greater freedom to alter relative wages during periods of rapid inflation, when such changes do not require cuts in anyone's nominal wage. Evidence that the dispersion in the growth rate of real wages across occupations was positively related to the rate of inflation would lend credence to this hypothesis, but I know of no such evidence. Two-tier wage agreements under which newly hired workers are paid on a lower schedule than members of the incumbent work force have been negotiated with some unions in recent years. The obvious problem with these agreements is that someone who is initially glad to be hired into a job at a given wage is likely eventually to become resentful of the fact that others performing exactly the same work are paid more simply because they were hired under a different regime. Indeed, there is anecdotal evidence that many of the two-tier wage schemes negotiated during the early 1980s are now being dismantled, at least in part because of their adverse effects on employee morale (*Business Week* 1987; *New York Times* 1987). Nonunion employers who seek to alter relative wages by paying new employees on a lower scale are likely to face similar problems.

While some firms may be able to get away with paying high wages to some employees and low wages to others, over the longer run this seems likely to cause morale problems. Moving work outside the internal labor market permits the firm to take advantage of low market wage rates for certain types of work without violating internal equity constraints.

Specialized Services

A final important reason for contracting with outsiders is that they may have specialized equipment or skills that are lacking within the organization. The essential consideration here is the degree to which there are economies of scale in the provision of the service in question. For example, it may not be cost effective for a small- or medium-sized organization to have an in-house computer software engineering department. Even if the firm could keep one or more software engineers busy, much of the day-to-day work would likely be rather routine. More complex problems would be outside the experience of the in-house staff. The firm might well be better off placing greater reliance on the resources and experience of a software consulting firm rather than trying to maintain an in-house department. This motivation is distinguished from the two previous motivations by the fact that technological, rather than labor market, imperatives are operative.

Evidence on Employers' Motivations for Using Market-Mediated Work Arrangements

Having briefly sketched out several plausible motivations for employers' reliance on market-mediated work arrangements, I turn now to an investigation of their importance. This discussion draws on several different sources of information. First, to assess the hypothesis that the use of market-mediated work arrangements serves primarily to buffer firms' regular employees from changing demand conditions, I examine the seasonal and cyclical variation in various categories of business service employment relative to the variation in overall employment. Second, to assess whether such work arrangements have been adopted primarily as a means of cutting per-hour labor costs, I consider available information on labor compensation in the business service sector relative to labor compensation for workers doing similar jobs elsewhere in the economy. Third, I explore the relationships between organizational characteristics and the use of various market-mediated work arrangements. Finally, I examine the reasons for using market-mediated work arrangements given by the respondents to the BNA-sponsored survey described earlier in this chapter. While none of the available sources of information offers a definitive answer to the question at hand, the available bits and pieces do make an interesting collage that adds up to a reasonably coherent picture of the factors underlying employers' use of market-mediated work arrangements.

Seasonal and Cyclical Variability in Business Service Employment

If business service firms were absorbing seasonal fluctuations in other firms' work loads, one might expect business service employment to be more seasonal than employment in the rest of the economy. Similarly, given that employers' labor demands tend to move together over the business cycle, one might also expect that, if a particular sort of contractor were being used as a buffer against cyclical work load fluctuations, those contractors' employment should be highly cyclical.

These issues are examined in table 4.4. The first column in the table reports the standard deviation of the mean change in ln(employment) across quarters, for total business service employment and for selected business service industries' employment, based on data from the BLS payroll survey for the 1972:1 through 1986:1 time period.[7] The same measure of the seasonality of employment growth rates is also reported for total nonagricultural payroll employment. Perhaps surprisingly, total business service employment is actually less seasonal than total nonagriculatural payroll employment, as is employment in most of the three-digit business service industries for which data are available. Only in the personnel supply services sector, which is dominated by temporary help firms, is employment substantially more seasonal than employment in the rest of the economy.

The second column of the table summarizes the results of equations fit with seasonally adjusted changes in ln(employment) on the left-hand side and a constant plus the current and four lagged values of the change in the deviation of seasonally adjusted ln(GNP) from its trend (GNPGAP) on the right-hand side. The sum of the coefficients on the GNPGAP variables in a particular equation is a measure of the cyclicality of the industry's employment. Inspection of the table reveals that employment in the business service sector as a whole is substantially more cyclical than overall employment. This above-average cyclicality is wholly attributable, however, to the tremendous cyclicality of the personnel-supply industry, which, as just noted, is dominated by temporary-help firms. Every one percent change in the deviation of ln(GNP) from its trend value produces a 0.85 percent change in total nonagricultural payroll employment, but a 3.45 percent change in SIC 736 employment. In contrast, none of the other three-digit business service industries for which time series data are available has employment that is significantly more cyclical than total nonagricultural employment.

It is possible—and indeed likely—that users of agency temporaries face more variable demand than other organizations. But personnel supply services employment, the closest one can get in a long time series to temporary-help agency employment, is so strongly seasonal

Table 4.4
Seasonality and cyclicality in business service employment

	Standard deviation of mean unadjusted employment growth rates across quarters	Estimated proportional response of employment to changes in GNP over four quarters
Business services (73)	1.16	1.143 (.145)
Advertising (731)	.42	.544 (.187)
Credit reporting and collection (732)	1.29	.832 (.269)
Mailing, reproduction, and stenographic (733)	1.80	1.011 (.278)
Services to buildings (734)	.94	.959 (.228)
Personnel supply (736)	3.25	3.453 (.428)
Computer and data processing services (737)	.42	.913 (.223)
Total nonagricultural payroll employment	1.37	.852 (.058)

Note: The numbers in the first column were calculated using seasonally unadjusted data on the quarter-to-quarter change in ln(employment) for the time period 1972:2 through 1986:1. Each change in ln(employment) series was then seasonally adjusted by subtracting from each observation the difference between the mean value of the series in the relevant quarter and the mean value of the series across all quarters. The adjusted change in ln(employment) series were used as dependent variables in regressions containing a constant plus the current and four lagged values of the change in the deviation of seasonally adjusted ln(GNP) from its trend (GNPGAP). The numbers reported in the second column are the sums of the estimated coefficients on the GNPGAP variables and, in parentheses, the standard errors of the sums.

and so strongly cyclical as to lend support to the conclusion that agency temporaries are filling a buffer role for user firms.

Business Service Sector Compensation

Another question of interest is how the labor costs per unit of output associated with work performed under different arrangements compare. Unfortunately, this sort of information is not readily available. What is available is some sketchy information on the per-hour costs associated with work performed under different arrangements.

For a firm that is thinking about contracting work out versus doing the work in-house, there is likely to be an incentive to contract out if the hourly compensation rates paid by the outside contractor are lower than those paid within the firm. Although the contractor will add a markup to direct compensation expenses to cover other costs of performing the work, the firm also would have to bear these other costs even if the work was done in-house. Moreover, in both cases, the people performing the work will be experienced at it. All of this implies that differences in hourly compensation rates are likely to translate into differences in per-unit production costs.

The situation is rather different for a firm that is considering using temporary workers in place of regular workers. Unlike a firm that contracts out work, a firm that uses a temporary worker must provide any materials and equipment that are needed for the work to be performed and also supervise the work, just as if it were being done by a regular employee. Moreover, a temporary is likely not to be experienced at the work he or she is expected to perform and may not be very proficient at it. Evidence that temporary workers are paid more than regular employees would establish fairly persuasively that using temporaries raises per-unit production costs, but evidence that temporary workers are paid less than regular employees would not establish the opposite conclusion. Indeed, even if the total per-hour cost of using a temporary, inclusive of any agency markup, were less than the per-hour compensation of a regular employee, it might still be more costly to use a temporary than to have work done by a regular employee.

Table 4.5 presents some evidence on selected occupational average hourly wage rates for the business service sector, exclusive of personnel supply services, for the manufacturing sector and for the economy as a whole, based on a data file that makes use of all

Table 4.5
Mean wages in selected occupations: business services, manufacturing, and the nonagricultural private sector

	Business Services[a]	Manufac- turing	Overall
Engineers and architects	$16.03	$14.78	$14.80
Mathematical and computer scientists	14.73	13.96	13.80
Engineering technicians	9.60	10.01	9.86
Computer equipment operators	7.20	8.19	7.54
Financial records processing personnel[b]	7.84	7.24	6.75
Information clerks[b]	5.18	5.99	5.61
Mail clerks and messengers	5.10	6.47	5.80
Guards	5.04	7.18	5.72
Building service personnel[b]	5.23	6.57	5.25

Notes: These tabulations of occupational wages by industry were made using a special 1983 Current Population Survey extract containing data from all twelve monthly surveys, kindly made available by William Dickens and Lawrence Katz. All reported mean wages were based on at least fifty observations.
a. Business services consists of SIC 73, exclusive of SIC 736.
b. "Financial records processing personnel" consist of bookkeepers, accounting and auditing clerks, payroll and timekeeping clerks, and billing clerks. "Information clerks" include interviewers, ticket agents, and receptionists. "Building service personnel" include maids and housemen, janitors and cleaners, elevator operators, and pest control personnel.

available information on private-sector wages from the twelve monthly Current Population Surveys (CPSs) administered during 1983. The construction of this data file is described in Dickens and Katz (1987). The occupations for which data are reported were selected by a two-step procedure. First, I identified a dozen reasonably homogenous occupational groupings that I also expected would be well represented within the business service sector. Mean wages are reported for the nine of these twelve occupations for which the data file contained at least fifty observations within the business service sector; the three excluded occupational groups were nonfinancial records processing clerks, office machine operators, and communications equipment operators. The tabulations include both union and nonunion observations.

The data reported in table 4.5 indicate that average wages for less-skilled workers (information clerks, mail clerks and messengers, guards, and building services personnel) employed in the business service sector are from 15 to 30 percent lower than average wages for workers holding similar jobs in manufacturing and are also lower than average wages for the private sector as a whole. The differential between business service sector wages for these jobs and the wages paid to unionized workers in other sectors is almost certainly even larger. But in more highly skilled jobs, rates of pay in business service firms are comparable to or higher than rates of pay elsewhere.

The data in table 4.5 do not include employer expenditures on employee benefits. Some pertinent information on the probability of pension coverage and on the probability of health insurance coverage is reported in table 4.6. Every March for the past several years the CPS supplement has asked whether individuals were covered by a pension plan or by a health insurance plan provided by their employer at any point during the previous year. The same supplement also asks for the industry and occupation of the longest job held during the previous year. If one is willing to assume that the pension plan and health plan answers generally reflect the situation on the longest job the individual held, one can compute coverage probabilities for occupation by industry cells.

The data in table 4.6 are based on the March 1985 and March 1987 CPS surveys. The two files were pooled to increase sample sizes. (Picking files two years apart avoids overlap in the two survey samples). The pattern of benefit coverage is generally consistent with the pattern of wage differentials in the previous table. Business service sector employees in low-skill occupations (information clerks, mail clerks and messengers, guards, and building service personnel) are less than half as likely as manufacturing-sector employees in the same occupations to have health insurance coverage through their employer and only 25 to 35 percent as likely to be covered by a pension plan. They are also much less likely to have health and pension coverage than the average private-sector employee. The differences between business service sector coverage probabilities and those in other sectors are generally much less pronounced for those in higher-skill occupations.

If business service sectors workers employed in low-skill occupations were substantially less productive than their counterparts in other sectors, contracting low-skill work out to the business service sector might be unattractive in spite of what the data suggest are substantially lower compensation costs there. Conversely, if high-

Table 4.6
Probabilities of pension plan and health insurance coverage for selected occupations: business services, manufacturing, and the nonagricultural private sector

	Business Services[a]		Manufacturing		Overall	
	Health	Pension	Health	Pension	Health	Pension
Engineers and architects	91	77	95	80	90	75
Mathematical and computer scientists	79	46	93	76	86	71
Engineering technicians	70	51	90	68	78	59
Computer equipment operators	62	42	81	57	72	53
Financial records processing personnel[b]	49	26	73	45	58	36
Information clerks[b]	23	12	65	33	46	29
Mail clerks and messengers	25	9	52	36	67	62
Guards	34	17	72	61	42	31
Building service personnel[b]	25	12	65	46	43	29

Notes: These tabulations were made using March 1985 and March 1987 Current Population Survey data. Occupation and industry are for the longest job held during the previous calendar year. The pension and health insurance questions refer to coverage on any job held during the year. All reported proportions were based on at least fifty observations.
a. Business services consists of SIC 73, exclusive of SIC 736.
b. "Financial records processing personnel" consist of bookkeepers, accounting and auditing clerks, payroll and timekeeping clerks, and billing clerks. "Information clerks" include interviewers, ticket agents, and receptionists. "Building service personnel" include maids and housemen, janitors and cleaners, elevator operators and pest control personnel.

skill business service sector employees were more productive than their counterparts elsewhere in the economy, firms might actually reduce their labor costs by contracting out to business service firms even though the business service firms paid their more highly skilled workers higher wages. At least at the low-skill end of the occupational spectrum, I find it implausible that productivity differences among those performing similar work could be large enough to offset the wage and benefit differentials revealed in the data just examined. Moreover, at both the low-skill and the high-skill end of the occupational spectrum, the observable characteristics of workers within the occupations I have examined are surprisingly similar across sectors.[8] All in all, the CPS data suggest that reducing wage costs is an important motivation for contracting out tasks with low skill requirements, but is probably not a motivation for contracting out high-skill work. For high-skill work, other explanations, such as special expertise possessed by the outside contractor, must be appealed to.

What about the relative hourly costs associated with using temporary workers rather than relying on regular workers? Here, the CPS data are less useful. Temporary-help agencies typically charge users an additional percentage fee on top of the amount the temporary worker is paid, so that there is a wedge between the wage the worker receives and the cost to the user organization. Agency temporaries might report lower wages than regular employees doing similar work, but still cost employers more. In addition, in the CPS data there is no way to identify temporary workers hired onto organizations' own payrolls. Table 4.7 summarizes respondents' answers to a series of questions asked on the survey I conducted in cooperation with the BNA concerning the relative per-hour costs of employing temporary workers compared with the per-hour costs of employing regular employees. A strong plurality of users of agency temporaries reported higher per-hour costs than associated with regular employees; only about a quarter reported that per-hour costs were lower. However, a majority of users of short-term hires and a substantial fraction of users of on-call workers reported that these temporary workers received lower per-hour compensation than regular employees in comparable jobs.

While this is interesting information, it does not establish that using short-term hires and on-call workers lowers per-unit production costs. To draw any conclusions about per-unit production costs, one would also need information on relative productivities. Collect-

Table 4.7
Costs of using temporary workers compared with costs of using regular workers

| | Percent of users reporting direct costs of temporary workers versus regular employees | | |
	Agency temporaries	Short-term hires	On-call workers
Generally higher	42	6	11
Generally about the same	30	33	46
Generally lower	27	60	43
Sample size	330	273	156
Number of users	339	282	161

Note: The tabulations reported are based on responses to the Bureau of National Affairs survey described in the text. The question asked about agency temporaries was, "Is your hourly cost for agency temporaries generally higher or lower than the hourly pay and benefits costs for regular employees in comparable positions?" The questions about short-term hires and on-call workers substituted "your hourly pay and benefits cost" for "your hourly cost." Only those respondents who reported use of an arrangement were asked about its cost.

ing this sort of information was beyond the scope of the BNA survey. As suggested above, if short-term hires are unfamiliar with the tasks they are asked to perform, their productivity may well be lower than that of regular employees. This may offset the cost savings associated with their lower hourly compensation. The fact that temporary workers' assignment durations are typically quite short is consistent with the view that it is not cost-effective to use temporaries in place of regular workers for ongoing tasks.[9] At a minimum, then, the data suggest that reducing hourly compensation costs is not generally a motivation for reliance on agency temporaries; whether use of other categories of temporaries reduces unit labor costs remains an open question, though I suspect it does not.

Organizational Characteristics and the Use of Market-Mediated Work Arrangements

The BNA survey data mentioned earlier also provide an opportunity to explore what organizational characteristics are associated with each of three categories of market-mediated work: use of temporary work-

ers; production subcontracting; and contracting out for business/
administrative support activities. If these arrangements serve mainly
to absorb work load fluctuations, one would expect organizations
with highly seasonal or highly cyclical demand to make greater use
of them. If reducing per-unit costs were an important motivation for
moving work outside the internal labor market, one would expect
high-wage organizations to do more of it. In the absence of a good
direct measure of firms' relative pay levels, whether the firm is unionized may proxy for whether it is a high-wage employer. However,
the presence of a union in the workplace may also constrain employers' ability to restructure work as they might otherwise like. A finding
that unionized firms make greater use of a particular market-
mediated work arrangement would strongly suggest that reducing
per-unit costs was an important motivation for that use; the opposite
finding would not permit the opposite conclusion.

The first column of table 4.8 reports a model with the intensity of
the organization's use of temporary workers as the dependent variable and various organizational characteristics on the right-hand side.
Because of incomplete reporting by some respondents, this equation
was fit using a tobit procedure that allowed for both lower and upper
truncation of the dependent variable (see Abraham 1988 for details).
The second and third columns report probit models intended to
capture the factors that affect whether organizations engage in subcontracting and contracting out. Unfortunately, the survey did not
yield good information on the extent of organizations' reliance on
these market-mediated work arrangements, so that it was not possible to model this empirically.

All models include dummy variables that capture whether respondents considered their organization's demand to be either highly or
somewhat seasonal, or highly or somewhat cyclical. Both the seasonality and the cyclicality of the organization's demand appear to affect
its use of temporary workers, but neither appears to affect the probability that it subcontracts production work or that it contracts other
work out.

All models also include a dummy variable equal to one if the
respondent thought that his or her organization's pay and benefits
package was in the top 10 percent of the local area distribution. This
variable was not statistically significant in any of the three equations.
However, it may not be a very good indicator of firms' actual wage
policies: almost a third of respondents reported that their pay and

Table 4.8
Organizational characteristics associated with the use of temporary workers and outside contracting

		Dependent variable		
	Mean [s.d.]	Temporary worker use intensity	Business/administrative support contracts	Production subcontracting
Demand highly seasonal (yes=1)	.032 [.175]	1.493 (.543)	.133 (.414)	-.220 (.383)
Demand somewhat seasonal (yes=1)	.331 [.471]	.125 (.354)	-.209 (.147)	-.134 (.147)
Demand highly variable from year to year (yes=1)	.074 [.261]	1.712 (.577)	.005 (.287)	.421 (.292)
Demand somewhat variable from year to year (yes=1)	.648 [.478]	.411 (.491)	-.090 (.158)	.117 (.157)
Compensation reported in top 10 percent of distribution (yes=1)	.323 [.468]	.011 (.303)	-.051 (.143)	.079 (.142)
Proportion of nonexempt work force unionized	.194 [.326]	-1.333 (.481)	.521 (.212)	.605 (.211)
Manufacturing (yes=1)	.577 [.495]	-.049 (.306)	-.008 (.139)	-.056 (.142)
Constant	—	1.404 (.453)	.230 (.143)	-.194 (.142)
ln(likelihood)	—	-741.99	-255.45	-258.06

Note: The models reported were estimated using data from the Bureau of National Affairs survey described in the text. The data set contained information not only on whether the organization used temporary workers (agency temporaries, short-term hires, or on-call workers), but also on the intensity of their use. For administrative/business support contracting and production subcontracting, I have reliable information only on whether contracting out occurred. The temporary worker use-intensity model was fit using a tobit procedure that allowed for both lower and upper truncation of the dependent variable. The two contracting-out models were fit using a probit procedure. The numbers shown in parentheses are standard errors. The sample size for all equations was 381.

benefits package was in the top 10 percent of the distribution. Alternatively, the very high proportion of respondents reporting that they offer above-average compensation may say something about the nature of the survey sample.

Another explanatory variable included in all models is the proportion of the organization's nonexempt work force that is covered by a collective bargaining agreement. As noted earlier, this variable may proxy for whether the firm is a high-wage or a low-wage employer, though interpretation of the union coefficient is complicated by the fact that the union may be able to prevent assignment of work to outsiders. The union variable's coefficient in the temporary-help equation is strongly negative. It is not possible to tell whether union employers could have reduced their per-unit labor costs by making greater use of temporaries, but one can conclude that unions are quite effective at stopping employers from bringing outsiders in to do work on the organization's premises. In contrast, the union coefficients in both the subcontracting and the contracting-out equations are strongly positive. This suggests that the desire to reduce hourly labor costs is an important factor behind the use of these arrangements and, in addition, that unions are not very effective at preventing employers' efforts to circumvent negotiated contract terms by having work done off the premises.

Employers' Stated Reasons for Using Market-Mediated Work Arrangements

The evidence just described permits some indirect inferences concerning employers' use of market-mediated work arrangements. An alternative approach, less favored by economists, is simply to ask employers what their reasons for using these arrangements are. The BNA survey included questions about employers' motivations for using temporary workers, production subcontracting, and the contracting out of administrative and business support work. The answers to these questions, summarized in table 4.9, are broadly consistent with the evidence already discussed.

Some 90 percent of users of temporary help (which here includes agency temporaries, short-term hires, and on-call workers) report reasons related to workload fluctuations—special projects, seasonal needs, and providing a buffer for regular staff against downturns in demand—as factors in that use. The list of possible reasons that

Table 4.9
Reasons for use of temporary help, administrative/business support contracts, and production subcontracting

	Temporary help[a]	Business/administrative support contracts	Production subcontracting
Special projects	77	—	—
Seasonal needs	52	—	36
Short-term or irregular work	—	28	13
Provide a buffer for regular staff against downturns in demand	22	10	41
Any of the above	90	33	41
Lower cost due to lower wages paid by contractor	—	26	32
Lower cost due to other factors	—	29	38
Either of the above	—	44	53
Special expertise of temporary worker or contractor	29	65	55
Prefer not to hire regular employees for some ongoing jobs	20	33	28
Fill vacancy until a regular employee is hired	60	—	—
Fill in for absent regular employee	80	—	—
Identify good candidates for regular jobs	23	—	—
Unable to recruit regular employees to perform work	—	12	7
Sample size	412	202	169
Number of users	413	252	181

Notes: The numbers reported are percentages based on responses to the Bureau of National Affairs survey described in the text. "—" means not included in the list of reasons respondents were asked to choose from.
a. "Temporary help" refers to agency temporaries, short-term hires, and on-call workers.

respondents were asked to choose among did not include "labor-cost savings" but did include "special expertise of the temporary worker." Relatively few respondents cited temporaries' special expertise as a reason for using temporary workers.

In contrast to the reasons given for the use of temporary workers, only 41 percent of those who subcontract production work and only a third of those who contract out for business/administrative support services mention work load fluctuations—short-term or irregular work or providing a buffer for regular staff against downturns in demand—as a reason for their contracting activity. These respondents were somewhat more likely to cite "lower cost due to lower wages paid by contractor" and "lower cost due to other factors" as reasons for their contracting activity, and those contracting out either for security services or for cleaning services, where the least-skilled workers would probably be employed, were significantly more likely to mention lower wage costs as a motivation for their contracting out. But the most often-cited motivation for contracting out is the special expertise possessed by the outside contractor, cited by 55 percent of those who subcontract and by 65 percent of those who contract out for administrative/business support services.

Taken as a whole, the evidence just presented points to quite different motivations for employers' use of different sorts of market-mediated work arrangements. Temporary employment—including both agency temporary employment and hiring of temporaries onto organizations' own payrolls—is the only category of market-mediated work for which buffering regular employees from fluctuations in demand appears to be a primary employer motivation. For business services requiring relatively low skill levels, wages and benefits in the business service sector appear to be substantially less generous than elsewhere in the economy and employers appear quite likely to view savings on labor costs as important in their contracting-out decisions. Labor-cost savings are also cited as important by a substantial fraction of organizations that subcontract production work. The ability of contractors to provide specialized services that cannot be economically provided in-house has been conspicuously absent from popular discussions of market-mediated work arrangements. It is therefore all the more striking that so many organizations cite contractors' special expertise as a reason for their contracting-out activity.

Why Has the Use of Market-Mediated Work Arrangements Grown?

The previous section has presented considerable information pertaining to employers' motivations for using various market-mediated work arrangements. An equally interesting question is what accounts for U.S. employers' growing use of these arrangements over the past decade or so. Hard evidence on the latter issue is quite difficult to come by, but some clues concerning the factors that have been at work can be found. I start from the premise that the most plausible explanation for the growing use of market-mediated work arrangements is that the central motivations for their current use have become more compelling over time. Taking this premise as a starting point, any development that might have increased the attractiveness of using temporaries to buffer the regular work force would provide an appealing explanation for the growing use of temporary workers. In the same spirit, evidence of a widening wage or benefit cost gap between firms contracting out work and firms performing contract work would offer a natural explanation for the increased contracting out of less-skilled work.

The theoretical discussion earlier in the paper suggests at least four developments that could have made using temporaries to buffer the regular work force more attractive to U.S. employers: increases in the variability or uncertainty of product demand; increases in the costs of hiring and firing regular employers; increases in regular employees' relative wages; and reductions in the firm-specificity of regular employees' skills. Readily available evidence suggests that at least the first two of these could have been important. I have no good basis for assessing the potential importance of the latter two possibilities, though this would be an interesting subject for future research.

With respect to the variability of demand for employers' products, there is considerable evidence of increased volatility in the macroeconomic environment since the early to mid-1970s. The shift from a fixed exchange rate system to the current flexible exchange rate system in 1973 seems likely to have contributed significantly to this volatility. Recent experience makes it all too clear that fluctuations in exchange rates can cause enormous problems for U.S. exporting industries, in particular, and for the U.S. economy as a whole (see, for example, Piore and Sabel 1984). Evidence on the rate of structural change in the economy is more mixed. There is little evidence that growth is more unevenly spread across industries than used to be the case, at least not once aggregate conditions have been taken into account. There is, however, some indication that product life cycles have shortened significantly in the past twenty years. Shorter product life cycles create the need for more frequent retooling and are likely also to create significant uncertainty concerning labor demand (Osterman 1988).

There is also reason to suspect that it has become more expensive for U.S. employers to adjust the size of their regular work forces. While U.S. law and practice with respect to job security still gives employees very limited "property rights," recent changes have made it more difficult to lay off workers. An important development has been the passage of equal employment opportunity legislation that prohibits dismissal of employees because of their sex, race, color, creed, or, most important in the present context, age. Any employer who carries out a large-scale layoff runs a significant risk of being sued by former employees who believe that discrimination was a factor in their being let go. The number of cases charging age discrimination in dismissal or layoff decisions has risen particularly rapidly, from about 5,500 in 1980 to more than 13,000 in 1986. Settlements can be expensive; the Equitable Life Assurance company, which was involved in a lawsuit involving a mass layoff that affected 360 workers over the age of forty, ended up with a $12.5 million liability.[10] And even if the employer "wins" a case, legal fees and adverse effects on other employees' morale may be quite costly. Casual observation suggests that many employers have deemed it worthwhile to offer expensive voluntary severance and early retirement programs rather than carry out layoffs; this must at least in part reflect the increased costs associated with reducing the size of the work force through layoffs.[11]

A recent development with similar, if as yet less dramatic, consequences has been the erosion of the employment-at-will doctrine. Under U.S. common law, employers have had the right to fire any employee, for any reason, at any time. As already noted, this right has been restricted by legislation that prohibits the use of certain specific criteria in firing decisions, but a series of judicial decisions handed down beginning in the 1970s have begun a potentially more fundamental attack on the at-will concept. In some cases, judges have gone so far as to hold that employers' assurances to employees concerning their jobs created an "implicit contract" that the employer was obligated to uphold (BNA 1982a). While there have been relatively few cases of this sort, they have received enormous publicity and have surely contributed to employers' perceptions that the use of dismissals and layoffs can be very expensive.

The second major issue to be addressed is whether contracting out to take advantage of lower labor costs at other firms has become more attractive. Evidence that the dispersion of wage rates across sectors has increased would suggest that it has, since there would be a larger potential gain to firms at the top of the wage distribution that contracted out work to firms at the bottom. Bell and Freeman (1985) document a significant increase in the dispersion of wage rates across industries during the 1970s and early 1980s. They show further that this widening wage dispersion was attributable to the growth of high-wage industries' wages relative to low-wage industries' wages, so that there would have been an increased incentive for firms in high-wage industries to contract out work to firms in low-wage industries. Johnson (1983) provides evidence that the union/non-union wage differential rose significantly between the early 1970s and the early 1980s; this could have strengthened unionized employers' incentive to contract out work. The case that cost-cutting incentives for reliance on market-mediated work arrangements have become more important certainly could be strengthened. An obvious next step would be a more careful investigation of whether relative labor costs have risen at firms that have increased their contracting activity while falling at firms performing contract work. Nonetheless, the fact that sectoral wage differentials appear to have widened substantially over the period of interest is certainly suggestive.

Conclusion

This chapter has documented the extensive and growing reliance of U.S. employers on market-mediated work arrangements, including the use of temporary workers, production subcontracting, and contracting out for business support services. Rough calculations indicate that by 1986, temporary workers represented about 1.5 percent of the total work force and other business service employment accounted for another 4 percent or so of the total. A reasonable guess is that adding in production subcontracting might bring the total for all categories of market-mediated work up to somewhere in the vicinity of 10 percent of total employment. Moreover, all categories of market-mediated work appear to be growing more rapidly than employment elsewhere in the economy.

These and related developments have been the subject of considerable popular discussion, much of it quite misleading. The types of arrangements discussed here are often lumped together with part-time work under the label "contingent work." This label conjures up a picture of workers who are only loosely attached to their positions and who might easily lose them should economic conditions change. This picture does not in fact match up well with the evidence on employers' motivations for using market-mediated work arrangements presented in this paper. It is also questionable whether the contingent worker label should be applied to part-time workers. In preliminary explorations of part-time and full-time employment by industry, I found no evidence that the number of part-time employees fluctuated disproportionately over the business cycle.

Workers who fill the role of buffering regular employees from fluctuations in demand can appropriately be labeled contingent workers. The information we have examined suggests that only temporary workers belong in this category. Employers' interest in reducing hourly labor costs, another motivation that figures prominently in the popular discussion, does seem to play an important role in decisions to contract out for support services and to subcontract production work, at least in cases where relatively low-skilled work is involved. While internal labor market constraints do seem to play an important role in employers' decisions to use market-mediated work arrangements, a substantial fraction of both business service firms' employment and production subcontractors' employment is accounted for by the provision of specialized services that simply cannot be produced economically by their clients in-house.

The final issue taken up here is the noticeable increase in the use of market-mediated work arrangements in the past ten years. While the evidence considered supports no more than very tentative conclusions, there are some obvious suspects. Insofar as the growing use of temporary workers reflects increased demand for a buffer work force, the evidence points a finger at increased volatility in the economic environment and increased costs of hiring and firing regular employees. Widening labor cost differentials between high- and low-wage firms may help to explain the growth in such low-skill business service activities as mailing, reproduction and stenographic services, and building maintenance services. The question of why employment relationships are evolving as they are is certainly a question deserving of further study.

Appendix 4.A

Respondents to the survey concerning employers' use of market-mediated work arrangements conducted in collaboration with the Bureau of National Affairs that is discussed in the text were given the following definitions to guide their responses.

Agency Temporaries.
Individuals employed through a temporary-help agency to work for your organization. Examples: accountants, clerical help, laborers, maintenance workers, nurses.

Short-Term Hires.
Employees hired on the company payroll either for a specific period of time or for a specific project. Examples: employees hired during the Christmas season, students hired for the summer, employees hired for a one-time project or event. This classification includes freelancers hired by the hour or day, but does not include individuals in an "on-call" pool.

On-Call Workers.
Individuals in a pool of workers who are called in on an as-needed basis. Examples: laborers supplied by a union hiring hall, retirees who work for a few days a month.

Contract Work.
Production or service operations and administrative/business support activities performed under contract by other firms or individuals. Contract production/service operations include any work performed to your specifications that contributes directly to the products or services your organization sells. All other contract work should be reported as administrative/business support activities. Examples of other contracts include: cleaning, maintenance, security, food service, printing, duplicating, mailing, payroll processing, engineering, accounting, product testing, marketing studies, other management consulting, warehousing, shipping, and billing.

Notes

1. The internal labor market concept can be traced back to Kerr (1954) and Dunlop (1966), and is developed at length in Doeringer and Piore (1971). The importance of transactions costs as a determinant of organizational structure is stressed by Williamson (1975). Becker (1975) and Mincer (1974) discuss on-the-job learning. Lazear (1979) and Shapiro and Stiglitz (1984)

offer two quite different analyses of how wage policies in an internal labor market can influence employees' behavior.

2. See, for example, *Boston Globe* (1984), *New York Times* (1986), and *Business Week* (1986). More academic discussions include Mangum, Mayall, and Nelson (1985), Pfeffer and Baron (1986), Howe (1986), and Appelbaum (1987a, 1987b).

3. Perhaps the most important difference between the two series is that the BLS numbers are annual averages, whereas the BOC numbers refer to payroll employment during the week of March 12. In addition, the BLS survey questionnaire distinguishes between supervisory and nonsupervisory employment, while the BOC survey questionnaire does not.

4. Estimates of the proportion of hours worked accounted for by each type of temporary worker were based on answers to three questions: number of temporary assignments made during 1985; average assignment length; and year-end 1985 regular employment. The answers to the first two questions were used to construct estimates of the person-years worked by temporaries, which I then compared to the year-end level of regular employment. For details of these calculations and of the calculation using BLS data, see Abraham (1988).

5. The survey question concerning use of contracted administrative/business support services asked respondents to indicate the extent of their reliance on contractors to provide cleaning/maintenance, security, food service, printing/duplicating/mailing, payroll processing, engineering, and "other" services. Considerable initiative would have been required to list contracted activities in the "other" category; only about 15 percent of respondents did so. The 57 percent number in the text is best thought of as the percent of organizations contracting out for any of the six specifically-mentioned support services.

6. Abraham (1988) presents a simple model in which a firm facing variable demand must choose its desired level of regular employment, assumed to be fixed once chosen, and the extent to which it will rely upon supplemental staffing. That model can easily be modified to allow for hiring and firing of regular employees. A more realistic model would also explicitly consider the costs associated with other means of accommodating fluctuations in demand, such as varying regular employees' hours of work or varying inventory levels, and might also make decisions concerning investment in the regular work force endogenous. Introducing these additional complexities would certainly affect the specific solution to the firm's optimal strategy problem, but would not alter the qualitative conclusions just stated.

7. For mailing, reproductive and stenographic services, personnel supply services, and computer and data processing services, 1972 is the first year for which these data are available.

8. Business service sector employees actually tend to have slightly more education than employees holding similar jobs in other sectors. They are

younger than average, but are distributed similarly across race and sex groups.

9. The median respondent to the BNA survey reported a typical assignment duration of under one month for agency temporaries, one to three months for short-term hires and under a week for on-call workers. See Abraham (1988).

10. The data on number of charges refer to cases handled by the EEOC or by state agencies reporting to the EEOC. The information on the Equitable settlement was obtained directly from the EEOC.

11. See BNA (1982b) for a discussion of some companies' voluntary severance programs.

References

Abraham, Katharine G. 1988. "The Role of Flexible Staffing Arrangements in Short-Term Workforce Adjustment Strategies," in Robert A. Hart, ed., *Employment, Unemployment, and Hours of Work*, London: George Allen and Unwin, 288–311.

Appelbaum, Eileen. 1987a. "Restructuring Work: Temporary, Part-Time, and At-Home Employment," in Heidi Hartmann, ed., *Computer Chips and Paper Clips*, Vol. 2, Washington: National Academy Press, 268–310.

Appelbaum, Eileen. 1987b. "Contingent Jobs and Union Responses in the U.S." Philadelphia: Temple University Department of Economics Working Paper.

Becker, Gary S. 1975. *Human Capital,* second edition, New York: National Bureau of Economic Research.

Bell, Linda, and Freeman, Richard B. 1985. "Does a Flexible Industry Wage Structure Increase Employment?: The U.S. Experience," Cambridge, Massachusetts: NBER Working Paper No. 1604.

Blau, Francine. 1977. *Equal Pay in the Office.* Lexington, Massachusetts: D. C. Heath and Company.

Boston Globe. 1984. "Fear of Slowdown Causes Businesses to Limit Payrolls," May 10, 68.

Boston Globe. 1987. "Being a 'Temp' Takes on New Meaning," November 3, 29.

Bureau of National Affairs. 1982a. *The Employment-at-Will Issue,* Supplement to *Daily Labor Report,* Washington, D.C., November 19.

Bureau of National Affairs. 1982b. *White Collar Layoffs,* Supplement to *Daily Labor Report,* Washington, D.C., August 12.

Bureau of National Affairs. 1986. *The Changing Workplace: New Directions in Staffing and Scheduling,* Special Report, Washington, D.C.

Business Week. 1986. "The Disposable Employee is Becoming a Fact of Corporate Life," December 15, 52–56.

Business Week. 1987. "Why Two-Tier Wage Scales are Starting to Self-Destruct," March 16, 41.

Carter, Susan. 1988. "The Changing Importance of Lifetime Jobs," *Industrial Relations* 27, 287–300.

Dickens, William T., and Katz, Lawrence. 1987. "Interindustry Wage Differences and Theories of Wage Determination," Cambridge, Massachusetts: NBER Working Paper No. 2271.

Doeringer, Peter B., and Piore, Michael J. 1971. *Internal Labor Markets and Manpower Analysis.* Lexington, Massachusetts: Lexington Books.

Dunlop, John T. 1966. "Job Vacancy Measures and Economic Analysis," in *The Measurement and Interpretation of Job Vacancies: A Conference Report,* New York: Columbia University Press, 27–47.

Groshen, Erica. 1986. "Sources of Wage Dispersion: How Much Do Employers Matter?" Doctoral dissertation, Harvard University.

Howe, Wayne. 1986. "The Business Services Industry Sets Pace in Employment Growth," *Monthly Labor Review* 109 (April), 29–36.

Jacoby, Sanford. 1985. *Employing Bureaucracy.* New York: Columbia University Press.

Johnson, George. 1983. "Unionism in a Macroeconomic Context: An Exploratory Analysis," Ann Arbor: University of Michigan Department of Economics Working Paper.

Katz, Lawrence. 1986. "Efficiency Wage Theories: A Partial Evaluation," in Stanley Fischer, ed., *NBER Macroeconomics Annual 1986.* Cambridge, Massachusetts: MIT Press, 235–276.

Kerr, Clark. 1954. "The Balkanization of Labor Markets," in E. Wight Bakke et al., eds., *Labor Mobility and Economic Opportunity,* Cambridge, Massachusetts: Technology Press of MIT, 92–110.

Lazear, Edward. 1979. "Why is There Mandatory Retirement?" *Journal of Political Economy* 87 (December), 1261–1284.

Mangum, Garth, Mayall, Donald, and Nelson, Kristin. 1985. "The Temporary–Help Industry: A Response to the Dual Internal Labor Market," *Industrial and Labor Relations Review* 38 (July), 599–611.

Mincer, Jacob. 1974. *Schooling, Experience, and Earnings.* New York: National Bureau of Economic Research.

New York Times. 1984. "What's New in Temporary Employment," December 16, F15.

New York Times. 1986. "Part-Time Work New Labor Trend," July 9, 1.

New York Times. 1987. "The Two-Tier Wage System is Found to Be Two-Edged Sword by Industry," July 21, 1.

Osterman, Paul. 1988. *Employment Futures: Reorganization, Dislocation, and Public Policy.* New York: Oxford University Press.

Pfeffer, Jeffrey, and Baron, James N. 1986. "Taking the Workers Back Out: Recent Trends in the Structuring of Employment," Stanford, California: Stanford University Graduate School of Business Research Paper No. 926.

Piore, Michael J., and Sabel, Charles F. 1984. *The Second Industrial Divide.* New York: Basic Books.

Shapiro, Carl, and Stiglitz, Joseph. 1984. "Involuntary Unemployment as a Worker Discipline Device," *American Economic Review* 74 (June), 433–444.

U.S. Department of Commerce, Bureau of the Census. 1975. *1972 Census of Selected Service Industries, Area Statistics, SC72-A-52,* Washington, D.C.: General Printing Office.

U.S. Department of Commerce, Bureau of the Census. 1980. *1977 Census of Service Industries, Geographic Area Series, CS77-A-52,* Washington, D.C.: General Printing Office.

U.S. Department of Commerce, Bureau of the Census. 1984. *1982 Census of Service Industries, Geographic Area Series, SC82-A-52,* Washington, D.C.: General Printing Office.

U.S. Department of Labor, Bureau of Labor Statistics. 1985. *Employment, Hours, and Earnings, United States, 1909–1984,* Washington, D.C.: General Printing Office.

U.S. Department of Labor, Bureau of Labor Statistics. 1987. *Supplement to Employment, Hours, and Earnings, United States, 1909–1984,* Washington, D.C.: General Printing Office.

Williamson, Oliver. 1975. *Markets and Hierarchies: Analysis and Antitrust Implications.* New York: Free Press.

Yellen, Janet. 1984. "Efficiency Wage Models of Unemployment," *American Economic Review* 74 (May), 200–205.

Discussion

Ron Ehrenberg (Cornell) worried that there might be significant differences in the productivity of business service sector employees and those performing similar work in other sectors. This would mean that evidence on compensation, such as that presented in tables 4.5 and 4.6, is not sufficient to establish that even high-wage employers could save money by contracting out for janitorial, guard, or other low-skill services. Even though the observable personal characteristics of business service sector employees are similar to those of individuals in the same occupation employed in other sectors, Ehrenberg continued, they might differ in important but unobservable ways. Woody Powell (University of Arizona) speculated that organizational factors in addition to the purely economic forces identified in Abraham's paper might lead managers to use temporaries and to contract out work. For example, managers may face restrictions on total head count or total payroll in their departments, but be able to draw on other resources to pay temporaries or contractors. It is an open question, Powell continued, whether managers' responses to these constraints produce outcomes that are in any sense organizationally optimal.

Several participants criticized the paper's exclusive focus on the demand for temporaries and contracting arrangements, arguing that the supply of labor to different sorts of jobs also needs to be considered. Ehrenberg suggested that it might be possible to use regionally-disaggregated data on temporary-help industry employment to perform more formal tests of the hypothesis that this sector's growth is demand driven rather than supply driven. Werner Sengenberger (ILO) raised the broader issue of whether the growing use of temporary workers and contracting arrangements is good or bad for society. While he would concede that these arrangements may help the individual firm, the cost of their use may be more precarious employment for a significant fraction of the workforce. It is not clear that, from a societal point of view, this would represent a net gain.

5

The Evolving Role of Small Business and Some Implications for Employment and Training Policy

Gary W. Loveman, Michael J. Piore, and Werner Sengenberger

This chapter focuses on changes in the size distribution of production, explanations for these changes, and the implications for labor market organization in general and for the U.S. labor market in particular. It draws on material collected by the International Institute for Labour Studies of the International Labour Organization (ILO) through its program, the New Industrial Organization, with which we have been working for two years. That program is designed to explore changes occurring in the key institutional structures of advanced industrialized countries, various hypotheses about the root causes of such changes, and the similarities and differences across countries. The program is thus focusing not only on business organizations, but also on trade unions and institutions of labor relations, and on the economic activities of the nation-state and local and regional governmental units.

The first project in the New Industrial Organization program focused on developments in the small business sectors of industrialized economies. The material on small business that we draw on here is largely based on reports prepared for six countries: France, Italy, the United Kingdom, West Germany, the United States, and Japan. Reports were also prepared for three additional countries: Norway, Hungary, and Switzerland. The empirical results from this project, discussed below, suggest that there has been a trend in recent years toward increased employment shares for small enterprises and establishments. This recent trend reverses a long-standing trend in the opposite direction.

The next two sections of the chapter summarize briefly the main empirical findings from the project and consider possible explanations for them. The third section examines the employment and training implications that follow from one of the explanations for increased relative employment shares in small units of production: the rise of flexible specialization.[1] This section begins by articulating the ingredients required for flexible specialization, and then discusses how Italy, Japan, and Germany have, each in very different ways, provided these ingredients. In conclusion we consider the current structure of employment and training in the United States, and the lessons these three countries provide for the changes in that structure necessary to make flexible specialization more effective in the United States.

Major Characteristics and Trends in the Size of Business Organizations

The preliminary results of the country case studies mentioned above have been synthesized in a working paper by Sengenberger and Loveman (1988), and the completed case studies and the synthetic overview appear in Sengenberger, Loveman, and Piore (1990). The critical empirical results from that document are summarized in the tables in this paper. Unless otherwise specified, the sources for all the data are the individual country reports (see Sengenberger, Loveman, and Piore 1990). While the coverage across countries is incomplete and there are serious problems of comparability which make generalizations difficult, the following broad conclusions emerge from the data.

First, as shown in table 5.1 and table 5.2, there is substantial international variation in the distribution of employment by enterprise and establishment size. This diversity cannot easily be accounted for by obvious factors such as the size of the national economy or the size of single industries. For example, in the group of large national economies, the United States and the United Kingdom have comparatively large enterprises and establishments, while Japan and Italy stand out as the countries with the smallest employment units. Similarly, among the small countries, there exist both small and large average scale in the business structure. Sweden (not shown here) exceeds every other country in the average size of her enterprises.

Second, the most important and internationally robust conclusion to emerge from the data, documented in tables 5.3, 5.4, and 5.5, is that a decentralization of production to smaller units has occurred in recent years. In all cases for which the necessary time series data

Table 5.1
Employment shares by enterprise size (number of employees)

Country	Sector	Year	<20	20–99	100–499	500+
United States	T	1982		45.7[a]	13.0	41.3
	M	1982		17.6[a]	12.7	69.7
Japan	T	1985	37.1[b]	17.9[c]	17.3	27.0
	M	1983	27.8[b]	19.3[c]	19.6	33.3
France	T	1985	25.8	20.4	18.3	35.5
	M	1979	10.7	17.9	22.0	49.4
Germany	T	1970	21.7[d]	22.5[e]	16.9	39.0
	M	1984		15.6[f]	24.1[f]	60.3[f]
United Kingdom	M	1981		27.1[g]	36.9[h]	29.2[i]
Italy	T	1981	53.2	16.1	12.2	18.5
	M	1981	33.7	21.8	18.5	26.0

Notes:
T = Total economy
M = Manufacturing
a. 1–99 employees
b. 1–29 employees
c. 30–99 employees
d. 1–9 employees
e. 10–99 employees
f. Enterprises with less than 20 employees are not included in the sample.
g. 1–99 employees
h. 100–199 employees
i. 1000+ employees

exist, there is evidence that the employment shares of small enterprises and establishments increased from the early 1970s to the early 1980s. For most countries there is evidence of a "V" pattern, with small unit employment shares declining through the late 1960s or early 1970s and rising thereafter.

In the cases of Japan, Italy, and the United States, there has been a shift both toward smaller enterprises and toward smaller establishments that can be documented for the total economy and for the manufacturing sector. In other cases, the pattern is demonstrable only for enterprises or establishments or only for a particular sector. The magnitude of the shift to smaller units also varies widely by country, ranging from rather modest in Japan to quite large in the United Kingdom and Italy. The fact that a shift to smaller employment units is evident at both the enterprise and the establishment level suggests that changes in the organization of production, rather

Table 5.2
Employment shares by establishment size (number of employees)

Country	Sector	Year	<20	20–99	100–499	500+
United States	T	1985	26.9	29.0	23.9	20.2
	M	1985	7.4	20.2	33.8	38.6
Japan	T	1981	49.4	27.6	11.2[a]	11.7[b]
	M	1983	35.0[c]	21.0[d]	17.0[a]	27.0[b]
France	M	1981	21.8	23.0	27.1	28.1
Germany	T	1983[e]	27.3	22.4	22.6	27.1
	M	1970		33.4[f]	25.3	41.1
United Kingdom	M	1983		26.2[f]	27.0	46.8
Italy	T	1981	50.7	21.7	14.9	12.7
	M	1981	35.5	23.8	21.1	19.6

Notes:
T = Total economy
M = Manufacturing
a. 100–299 employees
b. 300+ employees
c. 1–29 employees
d. 30–99 employees
e. Data from Employment Statistics; excludes self-employed
f. 1–99 employees

than simply changes in the organizational structure of enterprises, have occurred.

A further robust result is that the vast majority of the growth in the small unit employment share came at the expense of the large unit share, while the medium-sized unit share was rather stable. Moreover, it is interesting that the shift from large to small units took place both in countries where total employment was growing vigorously, such as Japan and the United States, and in countries with essentially stagnant total employment, such as France, Germany, and the United Kingdom. In Japan, for example, the small enterprise share in total employment rose 3.8 percentage points from 1971 to 1979, while the large enterprise share fell 4 percentage points. Similarly, in France a small enterprise share increase of 7.2 percentage points from 1971 to 1985 was offset by a 7.1 percentage point decline in the large enterprise share.

The inverse relationship between small and large unit employment shares over the period from the early 1970s to the early 1980s raises an immediate red flag because it occurred concurrently with a substantial shift in employment from goods-producing industries to services-producing industries, and the latter are clearly composed, on average, of smaller enterprises and smaller establishments. An aggregate shift to smaller units could simply reflect a move from goods-producing industries to services with an unchanged size distribution in each sector. It is important to differentiate between changes in the overall size distribution of employment due to changes in the sectoral distribution of output and those due to within-sector changes in the size distribution of employment, since only the latter signify a change in industrial organization.

The OECD (1985) used statistical techniques to decompose changes in the very small enterprise employment share into compositional, within-sector, and interaction components. The results for total private employment in two countries covered in the present study, Japan (1973–1983) and France (1975–1981), suggest that from 45 to 75 percent of the increase in their very small enterprise employment shares was due to compositional shifts. Piore (1990) conducts a similar shift-share analysis on U.S. establishment employment shares for the period from 1973 to 1984 and finds that roughly one-half of the change in the small establishment share resulted from compositional shifts.

The OECD's more rigorous method of attribution has not been applied to the current sample, but a reasonable first pass at weighing the importance of compositional shifts can be had by examining employment share changes within more narrowly defined categories. Unfortunately, there is little disaggregated time series industry data available in the country case studies, forcing a reliance on data aggregated to the manufacturing and service industry levels. The time series data show that the trend of the 1970s and early 1980s toward employment in smaller units has also been present within manufacturing in Japan, Italy, France, Germany, the United Kingdom, and the United States at both the enterprise and the establishment levels.

Piore (1990) also performs shift-share analysis on changes in U.S. manufacturing establishment employment shares from 1974 to 1984. He finds that essentially none of the rise in the small establishment share was the result of interindustry employment shifts within manufacturing. Marsden's (1990) report on the United Kingdom shows that from 1979 to 1983 the share of employment in establishments with fewer than 100 employees increased within all twenty-two two-digit manufacturing and construction NACE codes. While the services data are too thin to support inference one way or the other, the

Table 5.3
Time series employment shares by enterprise size (number of employees)

	1958	1963	1967	1972	1977	1982	
United States							
Total							
S	41.3	39.9	39.9	41.3	40.1	45.7	
S+M	55.1	52.9	53.2	53.5	52.5	58.7	
Manufacturing							
S	20.6	19.1	16.3	16.2	16.2	17.6	
S+M	37.1	34.5	30.4	28.9	29.0	30.3	
Japan	1959	1965	1971	1977	1979	1982	1985
Total							
S[a]	46.7	43.8	45.5	46.5	48.3	49.3	
S[b]			53.3	56.9	57.3	56.6	55.7
S+M[a]	54.6	53.7	55.9	58.9	60.2	60.0	
S+M[a,c]			70.0	72.7	73.6	73.1	73.0
Manufacturing	1919	1935	1949	1955	1972	1979	1983[f]
S	45[d]	48[d]	51[d]	57[d]	43	49	47
S+M	75[e]	83[e]	75[e]	85[e]	63	68	67
France	1971	1979	1985				
Total							
S	39.0	43.4	46.2				
S+M	57.4	60.7	64.5				
Manufacturing							
S	26.4	28.6					
S+M	49.5	50.6					

	1907	1925	1961	1970	1980	1984
Germany						
Total						
S[g]	72.9	61.5	54.9	52.3		
S+M[h]	86.2	76.0	70.4	68.8		
Manufacturing[i]	1963	1970	1976	1977	1980	1984
S	13.5	12.0	12.7	15.3	15.0	15.6
S+M	38.5	36.0	36.8	39.0	38.8	39.7
United Kingdom[j]	1971	1973	1976	1980	1983	
Manufacturing						
S	15.5	15.3	17.0	18.8	22.0	
Italy	1951	1961	1971	1981		
Total						
S	60.2	63.5	61.6	69.3		
S+M	73.0	77.1	74.4	81.5		
Manufacturing[k]						
S	50.5	53.2	50.5	55.3		
S+M	67.4	72.0	69.2	73.9		

Notes:
S = <100 employees
S + M = <500 employees
a. *Basic Survey of Employment Structure*
b. *Annual Report of the Labor Force Survey*
c. 0–299 employees
d. 5–99 employees
e. 5–999 employees
f. From OECD (1985), chart 13
g. 1–199 employees
h. 1–999 employees
i. 1963–1976 data are *not* comparable with 1977–1983 data due to inclusion of the *Handwerk* sector only in the latter period. Also, data cover only enterprises with more than 20 employees.
j. From Storey and Johnson (1987), table 4
k. Excludes NACE divisions 21 and 23

Table 5.4
Time series employment shares by establishment size: total economy

Recent Data							
United States	1962	1965	1970	1975	1979	1982	1985
S	51.3	51.5	49.5	54.0	54.1	55.1	55.9
S+M	77.7	77.6	78.6	79.8			
Japan	1969	1972	1975	1978	1981		
S	70.1	71.5	73.8	76.1	77.1		
S+M[a]	83.1	84.2	85.6	87.5	88.3		
Germany[b]	1977	1979	1982	1984	1985		
S	47.0	47.9	49.0	50.2	49.6		
S+M	70.4	71.1	71.9	73.0	72.3		
Italy	1951	1961	1971	1981			
S	67.2	61.6	69.3	72.4			
S+M	82.6	82.2	85.0	87.3			
Historical Data							
Germany[c]	1882[g]	1895[g]	1907	1925	1933	1950	1970
S[d,e]	78.0	70.4	62.9	53.3	62.0	56.8	43.6
S+M[d,f]	88.1	84.4	79.7	69.9	76.4	73.0	63.2

Notes:
S   = <100 employees
S+M = <500 employees
a. 1–299 employees
b. Data from Employment Statistics
c. Census data
d. Includes the self-employed in the "small" category
e. 1–49 employees
f. 1–199 employees
g. No self-employed data for these years

Table 5.5
Time series employment shares by establishment size: manufacturing

United States	1909	1919	1929	1933	1939	1947	1967	1977
VS[a]	14	10	10	10	10	7	6	7
S[a]	38	29	29	31	30	25	23	25
	1974	1978	1982	1985				
S[b]	24	25	27	28				
S+M[b]	57	58	60	61				
Japan	1957	1962	1967	1971	1977	1980	1982	1984
S	59	52	53	51	56	58	56	55
S+M[c]	73	68	69	67	71	74	72	72
France	1906	1926	1931	1936	1954	1966	1974	1981
S	75	63	59	61	52	48	45	47
S+M	88	81	79	79	75	74	72	73
Germany[d]	1963	1970	1976	1977	1980	1984		
S	20	19	20	19	18	19		
S+M	48	47	48	48	47	49		
United Kingdom	1930	1948	1954	1963	1970	1974/75	1983	
S	29	27	24	20	18	20	26	
S+M	62	59	57	50	45	45	53	
Italy[e]	1951	1961	1971	1981				
S	54	57	55	59				
S+M	75	79	77	80				

Notes:
VS = <20 employees
S = <100 employees
S+M = <500 employees
a. Census of Manufacturers data
b. Country Business Patterns data
c. 1–299 employees
d. 1963–1976 data are not comparable with 1977–1984 data due to inclusion of the Handwerk sector only in the latter period.
e. Excludes NACE divisions 21 and 23.

available results suggest that there has been a meaningful shift to smaller units even after accounting for changes in the composition of output.

Another cause for concern that the increasing small unit employment shares do not reflect fundamental changes in industrial organization is that aggregate economic conditions generally worsened between the early 1970s and the early 1980s. Small unit employment shares often rise in recessionary periods as there is a shift of employment out of industries like capital goods or other durables that are primarily composed of large units, while new and small firm employment rises as workers seek alternatives to unemployment. Since much of the observed rise in small unit employment shares reported here coincided with recessionary conditions, it would be desirable to control for cyclical factors. Unfortunately, except for the United States, this has not been done.

In the United States' case, there is evidence for a shift toward smaller employment units even after controlling for cyclical factors (see Piore 1990). What may be more persuasive evidence, however, is the fact that the movement to smaller units took place across so many countries with widely varying macroeconomic circumstances, e.g., Japan, Italy, the United Kingdom, and the United States. Furthermore, the coincidence of change in employment shares with a deep recession does not imply that the change is purely transitory. The recession itself may have been caused by, or connected with, ongoing structural change. If an economic system is in crisis, structural change may proceed coincidentally with an overall economic downturn. If small unit employment shares remain high after an economy rebounds, the case for industrial reorganization is much stronger. Where recent post-recession data exist, such as for Japan, the United States, France, Norway, and Hungary, the evidence is indeed consistent with an industrial reorganization interpretation.[2]

Finally, the existence of comparable enterprise and establishment data is important for consideration of a closely related issue: decentralization of production within large enterprises. Declining large enterprise employment shares are not sufficient to demonstrate that such decentralization has occurred, since they are consistent with a declining number of increasingly large establishments. However, if the dynamics of establishment and enterprise size distributions in an industry both favor smaller units, then the hypothesis of decentralization within large firms gains further credence. The data, in fact, support such a hypothesis for most cases where comparable data exist, e.g., Japan, Italy, France, Germany, the United States, and the United Kingdom. Nonetheless, to make the case conclusive requires data on the average number of establishments per large enterprise. The British report (Marsden 1990) provides such data for the 100 largest British firms from 1970 to 1983. These data show an increase in the average number of establishments per large enterprise and a decline in average employment per establishment, thus demonstrating decentralization of large enterprises in the United Kingdom.

Space does not permit us to include the other findings from the country case studies here, but two additional points emerge that because of their particular relevance to subsequent parts of this chapter should be added.

First, there is a large and growing literature on the job-generation process covering a number of different countries. The methodology for these studies was pioneered by Birch in the United States, using a Dun and Bradstreet file of individual businesses, and has been replicated in a number of OECD countries including Germany, the United Kingdom, France, and Norway.[3] The data are difficult to interpret and the results controversial, but they are, at least, not inconsistent with the hypothesis that small enterprises have become increasingly important in job generation, although probably not as important as the initial Birch results for the United States implied.

Second, the country reports examined the question of employment conditions in small and large businesses. A subset of the results are collected in table 5.6, which shows that wages are an increasing function of enterprise/establishment size. In Japan, wages in small enterprises are just over half those in large enterprises. Wage differentials appear much narrower in Germany (and in all Scandinavian countries) where comprehensive industry-wide bargains are often applicable to all employers, particularly in industries with many small firms. The figures in table 5.6 differ so substantially in definition and coverage, however, that the only meaningful conclusion to be drawn may be that small units pay lower average wages than large units in all countries in the sample.

The time series evidence on wages by unit size is much more limited, with comprehensive data available only for Japan. Manufacturing establishment data are available for the United States, and more anecdotal evidence is available for the United Kingdom. The Japanese report (Koshiro 1990) presents three time series by firm size:

Table 5.6
Average wages by enterprise and establishment size (percentage of wages in largest employment size group)

Country	Year	Number of employees		
		10–99	100–499	500+
United States[a]	1983	57[b]	74	100
Japan[c]	1982	77	83[d]	100[e]
France[f]	1978	83	86	100
Germany[g]	1978	90	92	100
Italy[g]	1978	85	93	100

Country	Year	5–29	30–99	100–499	500+
Japan[h]	1984	59	70	83	100

Country	Year	10–49	50–99	100–199	200–499	500–999	1000
Germany[i]	1978						
blue collar		80	79	80	82	86	100
white collar		64	74	79	80	85	100

Country	Year	25–49	50–99	100–199	200–499	500–999	1000–1999	2000+
United Kingdom[j]	1980							
semi-skilled		76	86	85	91	94	97	100
skilled		82	88	86	94	95	97	100
clerical		82	86	87	89	89	89	100
middle management		82	85	85	87	92	89	100

United States[k]						
1974	78	71	73	80	100
1976	69	71	72	80	100
1978	65	66	70	79	100
1980	61	66	71	80	100
1982	62	65	71	79	100
1984	60	63	69	77	100

Japan[h]	5–29	30–99	100–499	500+
1965	66	78	87	100
1970	65	76	86	100
1975	65	76	86	100
1980	62	73	84	100
1984	59	70	83	100

United Kingdom[l]	25–99	500+
1970	85	100
1980	93	100

Notes: The Italian data, the first German and United Kingdom series, and the second United States series are for establishments; all others are for enterprises. For more information concerning the data, see the individual country reports in Sengenberger, Loveman and Piore (1990).

a. Usual weekly earnings for wage and salary earners in private nonagricultural sector
b. 1–99 employees
c. Monthly scheduled earnings for regular employees in private nonagricultural sector
d. 100–999 employees
e. 1000+ employees
f. Hourly pay, manual manufacturing workers
g. Hourly pay, male manual manufacturing workers
h. Average monthly cash earnings of regular employees in all industries except services
i. Total labor cost per hour in manufacturing, mining, and construction
j. Workplace industrial relations survey for whole economy, establishments
k. Annual payroll per employee in manufacturing establishments
l. Average weekly earnings for manual workers in engineering firms

average monthly regular pay; average hourly earnings; and average monthly cash earnings. The last series, shown in table 5.6, is consistent with the other two in showing a trend increase in size-related differentials. There is likewise a strong trend from 1974 to 1984 toward larger differentials for all U.S. manufacturing establishment size groups under one thousand workers. The only other intertemporal evidence comes from a comparison of 1970s and 1980s average weekly earnings for manual workers in engineering firms in the United Kingdom that shows a very significant decline in size-related wage differentials.

The evidence is thus inconclusive with respect to how size-related wage differentials have changed. These "gross" differentials are, in any case, an imperfect measure because they fail to adjust for differences in worker characteristics such as education and experience that may vary by firm size. It is well known, however, that at least in the United States, workers in small firms earn less than those in large firms even after adjusting for all relevant observable worker characteristics.[4] Koshiro (1990) examines similarly adjusted Japanese data and finds that, while significant size-related differentials exist even in the adjusted data, they declined over the period 1961 to 1984.

Typologies, Hypotheses, and Explanations

In order to interpret these structural patterns and trends, it is useful to develop a typology of small business in industrial economies and a set of hypotheses about how structural shifts in the economy are manifested across these various types. The structural shifts just documented should be considered along two dimensions: temporally, to account for the observed successive stages of decline and revival of small firms; and cross-sectionally, to explain the significant international dispersion in the share of small business employment. No standard typology emerges either from economic theory or from the writings on economic structure in other fields. But the existing literature, together with discussions with researchers associated with the ILO project, does suggest four sets of hypotheses about the evolution of economic structures in the course of economic development. These sets of hypotheses are not mutually exclusive, but they are distinct.

1. In the absence of any structural theory, one strand of thinking emphasizes the influence of the dynamics of growth and decline on

the dispersion of business units by size. In every industry there is presumably an optimal size for business units. At any point, units will be distributed around that optimal size due to accidental factors that make them temporarily larger or smaller.[5] There will also be a systematic distortion of the distribution over time due to the growth and decline of particular industries. In expanding industries, there will be many new firms growing toward the optimum; in declining industries, there will be many old firms shrinking away from the optimum on their way to oblivion. Hence, both new and older industries should have a relatively large number of smaller units. A shift toward smaller units in the overall distribution might be associated either with a cyclical downturn, in which more businesses were forced by economic events to operate below their "normal" capacity, or with rapid structural change, in which there was an unusually rapid shift in activity away from one set of older industries (reducing the size of existing firms below their optimal level) and toward a new set of industries (generating new firms which had not yet reached their optimum).

This "reversion to the mean" view cannot explain the wide international variance in the size distribution of employment, since it would lead one to expect a similar size distribution within similar industries.[6] The international variance in the size distribution of employment documented above must reflect historical and institutional differences ignored by the "reversion to the mean" view that influence the organization of production in important ways.

Furthermore, in and of itself the "reversion to the mean" view implies nothing about the wage levels, employment conditions, skill, or training patterns across firms of different sizes. We must look elsewhere to explain the general finding that small firms pay lower wages. If size-related wage differentials were small, one could argue that reduced wage levels, like reduced employment, were associated with transitory business difficulties, while high wages were associated with transitory business success. But this does not appear plausible for differentials of the size observed in the United States or Japan. Moreover, the fact that in some cases the shift in the size distribution of employment toward smaller units has been accompanied by a compression of size-related earnings differentials argues against this hypothesis. To the extent that the small firm sector was composed of a disproportionate number of firms in adverse circumstances, one would expect them to have trouble paying the market wage.

2. Classical economists, beginning with Adam Smith and continuing through Karl Marx, have developed the idea that the size structure of enterprises can be understood in terms of the economies of scale associated with the specialization of resources and the division of labor. Their views are consistent with the theories of mass production exemplified by the business practices associated with Frederick Taylor and Henry Ford. Technological progress, Smith and Marx argued, is dependent upon dividing the productive process into a series of discrete tasks and then creating inputs, in the form of narrowly trained labor and dedicated capital equipment, especially adapted for the performance of these tasks. The larger the scale of the production process, the more finely divided the number of productive tasks and hence the more specialized the resources. Justifying the investments in such specialized resources requires markets large enough to absorb the output produced and stable enough to keep the specialized resources fully employed. Large organizations are required to maintain markets with these properties, to mobilize resources on the scale required for investments of this magnitude, and to coordinate internally the pieces of the production process that are isolated from each other in the development of the production technology but so specialized that they have no independent meaning and no latitude for adjustment to variations in adjacent operations.

An economy dominated by these technological principles will require a complement of other productive activities that do not lend themselves to mass production and that take place in different and probably much smaller organizational entities. Such activities include catering to markets where demand is too volatile and/or too uncertain to justify investment in specialized resources; the production of the highly specialized machinery used in mass production; supplying new products and output in declining industries with markets too small to justify mass production; and the production of luxury goods whose value is associated with their relative rarity. These other activities are heterogeneous to the point that it may not be meaningful to think of them as all of a piece but, relative to mass production, they are sufficiently similar that one can reasonably talk about a dual economy, with a second or "peripheral" sector composed of smaller firms. In part, however, the small firms tend to be dependent on the large ones in the sense that the mass-production companies use them to handle the volatile portion of demand for their own products, to act as subcontractors, or to produce specialized capital goods. Increased volatility and uncertainty, or an increasing taste for non-standard, specialized goods, will tend to shift the distribution of production in the direction of the peripheral sector and, hence, toward these small businesses.

The structure of the labor market in an economy organized on these principles will not necessarily follow the firms' structure. Mass production tends to involve narrowly trained, semi-skilled workers. The work outside mass production tends to involve a broader range of operations and normally it requires more skilled labor. But, because a larger share of skilled labor is required and skilled workers are more expensive, there is also a strong incentive to separate skilled and unskilled work. Hence, one would expect this "peripheral" form of production to draw on two distinct labor market segments. One will contain highly skilled workers; for this segment, the expense of training creates an incentive to maintain continuity of employment. Another segment will contain unskilled labor; here, there may be little reason to maintain employment continuity. In practice, however, there may be a variety of social arrangements that conserve skilled labor despite employment variability or that provide employment continuity for unskilled workers.

A mass production economy may require some protection from the competition of low-wage, skilled workers. Mass-produced goods are, almost by definition, inferior to specialized commodities because the latter are adapted to particular needs. People presumably are induced to buy them because the economies of scale associated with their production render them considerably (and over time progressively) less expensive than specialized goods. If the skilled labor to produce the specialized goods were to be available at wages less than the semi-skilled labor required to mass produce, this structure would be seriously threatened. It should be noted that the threat is twofold: the specialized goods may become less expensive and hence more attractive than the mass produced goods; and, as customers desert the mass market, the economies of scale there are reduced and the cost of mass production increases.

This view of a capitalistic economy is generally termed "Fordist" or "dualist." It yields a family of hypotheses about the shift toward smaller units, including two central ones. First, the increasing flux and uncertainty of the business environment of the 1970s, symbolized by but not confined to the volatility in energy prices, induced a shift of economic activity toward the periphery. Second, increased rigidities in the primary sector associated with the labor unrest of the late 1960s, either by itself or in combination with the erosion of regulations controlling wages and working conditions in the secondary sector, produced an employment cost differential that offset the economies of scale associated with mass production. These two hypotheses seem to have been particularly consonant with developments in central Italy, but they also fit the stylized facts of developments in other countries, including the United States.

A variant on this proposition focuses more on cyclical events in the labor market. It asserts that the persistent slack in the labor market from the early 1970s onward, together with weaker worker resistance in small firms due to lower degrees of unionization, weaker employment security arrangements, and less stringent regulations, have pushed down small-firm wage levels and labor standards much more than those in large firms. This, in turn, has prompted a shift in employment to smaller units.

3. A third hypothesis about the rise of small business focuses upon a more fundamental breakdown of employment in the modern industrial economy. This hypothesis begins with the observation that the unemployed represent essentially free resources and that their existence in an economy where unsatisfied wants remain is a paradox that must reflect a set of rigidities associated with the organization of modern capitalism. These rigidities need not be "artificial" and unnatural; rather, they might be the by-product of social and institutional structures critical to effective economic performance. Nonetheless, when both unemployment and unsatisfied wants exist on a large scale, one would expect new organizations to develop that bring the two together. This argument can be used to account for changes in the number of self-employed persons, which started to grow again in many countries in the 1970s after a long period of steady decline. It is also the essential intuition behind theories of an underground economy. The business units in such an underground economy need not logically be smaller than those in the regular economy, but small units are less visible and, thus, more apt to be tolerated by the institutional and legal framework of the above-ground economy.

4. A fourth family of hypotheses suggests that innovations in production technology, particularly those associated with the computer, and/or innovations in organizational theory have reduced or eliminated the economies of scale associated with the mass produc-

tion of long runs of standardized products. This has led to the emergence of new organizational structures that offer alternatives to the vertically integrated, hierarchical corporation. A variety of different terms are used to characterize these structures—network organization, the federal company, the "system motif," and "clans"—but all these terms seem to refer to comparable developments and to imply a shift toward smaller business units.

To this point, various possible explanations for the growth in small unit employment have been presented as competing alternatives. *The Second Industrial Divide* (Piore and Sabel 1984) develops an argument that suggests that these hypotheses should not be treated as distinct alternatives but should be viewed as "historically nested." This argument accepts the proposition that the structure of capitalist economies has been dictated by the exigencies of mass production and the drive to obtain progressive increases in efficiency through the division of labor and the specialization of resources. It also accepts that the shift toward smaller units initially reflected the attempt to accommodate changes in the economic and social environment during the 1970s through an expansion of the peripheral, or secondary, sector. But it views mass production as essentially an engineering and organizational ideology rather than a reflection of the nature of the world or of capitalism itself. Once economic activity lodged itself in smaller units, these units began to evolve their own organizational styles and to drive new technologies in directions which favored their own activities. The result has been the emergence of a new technological paradigm termed, in *The Second Industrial Divide*, flexible specialization.

In this alternative, smaller units can play a dynamic, independent role. Singly or in some organized combination they are capable of generating products for their customers, and wages and working conditions for their employees, that constitute a viable alternative to mass production.

The emergence of this alternative appears to offer a choice, in the sense that if the implications and requirements of the two technological paradigms were clearly understood, any given society could pick the one more compatible with its values and/or structural advantages. The choice may, however, be illusory: mass production depends on large, growing markets. As an alternative technology develops and becomes capable of generating specialized products and selling them at competitive prices, it may cut progressively into mass markets, making it impossible for mass producers to maintain the scale of production they require to operate effectively. In this case, all producers would be forced to shift toward flexible specialization in order to survive.

In either case, whether because a system of flexible specialization offers the choice of an alternative to mass production, or because, in the long run, productive efficiency will depend on it, it is important to know how the new structures can be made to operate effectively.

The components of an effective regime of flexible specialization are not, however, well understood at present. *The Second Industrial Divide* offers a series of hypotheses about this. Most industrial countries offer some examples of enterprises and/or regions that are thought of as characteristic of the "new industrial organization," but even the key actors in them do not appear to fully understand the nature of their success. It is apparent, however, that these new entities are complex structures and that no single element alone is responsible for effective operation. Because of the unresolved state of the theoretical debate and of our empirical understanding, we cannot fully address this issue here. Nonetheless, given the scope of this book, we have separated out—albeit somewhat artificially—the employment and training dimension of flexible specialization and will examine that issue in the remaining sections of this chapter. We have chosen to focus our attention on Italy, Germany, and Japan. The data in the first section of this paper showed that each of these countries has had a large and growing share of employment in small units of production. Moreover, each has, in a very different way, generated the trained work force necessary for flexible specialization. Accordingly, their experiences may be useful in thinking about the employment and training requirements for flexible specialization in the United States.

The Employment and Training Implications of the New Industrial Organization

In the labor market, flexible specialization appears to require at least two ingredients. One is a peculiarly skilled labor force that combines hands-on production experience (i.e., practical education) with certain components of a more formal education that enable workers to actually create new products and to follow (or generate) shifting market demands. The three countries that seem to have been most successful with these new approaches—(central) Italy, Germany, and Japan—have each had a different approach to the development of this kind of work force.

The other important element for flexible specialization is an inter-firm organization in the labor market that allows the efficient exchange of labor resources across individual employers to cope with changes in labor demand, fluctuating skill requirements, or techno-logical innovation. In Italy and Germany these requirements are met mainly through more or less institutionalized occupational labor mar-ket structures, comprising many small firms in local labor markets. In the case of Japan, they are provided largely by the exchange arrangements between large and small firms under which the large enterprises transfer skill and know-how to dependent small firms.

Italy

In central Italy, the new pattern of technological development has occurred in industrial districts composed of numerous small firms. The firms are interdependent and mutually supportive, sharing infor-mation and technology but also drawing on each other's special expertise through complex contracting and subcontracting arrange-ments. The informal social arrangements that undergird these inter-firm relationships are supplemented by a variety of supporting institutions that facilitate cooperation and provide business services through employee associations, trade unions, and municipal govern-ments. Although some of these districts can be traced back in history, their current dynamism is the product of a process beginning in the late 1960s by which large companies sought, through subcontracting to less protected institutions, to escape legal, collectively bargained, and/or customary restrictions, and enhance their flexibility. The small firms then sought to overcome their subordinate position by exploit-ing niches in the international marketplace. New technologies and organizational forms emerged as a by-product of this dynamic.

Several of the industrial districts in central Italy have a longstand-ing craft tradition and an institutional heritage that includes munic-ipal technical schools. But the broad-based labor force with both formal education and extensive shop experience that makes these developments very widespread in central Italy, even outside tradi-tional craft districts, appears to be an accident of history. The small firms themselves were founded by skilled but basically uneducated workers dismissed by the larger companies as part of the political adjustments and economic rationalizations of the 1950s and 1960s. These entrepreneurs limped along in the 1950s and 1960s, operating largely with family labor and employing their children after school and during vacations. Through that employment, the children acquired shop experience. But the children also profited from the postwar expansion of Italian education. They graduated from the formal educational system, which, despite its reputation for large classes and poor-quality instruction, gave them broad exposure to modern technology and to the international marketplace. The very high youth unemployment rate of the 1970s, however, forced these children to remain in their families' firms. And the wave of subcontracting in the 1970s—a product of the same rigidities in large companies that drove up the youth unemployment rate in Italy—coincided with the transfer of control from the uneducated fathers who had founded the companies to the children who had grown up in them. It was the children, taking advantage of their unique background, who developed and introduced advanced production technology and moved their family firms into the international marketplace.

The self-consciousness of these districts and the increasingly articulated understanding that they are developing around their own success is probably enough to ensure that the pattern of education and training that emerged as an accident in this generation will be repeated deliberately for the next. But for a model of how such a combination of formal education and practical shop experience can be produced deliberately through policy, one has to turn to Germany.

Germany

Flexible specialization is probably more extensive and more firmly rooted in Germany than in any other developed country. This certainly is true in respect to its history. The same point can also be made in a spatial or geographic sense. While in Italy flexible specialization appears limited to a number of regions and provinces, in Germany, owing to nationwide organization and uniform regulation, it extends more or less over the entire country. There were two historic spells when mass production and Fordism made some headway, namely in the 1920s and the 1960s. During these periods, the labor force was expanded through the addition of foreign unskilled and semi-skilled labor, and attempts were made to stabilize consumption through macroeconomic regulation. But overall, mass production never took hold in Germany to the same extent that it did in countries like the United States, the United Kingdom, France, or Sweden.

Several indicators support this proposition. First, in traditional sectors, but also in some more modern sectors, the craft system has remained strong. For example, in the food sector, especially in baking and meat processing, production is still dominated by thousands of small craft firms that produce a large array of specialized fresh products for very limited local markets. Second, looking at the German industrial structure over the past ten to twenty years, it is notable that the country has moved out of labor-intensive mass production, but retained and even strengthened its base in the areas of specialized skill and know-how intensive commodities and services. This tendency is reflected in the foreign trade balance, which is heavily negative for labor intensive products such as shoes, leather, clothing, and electronic consumer goods, but strongly positive for investment goods, such as machine tools. Third, even within the traditional mass-production industries, such as automobiles and electrical machinery, German industry has leaned toward the high cost, high quality, differentiated or luxury goods segment. For example, while the mass production of cars spread in the United States, the United Kingdom, and France during the 1920s, Germany produced fewer, more expensive cars and lagged behind in mass motorization. Evidence of these differences remains today.

There are several institutional peculiarities of both the German product market and the German labor market that help to explain the prevalence of flexible specialization. Focusing on the labor market, there is first the vocational training system that generates, for the large majority of workers, comprehensive, general occupational skills. These skills are combined with practical shop experience, which is conducive not only to the production of quality goods but also to rapid adjustment to new products and processes. Nearly all young workers leaving school at the age of 16 or later undergo at least three years of apprenticeship training, which takes place partly in firms and partly in vocational schools and is organized according to nationally uniform, detailed curricula developed by the Federal Vocational Institute. Examination and certification of the skills and competence of the trainees is done by the Chamber of Industry and

Commerce for apprentices of large firms, and by the craft chambers for apprentices of small firms. However, the training and the level of public financial support for trainees and training institutions are regulated under federal law.

The training system is related, in part, to the survival of the crafts, but it also extends into industry and services. Unlike other countries where apprenticeship has been more or less controlled by the unions, in Germany employers and subsequently tripartite commissions have taken control of the apprenticeship system. This may have been the reason that craft-related worker training endured better than in other nations.

A second crucial precondition for flexible specialization on a large scale seems to be uniformity of wages and other terms of employment across regions, industries, and firm sizes. In Germany, this uniformity reflects extensive legal regulation, comprehensive bargaining units, and legally enforceable labor contracts. As nearly all employers face approximately the same level of labor costs for the same level of skill and it is difficult to escape or undercut this standard, a low labor cost strategy is not feasible. This may explain the relative lack of mass production and it may also explain why decentralization and fragmentation of large corporations have been rather limited in Germany.

Given comparatively small size differentials in labor costs, small German firms have to attain the same productivity and innovation levels—or other competitive achievements—as the large German companies in order to stay in business. How can they do this given their poorer capital and managerial resources? A clue presumably lies in the strong tradition of collective business organizations and associations in Germany, which allows the individual small firm to overcome the resource and power gap. Again, the crafts serve as a historical model for this form of business organization. Joint purchases of materials, joint research and development, joint worker and management training, joint marketing, and so on, help to compensate for limited economies of scale at the individual firm level. Collective organization also provides a powerful political lobby on both the regional and the national level.

Japan

Most discussions about Japan emphasize the quality of the formal educational system. The precise role of formal education in Japanese industrial success in general, and the kind of innovation and adaptability associated with flexible specialization in particular, is debatable. Formal education in Japan is extensive and intense by American standards, but the complexities of the language, especially the written language, mean that a good deal more time in school is required to produce general literacy than is true in the United States and Western Europe. In addition, much of Japanese education appears to involve learning by rote, to serve as a screening device for entrance into good jobs, and to be motivated more by aesthetic, as opposed to practical, considerations. Students and employers alike claim that very little of what is learned in school is useful on the job.

On the other hand, the large Japanese companies that have been most successful in international competition provide very extensive job training in-house once workers are hired. This company training includes both classroom and on-the-job instruction. Schooling may provide a critical foundation upon which this post-employment learning is built. It may also be important in the capacity of smaller enterprises, which do not and cannot provide in-house training, to follow the lead of the larger companies. But these are not hypotheses that emerge spontaneously in discussions with the Japanese about their own production system.

Paul Osterman (1988) develops the notion of an employment system as a series of interconnected and mutually supportive institutional structures and identifies the Swedish system as an alternative to the German and Japanese models. In Sweden, the nation-state assumes responsibility for the training adjustments that the German system handles through apprenticeship and the Japanese handle within the company. Overall, there is more emphasis in Sweden on adult training and retraining than on basic vocational training for youth. The Swedish model, however, appears more suited to mass production than to flexible specialization. The state assumes responsibility for labor mobility and trains displaced workers, but largely after the fact. Moreover, the Swedish programs are shorter and more removed physically from the shop itself than is the case in Germany or Japan. Thus, it is hard to see how the state can, in this way, provide the critical components of shop-based craft skills, especially to the displaced workers who are, by and large, older than the craftspeople trained in Germany and Japan.

The Structure of Education and Training in the United States

Employment and training in the United States do not lend themselves to the kind of neat, orderly descriptions that analysts seem to be able to abstract for Germany, Japan, and Sweden. Preparation for jobs appears to take many more forms and to be more erratic compared to that in these other countries. The formal educational system in the United States is extensive and important, but very difficult to summarize. In principle, there are three levels of formal schooling: primary, secondary, and university. But university education is in turn divided into undergraduate and graduate levels, and there are now two-year as well as four-year undergraduate programs and a variety of postgraduate programs including professional degrees (two to three years) and scholarly training. These degree levels are standard throughout the country, but the quality of the degree varies with the reputation of the school that grants it. Foreign students almost uniformly report that American education is more practical and more employment-oriented than their own.

The United States also has, however, very extensive employer-provided training, including both classroom and on-the-job learning. On-the-job training is sometimes formal and sometimes very informal. In principle, and in its administrative structure, the formal educational system is completely separate from employer training, but the two do not operate independently. Employer training is generally designed to supplement skills offered on the open labor market. Both hiring standards and employer training vary with other market conditions and hence with the availability of workers already trained in the schools or by the other establishments in the local labor market. Employers also sometimes rent facilities and hire instructors from the schools to provide their own training. In certain communities, schools are "sponsored" or captured by a local employer, who dictates the curriculum, provides instructional material (occasionally also instructors), and hires a portion (normally the best-qualified portion) of the graduates. Like in-house employer training, the strength of these arrangements varies with labor market conditions.

There are also a whole variety of technical courses offered in community colleges and proprietary schools that do not fit into the generally recognized structure of credentials but that are important in certain occupations and preferred in a fair number of them. Such programs are, for example, central in most local markets for barbers, beauticians, and medical technicians, and peripheral in training cooks, printers, and photographers.

The system is further complicated by the structure of educational finance and by the role of research in the educational system. The contribution of public funds to education and training is enormous, even at the university level. But even in public institutions, individual students' tuition payments are very high relative to those in other countries. The role of tuition is complicated by the substantial number of students who receive scholarships or subsidized loans not only from public funds but also from employers and from foundations and institutional endowments. It appears that the portion of education paid for directly by the worker is greater in the United States than in Europe or Japan. However, the complex financing of public education and the variety in, and cyclical sensitivity of, in-house employer training, renders such calculations virtually meaningless. Furthermore, American education, especially at the highest levels, is heavily involved in research, much of which is applied in the sense that it yields an economic return. This involvement in research is one of the factors that gives the educational system a practical orientation, but, because of the cross-subsidization between the education and research budgets, it also makes it very difficult to calculate the cost of education.

Finally, it is important to recognize the strategic role of immigration in the way that the U.S. labor market operates. Quantitatively the bulk of foreign workers in the United States enter at the bottom of the labor market, but skilled immigrants play an important role as a labor reserve and make the supply of labor in many occupations extremely elastic at the current wage. The "elasticity" of credentials and employment requirements makes it possible to draw on this foreign labor supply, including but not limited to the numerous foreign students trained in the United States who, as a result, have American credentials.

What makes this whole patchwork effective is an extremely pragmatic approach to labor market qualifications. There are a whole variety of "equivalency" programs through which a worker can obtain a missing credential or piece of a credential. Employers are willing to supplement, and adept at supplementing, the market with more careful screening or internal training when they need to do so.

Borrowing from Abroad

Given the complexity of current American practice and the distance between it and any foreign system, it would require enormous conviction about the superiority of foreign practice to attempt to impose it here. It is also not clear that any such attempt could ever be successful. Nonetheless, useful lessons can be drawn from both the German and the Japanese systems. As noted earlier, the principal interest of both systems is, first, that they provide ways of combining formal education and practical on-the-job experience, and, second, that they involve interfirm structures. The combination of formal education and practical experience appears particularly valuable in a world of flexible technologies and markets that demand continual product variation. Interfirm structures seem important not only for economies characterized by industrial districts composed of interdependent small firms, but also for economies in which even very large firms are involved in close collaborations with other firms—small subcontractors and even larger competitors—that involve interchange of workers.

The German apprenticeship option offers an attractive combination of theory and practice, but more as a general model than as a precise set of institutional specifications. The United States already has an apprenticeship system supervised and accredited by the federal government. That system covers only a limited number of occupations and, even for these, it has never provided more than a small minority of the trained work force. But in those occupations encompassed by the federal apprenticeship systems, the system serves to *define* craft training, and people who enter the craft in other ways do so by attaining the "equivalent" of the qualifications that formal apprenticeship provides. The German experience suggests that public policy should concentrate on perfecting the existing system, upgrading the content of the curricula, experimenting with new techniques for incorporating both the practical and the theoretical components, and extending the program to new occupations. But the complexity of the U.S. structure suggests that public policy should not aim at universal apprenticeship programs. Workers will continue to be trained in other ways as well. If improvements in apprenticeship are to influence the system as a whole, funds must also be devoted to perfecting "equivalency" programs that enable people who have obtained one or another of the elements of apprenticeship in these "other ways" to round out and complete their training. In other words, apprenticeship will be effective only so long as it leads the system, and policy thus must focus simultaneously on the example offered and on the number, willingness, and capacity of others to follow.

It is a little more difficult to see how to strengthen interfirm linkages such as those that undergird the German apprenticeship system or the less formalized (or at least less formally recognized) labor exchanges among Japanese firms. Apprenticeship, like education and training more generally in the United States, is geographically based and operates through local institutions. When federal funds are involved, they are generally provided to these local institutions. This fits well with the nature of industrial districts. U.S. apprenticeship, however, has depended heavily upon trade unions as impetus for its organization, in the actual process of administration, and to protect worker interests where there are strong employer organizations. In the first two respects, trade unions have probably been more important in the United States than in Germany. The increasing weakness of the U.S. labor movement thus creates a vacuum. Organizationally, that vacuum could probably be filled by business groups, operating either directly or through state and local government, but that solution would seem only to aggravate the problem of protecting worker interests in the context of training provision. The problem here is not trivial. Historically, the chief axis of conflict has been the "breadth" or "generality" of training. Workers have pressed for the development of broader, more transferable skills, while business, wishing to reduce the possible leakage of trained laborers, has preferred narrow training with limited applicability in other industries and areas. At the present time, workers' interest in broad training coincides with the pressures of the global marketplace and the requirements of new technology and, therefore, with societal interests. At the moment, given the weakness of the U.S. labor movement, the best situation that can be imagined is one in which the federal government preserves a place for worker representation when it funds local programs and pressures directly for broad training.

To the extent, however, that institutional adaptation is coming not through industrial districts but through a transformation to an economy comprised of large, geographically dispersed corporations with extensive links to suppliers and satellites, the education and training system is ill-adapted to its new world. However, a change of this kind will involve institutional adjustments that extend considerably beyond the education and training system. In this new world, the idea—rapidly becoming a cliché—that workers will spend less of their work lives in any one company and must learn to negotiate the open labor market is only half true. The true half is that time spent in any one company is likely to fall. At the same time, mobility across firms may not involve an open labor market at all, but rather a highly structured and relatively closed system composed of a definite set of allied enterprises. Such a pattern poses problems for union representation, pensions, and other benefit systems (even workers' compensation and unemployment insurance) as well as for education and training. It will require us to invent a whole new set of legal frameworks and institutional structures. Even if foreign experience were to provide a complete solution to the training problem, that solution would be at best only an element of the broader picture into which it would have to fit.

Notes

1. Flexible specialization refers to the production of specialized products made in small quantities using flexible capital equipment and generally trained workers.

2. See Sengenberger and Loveman (1988) for the Norwegian and Hungarian data.

3. See Birch (1987), and, for a summary of European job generation studies, Storey and Johnson (1987).

4. See Brown and Medoff (1989) for detailed empirical work on size-related wage differentials.

5. See Leonard (1986) for a formal exposition of this "reversion to the mean" hypothesis, with empirical testing on U.S. data.

6. Also, empirical work by Hall (1986) on U.S. manufacturing does not support this explanation of firm size dynamics.

References

Birch, David. 1987. *Job Creation in America*. New York: Free Press.

Brown, Charles, and Medoff, James. 1989. "The Employer Size–Wage Effect," *Journal of Political Economy* 97 (October), 1027–1059.

Hall, Browyn. 1986. "The Relationship Between Firm Size and Firm Growth in the U.S. Manufacturing Sector," Cambridge, Massachusetts: NBER Working Paper No. 1965.

Koshiro, Kazutoshi. 1990. "Small Business and the Labor Market in Japan: The Interrelationship Between Large and Small Enterprises Since 1970," in Sengenberger, Werner, Loveman, Gary, and Piore, Michael, eds., *The Reemergence of Small Enterprise: Industrial Restructuring in Industrialized Countries*, Geneva: International Institute for Labour Studies.

Leonard, Jonathan. 1986. "On the Size Distribution of Employment and Establishments," Cambridge, Massachusetts: NBER Working Paper No. 1951.

Marsden, David. 1990. "Small Firms and Labor Markets in the U.K.," in Sengenberger, Werner, Loveman, Gary, and Piore, Michael, eds., *The Reemergence of Small Enterprise: Industrial Restructuring in Industrialized Countries*, Geneva: International Institute for Labour Studies.

Osterman, Paul. 1988. *Employment Futures: Reorganization, Dislocation, and Public Policy.* Oxford: Oxford University Press.

Piore, Michael J. 1990. "The Changing Role of Small Business in the U.S. Economy," in Sengenberger, Werner, Loveman, Gary, and Piore, Michael, eds., *The Reemergence of Small Enterprise: Industrial Restructuring in Industrialized Countries*, Geneva: International Institute for Labour Studies.

Piore, Michael J., and Sabel, Charles. 1984. *The Second Industrial Divide.* New York: Basic Books.

Sengenberger, Werner, and Loveman, Gary. 1988. "Smaller Units of Employment: A Synthesis Report on Industrial Reorganization in Industrialized Countries," Geneva: International Institute for Labour Studies Discussion Paper DP/3/87, revised.

Sengenberger, Werner, Loveman, Gary, and Piore, Michael, eds. 1990. *The Reemergence of Small Enterprise: Industrial Restructuring in Industrialized Countries*, Geneva: International Institute for Labour Studies.

Storey, D.J., and Johnson, S. 1987. "Small and Medium-Sized Enterprises and Employment Creation in the E.E.C. Countries: Summary Report," Study No. 85/407, Brussels: Commission on the European Communities.

Organization for Economic Cooperation and Development. 1985. *Employment Outlook.* Paris, September.

Comment by Peter Doeringer

This paper represents a worthwhile effort to draw together the evidence on trends in employment by size of firm in industrialized countries. Two stylized findings are highlighted by the authors: (1)

despite wide differences among countries in the extent to which work is organized into large and small employment units, until the 1970s the scale of employment units in industrialized countries typically trended upward; and (2) thereafter, at least through the early 1980s, the trend reversed in favor of smaller firms. While the strength and universality of these trends may not be as great as the authors suggest, the data certainly reveal that there are issues concerning the small-scale sector that merit further attention.

The data, however, are far less interesting than the authors' interpretation of the recent trend toward small-scale units. They rule out factors such as changing industrial mix, cyclical changes in scale of production, and adjustments to temporary disequilibria in production scale. Instead, they favor explanations in which various structural factors—increasing market uncertainty, a widening gap between production costs in large and small firms, flexible manufacturing technologies, and new forms of work organization—have led smaller firms to supplant larger, more bureaucratic firms.

They also argue from limited case study data that there are signs of an emerging "new industrial organization." This involves the decline of the "Fordist" system—mass production based upon large firms, semi-skilled labor, and stable employment relationships—and the rise of a new and dynamic group of specialized and flexible producers who operate on a smaller scale, with a craft-oriented work force and a craft-based work organization.

There is no doubt that factors are at work to shrink the number of permanent jobs in large firms. For example, downsizing, subcontracting, plant closings, and the use of temporary labor have resulted in a reduction from 18.9 percent in 1970 to 12.2 percent in 1986 in the share of employment represented by Fortune 500 firms. Some of these changes, such as subcontracting and the use of temporary contract labor, have presumably contributed to the growth of small firms and of self-employment. It is also likely that increased regulation of employment in some countries and changes in technology or market strategies in others have helped smaller and more flexible enterprises to gain new footholds in the economy.

Nevertheless, open questions remain as to whether a common phenomenon is being observed across industrialized countries, whether structural or cyclical processes are at work, and whether the result of economic downsizing is to increase or decrease the skill level of jobs within smaller firms. Structural changes such as the growth of specialized markets and the introduction of flexible technologies could affect the small-scale sector as the authors predict. On the other hand, I would guess that economic recessions and increased flux would encourage a shift toward smaller firms using relatively unskilled labor as large firms seek to shed work that has the lowest value added. Structural effects of a similar kind should result from increased government regulation.

At this point, it is unclear whether the shift toward flexible specialization will materialize to the degree anticipated by the authors. We know almost nothing about the present volume of specialized production or the likely extent of future markets for specialized products. Moreover, the emergence of aggressive, entrepreneurial, and flexible small firms that seize markets from bureaucratic large firms or are invited to collaborate as equal partners with large firms that the authors envision is only one possible scenario for the future of specialized production.

Large firms may not passively accept having their market shares and profits eroded by small firms, but may seek to emulate and otherwise capture for themselves the benefits of flexibility. Some large firms are moving to establish, or to acquire through merger, smaller firms that can innovate and experiment with research and development applications. Others are opting for work teams, skill-based compensation, and various other types of flexibility in pay, benefits, and job assignment practices of the type often associated with smaller "flexible specialization" firms.

Alternative plausible scenarios for the future have different normative implications. For example, one possible "future" would consist of a growing number of small, flexible firms that can outperform the large, bureaucratic firms while providing good economic benefits and a rewarding work experience. Alongside these small firms would be large firms with flexible organizations and human resource strategies that marry the work cultures of the small firm with the management expertise and production resources of the large to provide flexible and rewarding employment.

If there is to be such a shift from mass production to flexible specialization, it will need to be accompanied by a series of changes in our labor market institutions. There will have to be a much broader skill base with a new role for apprenticeship training; craft unionism will have to become more important; and there will need to be greater portability of skills, fringe benefits, and employment rights as employment tenure in a single firm is replaced by greater job mobility within multi-employer groupings.

But there is also a less benign projection in which large firms will continue to pare costs to the bone and foster substandard employment through contingent work arrangements and subcontracting to small firms that provide neither the pay nor the work environment that meets large firm standards. In the latter case, public labor market policies will have more traditional objectives and the role of unions will be not to foster skill and flexibility, but to fight for their traditional economic goals of pay, fringe benefits, and job security.

To assess systematically the probabilities of such alternatives requires a research program that will explore within particular countries how the organization of production and work is changing, why it is changing, and what the consequences are of such change. That the authors are building such a program within the International Institute of Labour Studies is to be applauded.

Discussion

Sandy Jacoby (UCLA) noted that this paper, along with others presented at the conference, focused on changes that, while arguably important, are occurring at the margin. He cautioned against letting public policy be driven by developments that as yet affect only a very small fraction of the work force.

Chris Tilly (University of Lowell) noted the close connection between the hypotheses concerning the growth of small firm employment advanced in this paper and the hypotheses concerning the growth of temporary employment and contracting out put forward in Katharine Abraham's paper.

6

Employment Security and Employment Policy: An Assessment of the Issues

Paul Osterman and Thomas A. Kochan

In an uncertain economic environment, how can jobs be preserved? Is it possible to think beyond macroeconomic policy and fashion policies at the firm or market level that enhance security? These questions are taking on heightened interest as the external environment becomes increasingly turbulent. In particular, there is increasing pressure for policies explicitly aimed at enhancing employment security.

In its broadest sense employment security (we will define the term with more precision below) refers to the conscious efforts by firms and/or the government to avoid layoffs in the face of demand-side shocks. It can be contrasted with a hire/fire policy in which firms simply lay off employees if their services are not needed for current production.

There are numerous signals of this growing interest. A series of new collective bargaining agreements negotiated in the 1980s contain job security commitments in return for work-rule changes and wage concessions by labor. Other agreements establish joint union-management retraining programs aimed at maintaining employment by redeploying labor. The One-Hundredth Congress recently enacted plant-closing notification requirements. Finally, of course, the Japanese model of lifetime employment—albeit limited to a fraction of the labor force and now under increased pressure—has exerted a powerful pull.

Seductive as is the concept of employment security there is nonetheless ample cause for scepticism. One obvious concern is that it is a policy for good times only (and hence a policy without real content).

The research underlying this paper was supported by the Sloan School of Management's project Management in the 1990's.

For every IBM, Eli Lilly, or D.E.C. that has maintained the policy there is an Eastman Kodak or Data General that, faced with severe market problems, has abandoned employment security (Foulkes and Whitman 1985). The costs of employment security are rarely calculated by the advocates but may be substantial (Dyer, Foltman, and Milkovich 1985).

A second issue concerns the consequences of such a policy were it maintained. Would not, many ask, such a policy lead to a rigid labor market unable to adjust to change? If labor became highly immobile, economic performance would surely suffer. For those who take this position, the (supposedly) rigid European labor markets and recent efforts on the Continent to dismantle protective legislation are the counterpoint to the Japanese example.

Finally, there is a social policy concern. In many circumstances employment security is maintained by surrounding the secure core of employees with a periphery (part-timers, temporaries, and contract workers) who bear the brunt of fluctuations in employment. Is it desirable to create these two classes of employment? By what equitable principle can people be allocated to one or the other group? What are the long-term consequences of such a division? These concerns raise serious questions about employment security policy.

The purpose of this essay is to sort through these issues and attempt to provide a framework for analyzing current issues concerning public policies and private practices for promoting employment security. We proceed first by indicating why there is growing interest in the issue. We then place employment security in the larger context of shifts in internal labor market structures and human resource policies and discuss how those structures deal with environmental flux. Next, we draw lessons from two "cases"—a nonunion high technology firm that has undertaken extensive personnel policies in order to maintain employment continuity and the auto industry's recent union-management agreements along similar lines—and examine the role played by government programs designed to assist displaced workers. We conclude with an assessment of the future and desirability of employment security as a policy instrument.

The "Supply" and "Demand" for Employment Security

The "supply" of employment security seems to have diminished in recent years. That is, by a variety of indicators the labor market provides less security than in the past. One measure is the most traditional: job loss. In 1982 4.1 million workers lost their jobs due to permanent separations while another 2.1 million experienced temporary layoffs. More disturbing, the fraction of unemployment due to permanent job separations has increased. Whereas in the 1969–1971 cycle permanent separations accounted for 37.1 percent of nemployment, by 1987 they accounted for 48 percent (Bednarzik 1983). In addition, the fraction of the unemployed who had been jobless for more than fifteen weeks has grown steadily and stood at 26.7 percent in 1987.

Other measures also indicate that employment has become less secure. The geographic dispersion of employment growth has increased, suggesting growing mismatch in the labor market (see Osterman 1988; Medoff 1983), and there has also been heightened industrial dispersion, suggesting that increased growth in some industries coexists with accelerated decline in others. This is due to the well-documented shift of employment from blue-collar industries to services and to the uneven impact of technical change as it reduces employment in some sectors and increases it elsewhere. The quality of employment has also shifted in the direction of less security. For example, analysts, including Abraham (1988) and Osterman (1988), have commented on the rapid growth of the temporary-help industry and the increased use by employers of subcontracting and fixed-term employment contracts. These are practices that frequently reduce security. Finally, reports of growing white-collar layoffs, as firms prune middle management, suggest that the distribution of insecurity may be widening.

Layoffs, job loss, increased dispersion, and new employment arrangements are part of the story. However, in any healthy, dynamic economy we would expect many of these characteristics. Three aspects of the current environment make the problem more worrisome. First, the U.S. labor market seems poorly structured to assist experienced workers who lose their jobs in finding new ones. In principle, job loss might be relatively unproblematic if equal-quality new jobs could be quickly found. However, in reality the situation is quite different. Whereas the economy has done very well in accommodating new entrants, the reemployment rates and quality of the jobs found by job losers leave much to be desired. For example, recent data on prime-age dislocated workers show that 25 percent of men and 35 percent of women who lost their jobs more than a year earlier had failed to find any employment, and among those who had, another 25 percent experienced substantial earnings losses (see Osterman 1988). Hence the costs of job loss seem very high.

The second aggravating factor is that the labor force is becoming older as the baby-boom generation moves into middle age. As workers become older they become less mobile, less able to adjust to change, and more concerned with security.

Finally, the pace of technological change driven by advances in microelectronics is expected to accelerate in the future and to further reduce demand for semi-skilled and unskilled workers who are least mobile and experience the greatest economic losses from displacement. Industries such as autos and steel that face serious problems with overcapacity can be expected to pose especially difficult problems. Unless there is a significant increase in the rate of economic growth many of the workers in these industries will be displaced.

Hence heightened economic turbulence is occurring in a labor market that seems ill equipped to ease adjustment and to a labor force increasingly less able to adapt. It is not surprising that employment continuity and job security are of growing interest.

A Framework for Thinking About Employment Security

The variability of the firm's environment is a fact of life. What is at stake in a discussion of employment security is how firms respond to, or seek to absorb, that variability. One strategy is the "hire/fire" option noted above. While the "fire" component often receives the greatest notice, it is worthwhile noting that the "hire" action implies that companies rely on the external labor market (as opposed to extensive internal training or job ladders) to provide new skills. An alternative strategy is to let the wage structure absorb environmental uncertainty by, for example, sufficiently reducing the wages of those skills and occupations whose demand has fallen so that they can remain employed in the new conditions. This, of course, is the traditional economics view of the function of wages and lies behind recent calls (e.g., Weitzman 1985) for increased wage flexibility and profit sharing. Alternatively (or in a complementary way) a firm may seek to train its labor force to the point that skills are broad enough that the firm can internally redeploy labor in response to changing conditions. This strategy can deal with shifts in skill requirements and technologies but has a harder time coping with changing levels of demand and hence may be combined with the core-periphery model outlined above. Finally, a firm may attempt to gain partial control over its environment by improving its product development, production, and marketing efforts, and in turn linking these more closely to its human resource policies.

What the foregoing suggests is that employment security is best viewed as an element in a larger set of an organization's human resource policies. In turn, human resource policies are part of an even broader set of business and production policies. For the moment we will focus on how employment security fits into the set of human resource policies. In a later section we will return to a discussion of how it relates to the business and production policies of an organization.

The best way of thinking about this larger human resource system is in terms of the firm's internal labor market. The internal labor market is the set of rules or policies that govern the employment relationship, and thus to the extent that employment security is practiced, it must be understood as an element of those policies.

Although the term "internal labor market" is sometimes used to denote a particular pattern—the seniority-based, closed job ladder system that characterizes much of America's heavy industry—it is more useful to recognize that all firms have rules and procedures but that they may vary in important ways. The high turnover, dead-end clerical job is organized by a set of rules just as are more stable occupations, but the rules and procedures differ. Similarly, white- as well as blue-collar jobs are embedded in an internal labor market. For example, in many firms managers work in the same kind of structured job ladders as do skilled blue-collar workers, while computer programmers may move between firms with the same frequency as construction crafts people.

The core[1] firms in the American labor market have traditionally organized work according to the logic of one of two dominant models that we will call the *industrial* model and the *salaried* model. Our image of what work is like and how it must be changed are reflections of the strengths and weaknesses of these two paradigms.

The industrial model represents the manner of organizing blue-collar work that became the norm as a result of the unionization drives of the Great Depression and that was solidified in the era of postwar prosperity.[2] In this model, work is organized into a series of tightly defined jobs with clear work rules and responsibilities attached to each classification. Wages are attached to jobs, and hence an individual's wage is determined by his or her classification. Management's freedom to move individuals from one job to another can vary from situation to situation, but the typical case is that both promotions and lateral shifts are limited by seniority provisions and by requirements that workers agree to the shift. Finally, there is no formal job security, and it is understood that management is free to vary the size of the labor force as it wishes. However, when layoffs do occur they are generally organized according to reverse seniority.

Although the structure of this model emerged from the spread of unionism, it should not be construed as limited to such situations. Because of fear of unions, government pressures for uniformity,[3] and the growth of large firms using mass-production technologies and imitation, the model spread throughout the economy.[4] Hence a recent survey of nonunion firms found that seniority-based promotion and layoff systems were extremely common even in the absence of formal contracts (see Abraham and Medoff 1984, 1985).

This model has a strong internal logic. Because wages are attached to jobs it is necessary that the jobs be carefully defined so that there is common understanding concerning who is doing what work and hence is entitled to what wage. Similarly, while the system provides no overall job security (management can vary the size of the work force at will) individual security is based on a bumping system grounded in seniority; for that system to be effective careful job classifications are necessary.

For workers the system has the overwhelming value of creating security in the face of an insecure environment where the long-term trend in demand is growing but cyclical fluctuations can be expected to produce significant dislocation. Thus this system established individual property rights to highly valuable jobs and the value of the jobs increased with one's seniority. There are, of course, costs to this model, notably the difficulty of altering work organization in the face of changing technology or other pressures. This difficulty arises because of the logic of the system itself and because over time that logic takes on a moral legitimacy which adds to its weight. However, for a long time these difficulties have seemed minor compared to the logic and stability of the industrial model. One reason for this was that an expanding product market made stability and predictability the key strategic human resource management concerns. Flexibility in deployment and sometimes even cost are of second-order concern to management in this kind of market environment. We will see shortly that the priorities attached to these human resource objectives are changing in response to product market and technological changes that increase the importance of flexibility in deployment of human resources.

Most labor economics and industrial relations research has emphasized blue-collar work, and consequently it is more difficult to describe the salaried internal labor market model. However, understanding the model is important for three reasons: it describes the employment pattern of large numbers of workers, it extends beyond salaried work to a number of innovative blue-collar employment settings, and some of its characteristics represent the direction in which management is trying to push work in general.

The salaried model combines a more flexible and personalised set of administrative procedures with greater commitment to employment security. Although individuals have job descriptions, much as industrial employees have work rules, these descriptions are not intended to have legal or customary force. They are subject to revision by superiors and the employees are prepared to take on new activities as demanded. By the same token, the clearly defined job ladders and promotion sequences that characterize industrial settings are absent.

Flexible career lines and job descriptions are consistent with another aspect of this employment system: the greater role of individual considerations in wage setting. There is a considerably greater scope for merit considerations in pay setting, and the wages of two individuals in the same job can vary considerably.[5] Put differently, the pay system of industrial settings, in which the dominant consideration is job assignment, is far less prevalent in the salaried model.

If rigid job classifications and reliance on nonpersonalised procedures are the key to job security and worker acquiescence in the industrial system, what plays a comparable role in the salaried model? What closes the salaried model is employment security. In the classic salaried model, individuals, once they pass a probationary period, can expect long term employment with the firm. Unlike the industrial model, in which it is explicitly understood that the firm will adjust the size of the labor force in response to product market conditions or technological change, the implicit promise in the salaried system is that layoffs either simply will not occur or else that the firm will be strenuous in its effort to avoid them. The latter point that absolute promises are not necessary is important because without it the scope of the salaried model would be limited. What is crucial is that employees are sufficiently convinced of the sincerity of the firm's commitment to employment stabilization that they are willing to provide the degree of flexibility that is the firm's reward in the system. We will refer to the "security pledge," but this is merely shorthand for sufficient employer commitment to employment stabilization to obtain employee consent. Exactly what that level of security is will vary from situation to situation depending upon the nature of the industry, the firm's history, and other variables.

What is being "bought," then, is commitment, and the exact price will vary from situation to situation. However, the nature of the bargain is clear, as is the distinction between the salaried and the industrial model.

The salaried model clearly characterizes much white-collar work. The career patterns of most managers and many professionals who work in bureaucracies are accurately captured by the model. However, the salaried model is *not* simply another way of describing white-collar work. There have also always been a few American firms that have stood outside the mainstream industrial model for their blue-collar workers. In the 1920s the exception was termed "welfare capitalism" and represented an effort to develop an alternative to unions. In the post-war period the alternative has taken the form of applying the salaried model in a blue-collar setting. In return for flexible work rules and a willingness to accept managerial prerogatives with respect to deployment, these firms offer their workers employment security.

Clarifying the Concept

The foregoing discussion implies that employment security is best conceived as one element of a larger structure, that of the firm's internal labor market. This will prove a useful perspective because it provides a basis for fully evaluating the costs and benefits of policies toward employment security. Before proceeding to this point, however, there are several additional points that need to be made about the concept.

First, as we have implied throughout the discussion, employment security is not an absolute standard but rather represents a point on a continuum. If we think of one end of that continuum as a day labor shape-up in which there is no commitment beyond pay for that day's work, and if we identify the other end by the practices of the very few firms that have made commitments not to lay anyone off regardless of circumstances, then it makes sense to ask at what point between the two extremes an individual firm falls. For example, historically the automobile industry has been more at the hire/fire end, although it does provide more security than is found in a shape-up, while IBM is closer to the other extreme (although not at the extreme because its policies of forced transfers and incentive retirements amount to quasi-layoffs). Where to locate a given firm is a more relevant question than whether that firm has achieved the "ideal-type" of system.

A related complication is that, for the purposes of the salaried model, what is most central is that an employment security policy be perceived by the labor force as representing the "best efforts" of the firm. That is, the firm should be seen as making every effort to avoid layoffs; it is the degree of effort (or cost), not the ultimate absence of layoffs, that represents the key test. Hence, if external events force some involuntary terminations, that in itself is not sufficient to abrogate the firm's commitment to employment security nor necessarily to undermine the salaried model. Indeed, in some variants of the employment continuity idea, the firm's responsibility is limited to actions—such as the introduction of new technology or outsourcing—over which it has control. Adverse shifts in the product market are not seen as the firm's responsibility, and hence any resulting layoffs do not undercut the model.

A second important point flowing out of the foregoing discussion is that the analysis meets the challenge of those who argue that employment security is a "good times only" policy. That is, many commentators believe that there is little more to the policy than the ability of firms that are profitable and growing to maintain a stable workforce. There is obvious truth to this comment given the bold claims of firms which they renounce as markets turn against them. However, to a substantial extent the criticism misses a deeper point. Employment continuity is, as we keep emphasizing, one aspect of a larger system. A firm that adopts a genuine employment continuity policy must change how it does business along a number of dimensions, ranging from other personnel policies to (frequently) the interaction of design, manufacturing, and human resource strategy. The adoption of the salaried model and the new relationships among the elements of the enterprise signal a way of operating that extends beyond downturns and possibly beyond reductions in force. That is, a firm's inability to avoid all layoffs does not imply that the model is not viable. That determination rests on a broader assessment of all the elements in the system that constitutes the firm's internal operations, and the model may well survive downturns and layoffs.

Internal Versus External Security

A final distinction involves stepping back from the operations of the firm and asking about alternative ways an economy can provide employment security. Obviously one option—the one emphasized thus far—is for the firm to maintain employment levels. This we term "internal" security or employment continuity. A second broad option is "external" or "social" employment security. In this model, the emphasis shifts from maintaining employment at a given firm to assuring that when layoffs do occur the consequences are minimized. In an extreme case, if there were no adverse economic or social consequences of job loss, then the firm could establish a salaried internal labor market structure just as if the employer itself had provided the security. Such extreme security is, of course, highly unlikely, but, as in the rest of this discussion, what is at stake is a matter of degree.

Consideration of external security naturally raises issues of labor market organization and public policy. The conventional image of the American labor market is of high mobility and fluidity. However, most of that flexibility is due to the large supply of new entrants, young people, and women, who have provided ample flexible labor. For mature workers, the American labor market has, at least over the postwar period, been poorly structured to provide easy mobility. One of the main reasons is the structure of internal labor markets, which tends to restrict hiring to the bottom rungs, thus making it difficult for experienced workers to change employers. That mobility is difficult is shown by the problems that dislocated workers have in finding new jobs and the substantial earnings losses of those who do find new employment.

There are several alternative ways of enhancing external security. One strategy is to use the transfer system to reduce the negative impact on individuals who are forced to change employers. This, of course, is the function of unemployment insurance, although the system now is not fully meeting the task (in 1975, 78 percent of the unemployed received unemployment insurance, while in 1982 only 45 percent did).[6] Enhanced unemployment insurance payments and other welfare state provisions are therefore one possible direction and in some sense constitute an alternative to more direct or active labor market policy. A second approach is to use public policy to modify the manner in which layoffs occur and to provide enhanced services to the victims of layoffs. This logic calls for plant closing and layoff notification legislation, and expanded training for dislocated workers. Finally, a third approach is to attempt to enhance mobility prospects in the labor market as a whole by, for example, expanding the scope of placement and training programs, providing broader training before people enter the labor force, and augmenting the amount of general training that firms provide incumbent employees.

None of the foregoing ideas is easy or noncontroversial and each should be examined with the same care as are ideas for enhancing internal security. At this juncture it is merely important to establish the point that external security strategies represent another approach to the issue.

Assessing the Costs and Benefits

The discussion thus far has established that employment security or stabilization programs need to be viewed in the larger context of the firm's internal labor market. We have also developed a number of additional distinctions aimed at clarifying the concept. What we have not done is develop a framework or methodology for evaluating the public and private costs and benefits of an employment security policy, either of the internal or the external variety.

The difficulty of such an undertaking is illustrated by the diametrically opposite views of businesspeople who have been exposed to such policies. One line manager in a firm that has remained committed to the concept (see Foulkes 1980) commented:

Full employment—indeed job security—is the very foundation of increased productivity. If there ever came a time when we had to lay off people for lack of work, how could we ever convince them that we have a common interest in trying to put out more goods in fewer man hours.

Yet another manager, this time in a company that had long been an advocate of employment security and had recently abandoned it commented:[7]

A lot of people thought working at Polaroid was like having a government job. That just couldn't go on.

These two assessments address the same issue: the impact of employment security upon employee attitudes. Both views have face validity, and in a sense their resolution is an empirical issue. One would like to have data demonstrating how similar employees respond with respect to effort, commitment to the firm, and acceptance of new technology in different human resource or internal labor market environments. Sadly, of course, such ideal data are lacking, and the same is true for other arguments for and against employment security policy.

Another way of posing the empirical problem is to observe that, as we have tried to make clear, the choice is not between two policies in the abstract (employment security or hire/fire) but rather between alternative systems. A successful employment security system involves not only a particular configuration of the internal labor market of the firm but also, quite possibly, an alternate set of external labor market institutions to those we have now. It is very difficult to think of a successful methodology for assessing and comparing costs and benefits of alternative systems so broadly defined.

The empirical problems posed above are real, but it would not be acceptable to give up in the face of them. One of the frustrating aspects of the discussion of employment security to date is the absence of a way of resolving, or at least analyzing, the conflicting claims concerning the policy. As a partial solution we will examine two case studies in order to see what light they shed on the issues. These cases are chosen because, taken together, they touch upon the spectrum of relevant policies that firms might adopt to promote employment security. The first case is that of a large, private, non-union, high technology firm that, when faced with a downturn in its product market, undertook an extensive range of personnel actions aimed at maintaining its traditional nonlayoff policy. The second case concerns the job security aspects of recent union contracts in the automobile industry. Following these cases we review the range of public policies aimed at assisting dislocated workers.

Taken together, then, this should provide us with a good sense of what we can say about the benefits, costs, and implementation issues concerning employment security.

Employment Security at Digital Equipment Corporation (DEC)

DEC is a nonunion high technology firm with a long commitment, put in place by the founder, to employment security.[8] Virtually all staff described this as one of the key "values" of the company. However, several years ago the policy came under severe pressure from two sources. First, DEC found itself gradually becoming a high-cost producer as technical change reduced unit labor requirements, while staffing remained high. Second, sharp downturns in the product market resulted in several disastrous quarters. In response, the firm initiated a "transition" process. The goals of this effort were somewhat confused: in part it was aimed at rebalancing the labor force by altering the occupational distribution, and in part it was intended to simply reduce employment levels. It was also part of a larger effort to shift DEC's manufacturing strategy to reduce inventories and upgrade the priority given to controlling costs as opposed to achieving large production volumes on short notice. Regardless, the overriding purpose was to reshape the firm's human resource profile without resorting to layoffs.

Under the transition process, individuals were "selected" if there was surplus staff in their location. In situations in which an entire line was shut down all employees were selected. In other cases, specific people were selected by inverse performance ratings. Once selected, a person was exposed to various counseling and orientation sessions, given a chance (with company assistance) to find a new job within the firm, and provided support for outside job search. Retraining was offered to persons who could locate a job elsewhere in the firm. White-collar labor (so-called "indirect" labor) could only turn down one job offer elsewhere in the firm regardless of location, but blue-collar workers were not required to relocate. If, after a given period of time, a person could not find a job elsewhere in the firm or a job she or he wanted to accept outside the company, then that individual was placed in a pool and was expected to take on temporary work, part-time assignments, or community service while continuing to search. In several locations, when these pools threatened to become too large, the company also offered various incentive resignation plans.

The reason that this case is useful is that it enables us to draw lessons concerning the possibilities and limits of employment security policies at the firm level. The following seem to be the most important conclusions:

1. *The policy entails substantial resources and other organizational costs. Only a firm that is highly committed to such a policy is likely to undertake it.* We have been unable to quantify the costs of the program, but they are clearly very large. They include corporate staff who oversaw the program and collected data on it (at least four full-time staff for a two-year period), staff in each plant who managed the program locally (at least one and often more), substantial attention required of line managers in selecting, counseling, and seeking to place individuals involved in the program, training costs, incentive retirement expenditures, and—doubtlessly very large—the continued salaries of individuals involved in the program who remained on the payroll as they looked for other work either inside the firm or on the outside. Even a year and a half into the program there were still several hundred people in "hold" status who were collecting salary but generally not contributing to the firm.

It is certainly possible to argue that some of these costs are offset by gains from the policy. At the concrete level, DEC saved on unemployment insurance taxes and recruitment costs. At the most abstract level, DEC was clearly organized along the lines of the salaried model and, as would be expected, executives rationalized the policy by referring to the positive impact upon the morale of employees who were not directly involved. The problem with these offsetting benefits, however, is that they are very abstract. Either they are costs that are saved, and hence influence the bottom line only indirectly or over the long run, or else they are benefits that, when they do appear, will be difficult to attribute to the policy. By contrast, the costs are very real, visible in the short run, and quite attributable.

Our conclusion is that it is and will be difficult to convince a cost-conscious firm to enter into such a policy and commitment. In our case, DEC had a long-standing commitment based on the philosophy of the founder, and hence the basic thrust of the policy was not at issue, only how to implement it.

2. *It is clear, at least to those who managed the transition process, that if a firm wishes to avoid crises in the future, it must change in fundamental*

ways how it manages its business. In the past, the central value driving this firm's manufacturing strategy was to assure that the product would be shipped with minimum delays. Plant managers were evaluated on their ability to meet virtually any volume requirements that might arise: "The cardinal sin is not being able to ship. Don't run out of capacity and don't fail to deliver on time." This incentive structure created a particular set of human resource practices. Overstaffing was obviously desirable since it provided slack that could be used to meet peak demands. As new products came on line the tendency was to establish new production lines rather than risk disrupting production by integrating the new product into existing lines. This in turn led to distant relationships among marketing, design, and manufacturing divisions since manufacturing needs could be met at the last minute by acquiring new bodies. Marketing estimates were not trusted because it was more costly to a manager's career to be short of product than to be carrying inventories that exceeded actual demand. Thus, the pressure for overproduction added yet additional staff and costs to manufacturing.

For those managers who participated in the transition process (and not all did, since many plants were unaffected and the engineering and sales divisions were only lightly touched) all of these assumptions were called into question. One manager commented:

We learned a lot. For instance, take the 400 contract people we had before. We were actually less productive with more people. Now we don't allow people to fill up all the space. We no longer see "bigness" as goodness. Before I ever hire another direct labor person I better be damn well convinced that I have a job for that person as long as I'm around. I don't want to have to go through this process again.

At a deeper level the senior managers responsible for the transition process are also attempting to introduce new practices. For example, staff from manufacturing are working with product design people in order to limit the duplication of staff required to bring new products on line. There are efforts to expand training expenditures in order to create a more flexible labor force. This is particularly important given the experience of transition in which people proved more reluctant than expected to accept new training in the midst of a crisis. Finally, there is a reversal of policies that move production from plant to plant in order to maintain employment. However, the politics of these reforms are difficult because managers who participated in the transition process are true believers, while others resist restructuring their staffing and related policies.

With respect to our earlier discussion, all of this implies that maintaining a commitment to employment security in an environment in which that commitment is not protected by continuously expanding product demand requires restructuring the organization along a number of dimensions. This strengthens the point that for employment security to not be simply a "good times" policy, an alternative mode of planning and organization is required.

3. *Even with a high level of commitment the firm cannot provide employment security.* Despite the large expenditure of resources and extremely powerful company culture aimed at maintaining the security pledge, in the end the firm was forced to rely on a number of devices that shifted insecurity into the external labor market. Although no layoffs were implemented, and in this sense the formal definition of security was maintained, the firm did withdraw employment from 1,700 temporary and contract employees (these represented 30 percent of the total headcount reduction), and the firm also provided incentive retirements to over a thousand workers.

The elimination of temporary and contract employment is clearly a layoff in the economic sense of the term although the firm can maintain that these were not regular employees. The incentive retirement case is more difficult since the individuals voluntarily participated. Nonetheless, there was doubtless a concern that failure to participate would lead to adverse consequences (either layoffs or transfers to unacceptable locations), and some fraction of these separations must be seen as layoffs with a one-time buyout of the previous employment security commitment. In any case, despite the commitment of resources (and the underlying health of the product market) the firm was unable to maintain employment levels internally and had to shed labor. The subsequent fate of those who left is no longer of concern to the firm and, if anything, becomes a matter of public policy. Firms on their own cannot stabilize employment.

4. *Those regular employees who did leave the company as a result of the transition process were better equipped to do so than equivalent workers who experienced traditional layoffs.* These people were provided counseling, job search assistance, had some control over the timing of their exit, and were often given a financial cushion. In many respects this firm ran a process similar to that (discussed below) organized by worker assistance centers supported by public dislocated-workers programs.

Recent Union-Management Initiatives: The Case of the Auto Industry

With relatively few exceptions, the unionized sector has traditionally followed the hire/fire approach to employment security for blue-collar occupations. The system of multiple and highly detailed job classifications, each with its own wage rate, and the seniority rules governing the deployment of individuals across these jobs serve as major components of the "job control unionism" model described earlier. As is now well known, this model has been under severe attack in recent years as employers and unions search for ways to respond to market and technological changes that demand greater flexibility in the use and deployment of labor while at the same time reducing costs in a environment of heightened international and domestic competition (see Kochan, Katz, and McKersie 1986). The U.S. auto industry has been at the center of this transformation process both because it has been particularly hard hit by changes in its competitive environment and because its internal labor market system so fully embodies the features of the traditional system. In this section we will review a number of efforts of the major U.S. auto firms to adjust to these pressures with a focus on their attempts to cope with the employment security consequences of these changes.

The United Auto Workers (UAW) and the major auto firms pioneered in introducing a variety of job security provisions into their contracts in the 1950s and the 1960s designed to cope with cyclical unemployment. The most important of these provisions is the Supplementary Unemployment Benefits (SUB) program. The companies were required to contribute a given amount of money for each hour worked into a fund that workers could draw on to supplement their government unemployment insurance benefits during times of layoff. Over the years SUB benefits were expanded to provide up to 95 percent of take-home pay. SUB provisions were accompanied by a variety of severance pay plans, early-retirement benefits, and related income security protections. Since the auto industry experienced a steady rate of expansion over these years, most of the attention was given to protection against cyclical rather than structural changes in the industry or the economy. There was, however, an informal but unwritten agreement that new technology would be phased into operations gradually so as to avoid layoffs.

Employment and product demand for U.S. auto producers peaked in 1978. Since then, employment has been falling as a result of increased imports, changes in technology, and other reasons. The first major change in the contractual relationships governing employment security came during 1982 negotiations with the introduction of the concept of a Guaranteed Income Stream (GIS).

The GIS guaranteed jobs to workers with fifteen or more years seniority affected by a plant closing, provided the workers were willing to accept a transfer to another location. Those who were covered, but chose not to transfer, were eligible for a severance payment of 50 percent of their annual earnings for up to fifteen years or until their normal retirement date. In 1982 Ford and General Motors (GM) also agreed to establish joint human resource centers with the UAW, funded originally at five cents per work hour (subsequently raised to ten cents) to provide training, job counseling, and related labor market services to laid-off auto workers.[9] As the UAW company centers have evolved, their scope of training activities has greatly expanded to such areas as safety and health training, training for local union leaders, and a variety of other activities designed to supplement but not subsidize or replace the "normal" training activities of the companies. For example, in addition to the jointly sponsored training efforts, GM estimates that in 1986 it spent approximately $60 million in training the work force for one plant as part of a $300 million technological retrofitting and upgrading of the plant.

In 1984, negotiations of the UAW with Ford and GM added a jobs bank to their employment security package. The jobs bank provides that no worker with more than one year's seniority will be laid off because of technological change, outsourcing, or corporate restructuring. The trade-off for this employment commitment is that the companies retain a free hand to make outsourcing and technological change decisions. Employees are not guaranteed jobs in the event of market fluctuations or changes in demand for their products. Employees displaced by covered events are provided training and transfer options where jobs are available and are placed on a seniority list for recall as new openings became available. However, they are not required to terminate employment with the company if no job is available.

In 1987, Ford, GM, and the UAW essentially closed the circle by linking current and future employment security to a commitment from the union to accept flexibility in work organization. In essence, the parties put in place a plant-level decision-making process to complete their conversion from the industrial to the salaried model. The 1987 agreements specify "guaranteed employment levels" for each plant based on the current employment levels. Employees may still be laid off temporarily in response to reductions in product demand; however, the companies may not lay off current employees or permanently reduce employment levels because of technological change, outsourcing, or other managerial decisions. Instead, a gradual reduction in the guaranteed employment levels for each plant occurs with the "two for one" rule. That is, the guaranteed employment level is reduced by one for every two workers who retire. This attrition rate can be accelerated to a "one for one" ratio if plant management and the local union negotiate a special early retirement or other voluntary severance package.

To make these new agreements work, the company and the union have established joint plant-level committees. These groups will examine the full range of financial and other managerial information needed to assess the economic performance and competitive prospects for the plant and will recommend changes in technology, work practices (including expanded use of team forms of work organization), and related human resource policies.

The comprehensive nature of these employment guarantees and adjustment provisions clearly place strong pressures on the company and the union to adjust their other internal labor market practices in ways that depart from the job control model. It is not surprising, therefore, that we see both Ford and GM making efforts to reduce job classifications, adopt team forms of work organization, and reduce the number and levels of supervisors in their organizations. Recently, Chrysler has begun a major effort to do the same. What is less clear, however, is how far the parties have gone in modifying these internal labor market practices in existing facilities. The evidence available to date suggests the biggest changes in existing facilities have come when the plant was threatened with permanent closure or loss of a significant portion of its work. The more common pattern in existing facilities seems to be gradual, piecemeal movement toward a more flexible internal labor market system as new technology or other major changes in the plant are introduced.[10] The 1987 GM and Ford agreements now put pressure on the parties to spread this new model across all existing plants.

If these auto industry examples are representative of future developments, we are likely to see more complete adoption of the salaried model in settings where labor and management jointly plan or negotiate the terms of employment for completely new facilities and continued efforts to gradually move away from the job control model in existing union facilities as new technology is introduced. In both cases, we are likely to see expanded attention to the employment security and/or adjustment provisions needed to make these changes acceptable to workers and their union leaders.

Several additional tentative conclusions can be reached from this review of what is perhaps the most comprehensive set of efforts to address employment security within the unionized sector. First, the inclusion of these various programs and their funding within the collective bargaining process represents a powerful means of internalizing the costs of employment security and adjustment, since presumably the parties must trade off increased investment in employment security against increases in other areas of the wage and fringe benefit package.

Second, the long-standing virtue of collective bargaining as a means of tailoring the new benefit or activity to the needs of the specific firm and work force are not only present in these examples, but the parties have taken this advantage a step further by setting up joint union-management structures and organizations to implement and administer these programs on an ongoing basis. This should further increase the responsiveness of the programs by providing continuous input from worker representatives and management experts.

Third, while these efforts go quite far in protecting workers in specific facilities against managerially controlled shocks to their security, they do not provide an iron-clad employment guarantee. Employees will continue to be at risk from product market changes or industry-wide developments. In the case of the auto industry, the biggest future risk to employment security of U.S. workers is likely to come from the effects of the projected overcapacity that is building up. Current estimates from the MIT International Motor Vehicle Program (O'Donnell 1987) are that by 1990 the capacity of auto plants in the U.S. will exceed product demand by 4.2 million vehicles (more than 30 percent of the total U.S. market for autos). What this suggests is that company- or plant-specific jobs banks and adjustment programs may be insufficient, and that some industry-level planning and adjustment strategy may be needed.

In summary, then, labor and management in this industry have introduced a number of important innovations as they seek to enhance employment security as part of their strategies for adjusting to new technology and more volatile market conditions. As they do so, they are also making incremental (and in selected cases, whole-sale) changes in those internal labor market practices that are related to employment security. Yet despite these innovations, there are threats to employment security that lie beyond the control of any single company or union in the industry. Thus, at least given the current decentralized, company-specific institutional structure of these efforts, private initiatives are not enough. A role for public policy clearly remains.

Public Policy and Employment Security

A variety of public policy efforts have been or could be used to supplement the private initiatives reviewed above. In this section we review the lessons gained from experience with these public interventions.

The central policy response in the U.S. has been reactive, to provide services to displaced (or, in the current jargon, dislocated) workers in the hopes of preventing or compensating for employment and earnings loss. These efforts include the Trade Adjustment Assistance Act, the dislocated-worker provisions (Title III) of the Job Training Partnership Act, a number of efforts initiated by state governments (for example the California Economic Readjustment Team), and several demonstration programs—such as the Downriver Training Center—established by the Department of Labor. Taken together the aggregate dollar expenditure has not been large (for example, Title III in program year 1984 was budgeted at $223 million), but there have been sufficient programs in the field to permit some conclusions.

The current level of our knowledge about what works well and what does not is roughly equivalent to the state of affairs in the 1960s with respect to more conventional employment and training programs. That is, there are a number of "lessons from experience" or "best practices" that many observers would agree upon, but these have not been tested by rigorous evaluations. In particular, random-assignment control groups have been employed in only a few cases; hence we do not know, for example, how comparable people would do in the absence of particular interventions, or whether the common observation that placement and counseling have a larger payoff than training is due to self-selection.

With these caveats in mind, most observers would reach the following conclusions:[11]

1. Program interventions can help in the sense that reemployment rates of dislocated workers are increased by well-administered projects. This conclusion is not universal; some efforts (for example the second phase of Downriver) were disappointing, and it is, of course, contingent upon the state of the local economy.

2. Advance notification of plant closings and mass layoffs improves the chances of effective interventions by permitting longer lead time in training, placement, and counseling.

3. If the firm is willing to cooperate by permitting the establishment of an on-site worker assistance center, then the chances of success are higher. Inserting dislocated workers into ongoing operations of training centers and employment services is less effective. Part of the reason for this is that employees frequently lack what Shultz and Weber (1966) in their review of the Armour Automation program termed a "sense of mobility."

4. As the last point suggests, counseling and placement are frequently as important as retraining.

5. Whenever possible, jointly managed labor-management programs are desirable. The strongest evidence here comes from the widespread respect given to the Canadian Manpower Consultative Service, which is premised on establishing joint committees to manage shutdowns and large-scale layoffs.

Taken together these lessons, if implemented, would lead to a well-run response to specific events. There is no question that when faced with job loss such efforts should be implemented, and we would certainly support the expansion of resources directed to such ad hoc or reactive efforts. The harder question we need to ask is whether a collection of such efforts would constitute effective public policy with respect to the employment continuity issues we have raised. Our answer is no.

After-the-fact policy responses are inherently limited in their effectiveness. Instead we believe that (1) an effective policy must be more proactive in assuring that workers receive the general training needed to adjust to market and technological changes before the threat of job loss occurs; and (2) the provision of comprehensive labor market services to dislocated workers must be institutionalized so that employees believe in advance that services will be available if or when needed. As we argue in our concluding section, achieving these two features requires an integrated public/private approach to employment security.

Toward an Integrated Public/Private Policy Model

If our analysis is correct, then neither current public policy nor current private practice alone is adequate for addressing the employment security/internal flexibility goals of contemporary workers and employers. Therefore, in this concluding section, we outline an integrated approach in which public policy seeks to support and diffuse private-sector innovations that promote employment continuity and also supplements or complements private initiatives by filling the gaps these private initiatives are unable to fill.

Each of the two cases involving private-sector initiatives described above suggests that efforts aimed at enhancing employment security hold some promise but are incomplete. For example, DEC was able to achieve greater stability in employment levels than a hire/fire firm would have achieved, yet in the end some labor was shed into the external market. Those workers who were displaced fell into two distinct classes: temporary employees who were dismissed without any special services or benefits, and regular employees who received extensive labor-market adjustment assistance and financial benefits. For the temporary employees, private efforts were inadequate, and a stronger public employment policy would have been appropriate. For the regular employees, public policy could have played more of a safety net role. The broader issue is how to diffuse the "best practices" we have observed to a larger number of firms.

One lesson, therefore, is that no single approach to the issue will be adequate. Instead, what is required is a melding together of several private and public strategies. A second lesson is that there is no evidence that any approach can fully succeed in stabilizing employment and eliminating risk in the labor market. Indeed, it would be foolish to hold this out as a goal. Instead what we might aim for is to shift the balance somewhat in favor of reduced risk and in doing so to clear the way for the emergence of more flexible internal labor markets.

The first step in moving toward a more secure labor market is to reduce the number of workers who are displaced into the external market. The material presented above suggests several directions for accomplishing this. First, it would appear that an important goal is to expand the amount of general training that workers receive, both prior to employment and in the course of their jobs. This would accomplish several objectives. It would make employees better able to fill a range of jobs within the firm and hence would enable companies to rebalance their labor force with less resort to layoffs and new hiring. By making training a more regular part of a career, it would reduce the resistance to retraining that we observed among employees at DEC and that other observers have also noted. Finally, general training would enable those employees who are displaced to better find their way in the external market.

A second way of reducing the number of workers displaced is to move toward a number of reforms of internal management practices. In some firms these reforms need to take the direction suggested by the DEC case: a better integration of human resource planning with the design, manufacturing, and marketing functions. Indeed, the extent to which DEC was able to achieve this probably represents the most significant accomplishment of the transition process. In many respects, however, DEC is ahead of others in that, by virtue of its security commitment, it has achieved a flexible, salaried, internal labor market system. This is not universally the case; in other firms, particularly of the sort represented by the auto industry case, the internal reforms need to take the form of more flexible internal labor market rules given in return for a commitment to move away from the hire/fire management style. This in turn may require a much broader transformation of the industrial relations systems that characterize these companies. Here again the role for public policy is an indirect one, namely to actively encourage the diffusion of these industrial relations reforms and to eliminate barriers in current labor law that discourage these initiatives.

Some workers are displaced without benefit of any company-provided services. The temporary and contract workers in DEC and similarly situated employees elsewhere are examples. One appropriate response for these employees is a much stronger and more effective public training and job matching system, and we believe that it is important to move in this direction. At the same time, we also should recognize that much of the regulatory framework governing the labor market is premised on full-time "regular" employment being the norm. The expansion of various contingent arrangements poses a challenge to that framework and may undermine some protections currently afforded regular employees (particularly in the area of benefits, such as health care or training). It seems appropriate to begin to rethink whether to reduce incentives for contingent employment, and/or how to provide these employees with protections comparable to those enjoyed by other workers. The first step in constructing an informed policy in this area would be to develop a better data base that can track the labor market experiences of these workers over an extended period of time.

The general policy directions outlined above will, we believe, shift the balance in favor of a more secure and better functioning labor market. The difficult question is how to get from here to there. Some of our proposals face well-known obstacles. For example, firms will be reluctant to provide more general training for fear of losing their investment. A possible solution is to greatly expand vocational training in public schools (drawing in part from the German apprentice model) or to provide public subsidies for firm-provided, on-the-job general training. Both solutions raise a series of implementation questions requiring more careful study.

There are even more problematic issues raised by the proposal to diffuse the "best practices" described in the DEC and auto industry cases. How can public policy encourage private actors to alter their internal labor market practices? This question points to a disturbing gap in our understanding of how public policy interacts with private decision making and what levers are available to policy makers. Instead of a useful model or theory of how public policy can encourage diffusion of private practices, we only have a series of historical lessons. For example, it is clear that the National Labor Relations Act and the War Labor Board helped diffuse the postwar industrial relations system model. This success, however, obviously owed a great deal to intense grassroots pressure. The legislation drew upon existing practices (but, it is important to note, not all existing practices) and provided a framework within which those pressures could play out. In contrast, the equal employment opportunity example points to the possibility of a successful regulatory and, at least potentially, punitive framework. Again, however, these policies were clearly enacted in a climate made somewhat fertile by the civil rights movement. We also have examples of failures, such as the weak private response to the federal government's efforts to promote work humanization/quality of work life initiatives[12] of the 1970s, or efforts to encourage private systems of unemployment insurance in the 1920s.

A reasonable conclusion would seem to be that local experiments and a degree of grassroots support are necessary for effective diffusion. At the same time, public policy in not passive in that it can select or legitimate specific models and affect the costs associated with particular practices. Having said this, we believe that developing a deeper understanding of how government policies help diffuse private practices remains an important topic for future research.

In some instances, such as plant closing notification legislation, we are at the stage when federal action is appropriate. More generally, we believe that our understanding of what works best remains sufficiently primitive and the degree of support in the private sector sufficiently uncertain that the best approach is to encourage a wide range of local experiments. These could take a variety of forms and be supported by collective bargaining agreements, the public employment and training system, foundations, and state and local policy. The key to translating these experiments into a better informed and more effective public policy is to build a strategy for diffusion into this process from the start. This in turn will require that more attention be given to the social and political processes by which new practices get translated into acceptable norms of conduct by employers, workers, and unions. Although such a measured approach might seem too timid, we believe that over time, as we learn what works and how to diffuse good practices, we will be able to move toward a more secure labor market.

Notes

1. This term is used loosely to exclude what might be termed secondary labor patterns. That is, we are not interested here in understanding the low wage/high turnover sector in which many youth, immigrants, minorities, and women find themselves. This sector of the labor market is, of course, of central importance to issues of poverty and low income.

2. For a historical account of the emergence of this model see Jacoby (1985). The classic description of this way of structuring internal labor markets is found in Doeringer and Piore (1971).

3. For example, in the United States, unemployment insurance is structured to encourage layoffs and to discourage part-time employment.

4. For an account of the spread that links it to more general institutions of macroeconomic "regulation," see Piore and Sabel (1984).

5. For evidence that merit is important in these settings, see Osterman (1984).

6. See Burtless (1983).

7. *Business Week* (1985).

8. For a more detailed case study of DEC's employment security problems, see Kochan, MacDuffie, and Osterman (1988).

9. See Katz (1985).

10. See Katz, Kochan, and Keefe (1987).

11. See, for example, Hollenbeck, Pratzner, and Rosen (1984), Mathematica Policy Research (1985), Bloom (1985), and Abt Associates (1986).

12. See Bureau of National Affairs (1978).

References

Abraham, Katharine. 1988. "The Role of Flexible Staffing Arrangements and Employers' Short-Term Adjustment Strategies," in Robert A. Hart, ed., *Employment, Unemployment, and Labor Utilization*. Boston: Unwin Hyman, 288–311.

Abraham, Katharine, and Medoff, James L. 1984. "Length of Service and Layoffs in Union and Nonunion Work Groups," *Industrial and Labor Relations Review* 38 (October), 87–97.

Abraham, Katharine, and Medoff, James L. 1985. "Length of Service and Promotions in Union and Nonunion Work Groups," *Industrial and Labor Relations Review* 38 (April), 408–420.

Abt Associates. 1986. "Evaluation of the Worker Adjustment Demonstration. Cambridge, Massachusetts: Abt Associates.

Bednarzik, Robert. 1983. "Layoffs and Job Loss: Worker Traits and Cyclical Patterns," *Monthly Labor Review* 106 (September), 3–13.

Bloom, Howard. 1985. "Lessons from the Delaware Dislocated Workers Pilot Program." Cambridge, Massachusetts: Harvard University Kennedy School of Government Working Paper.

Bureau of National Affairs. 1978. "GAO Report Finds Productivity Center's Accomplishments Limited," *Daily Labor Report* No. 103, May 26, A5–A6.

Burtless, Gary. 1983. "Why is Insured Unemployment so Low?," *Brookings Papers on Economic Activity* (1), 225–249.

Business Week. 1985. "A Troubled Polaroid is Tearing Down the House that Land Built," April 29, 51.

Doeringer, Peter, and Piore, Michael. 1971. *Internal Labor Markets.* Lexington, Massachusetts: Lexington Books.

Dyer, Lee, Foltman, Felice, and Milkovich, George. 1985. *Employment Stabilization,* Ithaca, New York: Lee Dyer Associates.

Foulkes, Fred. 1980. *Personnel Policies in Large Nonunion Companies.* Englewood Cliffs: Prentice Hall.

Foulkes, Fred, and Whitman, Anne. 1985. "Marketing Strategies to Maintain Full Employment," *Harvard Business Review* 63 (July/August), 30–35.

Hollenbeck, Kevin, Pratzner, Frank, and Rosen, Howard, eds. 1984. *Displaced Workers: Implications for Educational and Training Institutions.* Columbus, Ohio: National Center for Research in Vocational Education.

Jacoby, Sanford. 1985. *Employing Bureaucracy.* New York: Columbia University Press.

Katz, Harry. 1985. *Shifting Gears.* Cambridge, Massachusetts: MIT Press.

Katz, Harry, Kochan, Thomas, and Keefe, Jeffrey. 1987. "Industrial Relations and Productivity in the U.S. Automobile Industry," *Brookings Papers on Economic Activity* (3), 685–715.

Kochan, Thomas, Katz, Harry, and McKersie, Robert. 1986. *The Transformation of American Industrial Relations.* New York: Basic Books.

Kochan, Thomas, MacDuffie, John Paul, and Osterman, Paul. 1988. "Employment Security at DEC: Sustaining Values Amid Environmental Change," *Human Resources Management* 27 (Summer), 121–144.

Mathematica Policy Research. 1985. *An Impact Evaluation of the Buffalo Dislocated Workers Program.* Princeton, New Jersey: MPR, March.

Medoff, James L. 1983. "U.S. Labor Markets: Imbalance, Wage Growth, and Productivity in the 1970s," *Brookings Papers on Economic Activity* (1), 87–128.

O'Donnell, John. 1987. "Brownfields, Transplants, and New Entrants: The Overcapacity Problem," Cambridge, Massachusetts: MIT International Motor Vehicle Program Working Paper No. 16.

Osterman, Paul. 1984. "White Collar Employment," in Thomas Kochan, ed., *Challenges and Choices Facing American Labor,* Cambridge, Massachusetts: MIT Press, 175–192.

Osterman, Paul. 1988. *Employment Futures: Reorganization, Dislocation, and Public Policy.* New York: Oxford University Press.

Piore, Michael, and Sabel, Charles. 1984. *The Second Industrial Divide.* New York: Basic Books.

Shultz, George P., and Weber, Arnold. 1966. *Strategies for the Displaced Worker.* New York: Harper and Row.

Weitzman, Martin. 1985. *The Share Economy.* Cambridge, Massachusetts: Harvard University Press.

Discussion

Harry Katz (Cornell) observed that, rather than lying along a continuum of employment security practices, firms appear to pick from only a few "packages." The paper identifies the "industrial model" and the "salaried model" as two such packages. Katz believes that additional models might be identified as well. Other work that Osterman and Kochan have done on recent developments at the same high-technology firm discussed in this paper, for example, suggests that this firm fits neither the industrial model nor the salaried model. Identification of feasible policy packages leads naturally to the question of why certain patterns exist but not others. For example, Katz continued, one might ask why limits on external flexibility seem to be associated with greater internal flexibility. The paper contains hints of an answer to this question. In any event, Katz concluded, it is clear that employment security practices have both advantages and disadvantages for firms. Further investigation of these would be valuable.

Robert McKersie (MIT) noted that, in today's environment, many employers have been able to extract a significant quid pro quo in return for strengthening workers' employment security, including increased wage flexibility and slower wage growth. Moreover, employers are beginning to develop a store of expertise on how to manage employment security policies. This is likely to have reduced the costs associated with their adoption. Osterman stated that while he believes economic conditions have changed over the past fifteen years in ways that make adoption of the salaried model attractive, the transition to this model may be very difficult.

Michael Wachter (University of Pennsylvania) expressed some scepticism concerning the attractiveness of the salaried model. He reasoned that the salaried model depends critically upon trust between the parties to the employment relationship and commented that, given asymmetric access to information, such trust is apt to be difficult to develop. Peter Philips (University of Utah) commented that movement toward the salaried model may be associated with the concurrent movement toward casualization of labor markets, insofar as greater security for some may necessitate greater insecurity for others. Kochan agreed with this observation and added that one of the important lessons of the case studies presented in the paper is that not everyone will benefit from the spread of the salaried model. Philips speculated that the spread of the salaried model and the accompanying growth of casual labor markets may be linked to the "disappearing middle" identified by researchers who have studied that evolution of the income distribution. Julianne Malveaux called for more attention by researchers to the connection between employment policy and social policy.

Sandy Jacoby (UCLA) wondered whether, as an empirical matter, there is in fact a trade off between employment security and various sorts of internal flexibility. It would be of interest, for example, to know whether salaried workers' wages are more flexible than other workers' wages. Werner Sengenberger (ILO) noted that wages and hours are not the only sources of flexibility. For example, if workers have polyvalent skills and can be deployed flexibly within the enterprise, excess labor might be used for new product development.

7 The Equity and Efficiency of Job Security: Contrasting Perspectives on Collective Dismissal Laws in Western Europe

Susan N. Houseman

Job security and collective dismissal law has been one of the most dynamic and controversial areas of labor policy in the United States and Western Europe in recent years. The Worker Adjustment and Retraining Notification Act of 1988 gives U.S. workers the right to sixty days advance notice in the event of a mass layoff or plant closure. Prior to this bill, in the United States only certain union workers had such protection through their collective agreements.

In contrast, worker rights to advance notice date back to the nineteenth or early twentieth century in many European countries. Like U.S. law, European collective dismissal law requires employers to notify workers, their representatives, and local authorities prior to layoff. It typically requires employers to inform and consult with worker representatives over the terms of the layoff. Most countries also have minimum severance payments or require pay in lieu of notice. The length of the notice period, the size of the severance payment, and the strength of the consultation requirement differ across countries. In addition to these basic provisions, public authorities have the power to approve or delay layoffs in some countries.

Ironically, as the United States was introducing notice requirements for the first time, many West European countries were weakening their employment protection legislation. These laws frequently have been blamed for high unemployment and economic stagnation in Western Europe, and the loosening of restrictions on layoffs has been widely seen as part of a broader strategy to stimulate the

I would like to thank Katharine Abraham, Michael Wachter, and other participants of the conference on New Developments in Labor Markets and Human Resource Policies, Massachusetts Institute of Technology, for helpful comments. Research support was received from the U.S. Department of Labor, the University of Maryland, and the European Institute for Advanced Studies in Management, Brussels.

European economies. Opponents of the U.S. requirements, including former president Reagan, have pointed to these developments abroad to argue that by strengthening workers' job security the United States is repeating Europe's mistakes.

Debate over the effects of dismissal law on the European economies and lessons for U.S. policy often are confused by conflicting assumptions about the economic impacts of such laws. The debate is further confused by a misunderstanding of what the European laws actually stipulate and how they are changing. This paper seeks to clarify the conclusions that can be drawn from economic theory concerning the impact of job security legislation; how the theory applies to the specific provisions of European law; and how and why European dismissal laws and systems of job security are changing.

The impact of collective dismissal laws on the economic efficiency of work force adjustment is ambiguous. There are cogent arguments for some government regulation in this area on the basis of efficiency. The focus of the public debate on the efficiency issues, however, obscures the more important distributional effects they are likely to have. Legal restrictions on layoffs may adversely affect employers by increasing the costs of adjustment they bear. Government programs and special features of European industrial relations, however, have helped mitigate the costs to employers of strong job security.

The more volatile and uncertain economic environment of the 1970s and 1980s has raised the costs to European employers of providing job security. Faced with rising labor costs, employers have sought to shift more of the costs of economic adjustment onto workers. The weakening of employment protection laws has been only one response to lower these costs. The rhetorical attacks on employment protection laws in Europe have been broad, but actual changes have been limited in scope. Changes have been intended to address specific problems of the laws in certain countries, rather than to alter worker rights in any fundamental way. New government assistance programs and increased flexibility in the deployment of the work force within the enterprise have lowered the costs to employers of using alternatives to layoff. These developments, rather than weakening job security, have involved the adaptation of government policy and private-sector practices in ways that support a system of job security in the new economic environment.

This chapter is divided into three main parts. The first part reviews various theoretical treatments of job security provisions and dismissal

law. Drawing on contract and property rights theories, I consider
two questions. First, under what conditions will private parties negotiate contracts with efficient job security provisions? Second, what
are the equity and efficiency effects of the advance notice, consultation, and severance payment requirements that are common in Western Europe?

The second part details dismissal law in selected West European
countries and discusses its efficiency and distributional implications
in light of the preceding theoretical discussion. The third part
addresses recent trends in employment protection law and job security in Western Europe. It assesses the extent to which these laws,
in fact, have been weakened; points to other developments that have
helped to strengthen job security in Europe; and draws implications
of recent experiences in Europe for U.S. policy.

Theoretical Treatments of Job Security

In this section I examine the nature of job security provisions in
efficient contracts and whether bargaining parties have an incentive
to negotiate efficient contracts. In light of these issues, I discuss the
conditions under which government regulation in this area may
improve economic efficiency. In addition, I emphasize likely distributional effects of restrictions on collective dismissal.

Efficient Contracts and the Scope for Government Intervention

If labor and capital are perfectly mobile and other market failures are
absent, then government restrictions on layoff may well impede the
efficiency of work force reductions.[1] Arguments that government
regulation of layoffs reduces economic efficiency often presuppose
that labor markets operate efficiently.

Labor and capital, however, are likely to be immobile, particularly
in the short run. Workers invest in firm-specific human capital and
develop financial and personal commitments that tie them to a particular geographic area. Similarly, once funds are invested in physical
capital, the use of that capital in other activities is limited. The immobility of labor and capital after their use has been determined gives
rise to quasi-economic rents. That is, the supplies of labor and capital
to the firm are less than fully elastic, and, in the extreme, perfectly
inelastic. In these circumstances, there are many ways to divide the

economic rents between labor and capital that are consistent with the efficient allocation of labor and capital to the firm. The division of rents typically is determined by some process of negotiation. Problems arising from asymmetries in the information available to workers and firms, however, may keep parties from negotiating efficient contracts and may provide some justification for government intervention.

In addition, there may be negative externalities to communities from mass layoffs that are not taken into account by labor and management during negotiations. Such externalities provide another justification for government regulation. Market failures related to asymmetric information and externalities that provide some rationale for government intervention are discussed in turn.

First, however, it should be noted that efficient labor contracts are likely to contain restrictions on layoff. When labor is imperfectly mobile, efficient contracts will jointly specify employment and compensation. If, for example, labor and management bargain over wage levels, but the employer is free to select the level of employment, any wage above the opportunity cost of labor will result in too little employment by the firm. If employment levels are stipulated as well, labor may be hired in order to maximize joint economic rents. In the event of a decline in demand, the negotiation of employment levels may effectively place restrictions on layoffs.

Conceivably, state-contingent contracts specified at the time the worker joined the firm could solve problems of bargaining over quasi-economic rents arising because labor and capital become less mobile once their use has been determined. Even if such contracts were feasible, the implicit contract literature shows that restrictions on layoff still are desirable.[2] Although the initial motivation of the implicit contract models was to explain the phenomenon of wage stickiness and to assess whether too many layoffs occur during declines in demand, the theory points to the efficiency of job security provisions in contracts. Firms, which are assumed to be less risk-averse than workers, offer a form of insurance against the losses of wage reductions or layoffs during downturns. Workers accept lower wages during periods of high demand in return for higher wages and severance payments during periods of low demand, compared to wages that would be set in spot market exchanges. This smoothing of wage levels requires the joint specification of wages, severance payments, and employment levels across states of nature; otherwise firms would hire too few workers during downturns.[3] In situations where we do not observe explicit contract provisions governing compensation and employment, presumably because of contracting costs, this theoretical literature assumes that implicit contracts exist, enforced not by law but by reputation.

Despite the theoretical efficiency of job security provisions, the available, albeit limited, evidence suggests that in the United States, where such provisions were completely unregulated until recently, they occurred only sporadically.[4] Various market failures provide one explanation for the absence of job security provisions. Private parties may fail to negotiate socially efficient contracts due to asymmetries in information and to externalities.

Firms typically possess better information on demand conditions than do workers. Firms may withhold information on pending layoffs or closures to avoid problems with employee morale and with suppliers and creditors. If they do, workers may overinvest in firm-specific human capital and underinvest in job search during the pre-layoff period.[5] This is likely to result in longer spells of unemployment and greater income loss.

Even if job security provisions are negotiated, asymmetric information may introduce problems in the bargaining process between workers and firms, resulting in excessive unemployment. Firms often have better information than workers about the state of demand in the industry and have an incentive to represent these conditions as worse than they actually are in order to extract concessions from workers. Conversely, workers, who have better information than firms about their alternative employment opportunities, have an incentive to exaggerate their job prospects. Such asymmetries in the information available to workers and firms may lead to too many layoffs or unnecessary plant closures.[6]

Finally, even if contracts are efficiently written, enforcement may be difficult, particularly when contracts are implicit rather than explicit. For virtually all of the nonunion sector and much of the union sector in this country, any contract governing job security arrangements has been implicit. Under an employment-at-will system, enforcement of implicit contracts "would have to depend on uneasy and slippery notions of 'reputation' as bonding equivalents" (Rosen 1984, 987). For example, suppose that an employer threatened to close a plant, extracted concessions from employees on the implied promise of job security, and then closed the plant anyway. The breaking of such an implicit contract generally is not punishable under the current employment-at-will doctrine operating in the United States.[7] Particularly when work force reductions are permanent, reputation is unlikely to be a reliable enforcement mechanism.

Problems of asymmetric information and opportunistic behavior may prevent workers and firms from negotiating efficient contracts, or under an employment-at-will system, from enforcing implicit contracts. These problems provide some rationale for government regulation. Private parties are unlikely to arrive at optimal contracts because of the high transactions costs of exchanging accurate information and negotiating explicit contracts. In some cases the government may assist parties in achieving efficient contracts by acting as a third-party enforcer. Legal requirements that firms provide workers with certain types of information, including advance notice of layoffs and relevant data on the economic conditions facing the firm, and that parties bargain in good faith, may help parties achieve an efficient exchange of information and negotiate efficient contracts.[8] Private parties may not be able to achieve this result on their own, for their promises of accurate information are not credible.

In addition to their direct impact on workers, layoffs may impose negative externalities on communities, due to the spillover effects layoffs have on a regional economy.[9] The adverse effects on the economy of an additional layoff are likely to be an increasing function of the size of the layoff. In this case, the efficiency argument for government intervention is clear cut. Mandatory advance notice gives workers and communities time to prepare for the impacts of layoff or closure, and thus time to reduce its economic impact. Ehrenberg and Jakubson (1988) liken mandatory advance notice and severance payments, which may raise the marginal costs of laying off workers relative to keeping them, to taxes; both are mechanisms to help internalize the external effects.

In sum, probable market failures arising from asymmetric information and externalities provide some rationale for government regulation to increase the efficiency of resource allocation. It also should be noted that, in the absence of such market failures, inappropriate government restrictions on layoff may have little adverse effect on resource allocation. Mandatory severance payments that deviate from efficient levels, for example, will be undone by firms and workers through the negotiation of wage levels, assuming that parties negotiate efficient contracts in which they maximize joint rents. Wages will be cut to compensate employers for the higher expected costs of severance payments. The result will be optimal resource allocation, despite inappropriate government regulation (Lazear 1988). In practice, advance notice requirements are similar to mandatory severance pay, because laws typically allow companies to provide pay in lieu of notice. Thus, while the benefits of mandatory severance pay and advance notice are potentially large, the risks of inappropriate government regulation are arguably small.[10]

The Distributional Impact of Restrictions on Layoff

Various market failures related to asymmetric information and externalities offer one explanation for why parties may not negotiate efficient contracts with job security provisions. Another explanation for the frequent absence of job security provisions in contracts and employer opposition to legislation in this area concerns the impact worker rights in jobs have on bargaining power and the distribution of income between workers and firms.

With factor immobility, workers and firms bargain over rents. As noted above, efficient contracts jointly specify wages and employment—or wages and severance payments, which also may have the effect of determining employment levels.[11] However, the simultaneous negotiation of wages and employment levels, as opposed to just wages, greatly extends the range of possible outcomes; in the extreme, the stronger party may extract all of the rents from the weaker one. Although the joint negotiation of wages and employment levels increases the total rents to be divided, one party may be made worse off (Leontief 1946). Thus, the Pareto improvement is only potential. Even in the absence of externalities and asymmetric information, therefore, parties may not have an incentive to negotiate efficient contracts, if the negotiation of severance payments or employment levels significantly alters bargaining power.

Job security legislation, which explicitly redefines worker and employer rights, may undermine employer bargaining power. In the context of standard bargaining models, legal requirements, such as mandatory severance payments, increase worker bargaining power by changing the threat point.

More subtly, a redefinition of rights may change expectations. Work on negotiation, including the seminal book by Schelling (1960), has emphasized the role expectations play in helping parties converge on a single solution from among an infinite number of possibilities. Bargaining power, then, is partly a function of expectations about outcomes. The morale problems or industrial actions encountered by an employer laying off workers depend on what is deemed socially fair. Employment protection laws may significantly affect job security by affecting perceptions of what is socially fair. The impact may be substantial even if the law does not impose any particular solution on parties, but merely requires employers to consult or negotiate with workers in the event of layoff. Negotiation of job security provisions undermines "managerial prerogative" to dismiss workers, in turn undermining managerial function and status. The very negotiation over such issues as severance pay, advance notice, and work force levels may raise worker expectations of job security and change perceptions of worker rights in their jobs. Such effects may explain in part why private parties often fail to negotiate job security provisions in the absence of government regulation and why employers typically have vehemently opposed employment protection laws.

The importance of rights, power, and distributional factors is evident in the academic legal debate over job security legislation in the United States. Recent arguments in the legal literature on employment-at-will and job security legislation tend to focus on rights and equity, not efficiency concerns. Opponents of any relaxation of employment-at-will and job security legislation have stressed the encroachment on managerial prerogatives; proponents have called for the equalization of bargaining power.[12]

Legislation with requirements to notify, inform, and consult may increase the efficiency of resource allocation by encouraging efficient bargaining. More important, by affecting bargaining power government intervention may alter the distribution of income.

Job Security in Western Europe

The efficiency and distributional impact of legal restrictions on layoff depends on the specific provisions of the law and on their interaction with other government policy and labor institutions. In this section, I review the development of job security legislation in Europe and the structure of current law. Historical background on the law is provided to emphasize the deep legal and social roots of job security in European countries. From this basis, I discuss some of the efficiency and equity implications of legal restrictions on collective dismissal in light of the theory presented above and relevant aspects of European industrial relations.

Dismissal Law in Western Europe

By the mid-nineteenth century, the United States and West European countries had established contractual concepts of the employment relation involving mutual and reciprocal rights and obligations on the part of employers and employees, thus ending the substantial legal advantages previously enjoyed by employers. Labor law and its subsequent evolution in the twentieth century, however, has diverged in fundamental respects on the two continents. Over time, labor law in Europe provided greater rights to employees, undermining concepts of mutuality and reciprocity between employers and employees. In the United States until recently, only workers in the unionized sector had gained substantial job rights.

The employment-at-will doctrine, the mutual right to terminate at will without notice or liability, has operated in the United States for the most part over the last century and is uniquely American.[13] Under employment-at-will, work for pay is treated as a pure exchange of service. Consequently, there is no real concept of job or of property rights in a job.

In most European countries notice requirements have always modified employment-at-will. For example, although Britain first passed advance-notice legislation in 1968, common law had required a notice period, as was deemed customary in the industry, since the nineteenth century. This period was usually one week with pay in lieu of notice, unless the quit or dismissal was for just cause. Courts in France in the nineteenth century ruled that the employment relation was a contract of indefinite term that could not be broken suddenly and in prejudicial fashion, and that the employee could receive damages and pay in lieu of notice. Similarly, under nineteenth century German law, parties had to give advance notice except under extraordinary circumstances. Originally, these terms were set by mutual consent and, due to the weakness of unions in the last century, tended to favor employers. A law stipulating a minimum notice period prior to dismissal for both white- and blue-collar workers was first enacted in 1926.[14]

Over time there has been a gradual erosion of the concept of mutual and reciprocal rights and obligations of employers and employees in favor of worker rights in Europe. The advance notice that employers were required to give employees prior to dismissal was lengthened, breaking the symmetry. Furthermore, workers received protection against unjust dismissal in a number of European countries in the nineteenth or early twentieth century. For example, an 1890 French law allowed employees to receive damage awards for unjust dismissal. German laws protecting workers against "anti-social" dismissal were passed in the 1920s. Outside the unionized sector, in the United States only workers in certain protected classes have rights against unjust dismissal.

Of principal interest for present purposes is legislation concerning collective dismissal for economic reasons. In Western Europe these laws, most of which were passed in the 1960s and early 1970s, build upon the legal framework of advance notice to individual workers. Representing the culmination of a long development of worker rights in jobs, this legislation reflects a historical, legal, and social perspective on the employment relation as a permanent one. Much of the legislation was patterned on provisions in collective agreements. Tables 7.1 and 7.2 summarize key provisions of collective dismissal legislation in selected West European countries. While the specifics vary across countries, the legislation typically contains provisions regarding advance notice, consultation, and severance pay. In many countries, the public authority also has special powers in the event of a mass layoff or plant closure.

A major component of all European collective dismissal law is the requirement that employers notify worker representatives and public authorities of planned layoffs. This notice supplements notice requirements to the individual workers affected by a layoff. Closely connected to advance notice are requirements that employers provide information to and consult with worker representatives on alternatives to layoff or on provisions to mitigate the economic costs to workers laid off. The strength of the consultation requirement varies considerably across countries. Only under West German law must workers and management reach agreement on a "social plan" that determines the conditions of layoff.

Laws in a number of countries also stipulate minimum severance payments[15] and give the government some power to intervene in the dismissal process. In some countries companies may provide severance pay in lieu of notice. In the Netherlands and until recently in France, a public authority had to approve all dismissals. In Belgium, West Germany, Luxembourg, and the Netherlands, the labor office may shorten or extend the notice period.

Efficiency and Equity Implications of the Law

The core elements of job security legislation in all West European countries require that employers give advance notice to workers, their representatives, and public authorities, and that they consult with work representatives in the event of mass layoff. In addition, many countries have minimum severance payments. The discussion below emphasizes three points. First, there are strong economic efficiency arguments supporting these basic elements of European collective dismissal law. Second and more fundamentally, government regulation may significantly affect how the costs of economic adjustment are shared, and thus how income is distributed, between workers and firms. Finally, certain institutional arrangements and government programs increase the efficiency of implementing European job security law and mitigate its costs to employers.

As was argued above, legal requirements that employers provide advance notice to workers and their representatives and otherwise inform and consult with worker representatives over work force reductions may improve the economic efficiency of labor contracts. Because of asymmetric information and opportunistic behavior, private parties may be unable to credibly exchange information and achieve efficient contracts. In this case, the government may act as a third-party enforcer.

Advance notice to government or mandatory severance pay may help correct any externality resulting from the fact that firms and workers do not fully take into account the spillover effects of layoffs on the regional economy. Advance notice allows local government to institute more efficient administrative procedures. With advance notice it can provide counseling, training, and placement services before the layoff, facilitating more extensive contact at lower cost. More generally, notice gives communities additional time to develop a strategy for dealing with a major job loss. Advance notice and severance payment requirements also may increase the costs to employers of laying off workers, thereby reducing layoffs and helping to internalize the externality.

Table 7.1
Legislation governing collective dismissals: employer's obligations to workers

	Advance Notice: Where Applicable	Period of Advance Notice	Minimum Statutory Severance Pay	Information and Consultation Requirements
Belgium	Redundancy over 60-day period involving: 10 people, establishments 20–99 workers; 10% work force, establishments 100–299 workers; 30 people, establishments ≥300 workers	30 days	½ difference between unemployment benefit and salary (subject to ceiling) generally for 4 months	Consult with works council or other employee representative
France	Redundancy involving 2 people within 30-day period	15 days to 14 weeks depending upon economic circumstances and scale of dismissal	1/10 monthly pay per year of service or 20 hours pay per year of service	Inform and consult with works council or other employee representative
West Germany	Redundancy in 4-week period involving: 6 people, establishments 20–60 workers; 10% work force or 25 people, establishments 60–500 workers; 30 people, establishments ≥500 workers	30 days after notification of public authority	None	Consult with works council; must negotiate a social plan

Luxembourg	Redundancy involving 10 or more workers in 30-day period; 20 or more workers in 60-day period	60 days	With tenure ≥5 years; varies from 1 to 3 months pay according to length of service; employer may extend notice period in lieu of severance pay	Consult with worker delegates, works councils, and signatory unions
Netherlands	Redundancy involving 20 or more workers over 30-day period	30 days	None	Consult with works councils and unions
United Kingdom	All redundancies for economic reasons covered	Varies according to number of workers affected: a) "at earliest opportunity", 1–9 workers b) 30 days, 10–99 workers c) 90 days, ≥100 workers	Varies according to age and service; for each year of service: a) between ages 18–21, ½ week's pay b) between ages 22–40, 1 week's pay c) between ages 41–65, 1½ week's pay	Consult any union recognized for bargaining purposes

Table 7.2
Legislation governing collective dismissals: role of the public authority

	Employer Obligation to Notify Public Authority	Public Authority's Power to Intervene in Dismissal Process
Belgium	Notify regional labor office of dismissal plan	Labor office may extend waiting period by up to 30 additional days
France[a]	Inform Labor Inspectorate of dismissal plan	
West Germany	Notify local labor office, generally after consulting worker representatives	Regional labor office may reduce or extend (up to 30 days) waiting period
Luxembourg	Notify local employment office of dismissal plan at time of employee consultations	Labor Minister may extend notice period up to 75 days
Netherlands	Notify regional labor office	Regional labor office must authorize plan; has power to vary length of notice period according to economic circumstances
United Kingdom	For dismissals involving 10 workers, notify Department of Employment	

Note:
a. Law requiring public authorization of dismissals recently abolished.

Labor and management may undo the effects of mandatory advance notice or severance pay that are set at inefficient levels in wage negotiations.[16] If the levels of advance notice or severance pay are set too high, then wages may be reduced by the expected amount of the costs to companies, leaving total employer labor costs and employment levels unaffected.

In addition to these theoretical arguments, it should be remembered that much of the employment protection legislation is the codification of national-level collective agreements. This fact in itself undermines the view that these laws constitute inefficient regulation imposed on private parties.

The most interesting and controversial provisions in West European employment protection law are requirements that employers inform and consult with worker representatives on possible layoffs. A consultation requirement was also the most contentious provision in recent U.S. advance-notice bills introduced in Congress and was struck from the final version. Consultation requirements effectively give workers some rights to negotiate both wages and employment levels. In West Germany, where parties must reach agreement on a "social plan," these rights are the strongest. The efficiency of such joint negotiation is well established theoretically. Riordan and Wachter (1983) have argued that the costs of negotiating and enforcing contracts specifying work force levels are too high given the problems of asymmetric information. However, if efficiency were the predominant concern, one would expect that both employers and workers would oppose consultation requirements. In fact, labor strongly supports such legislation.

As was discussed above, parties may not have an incentive to negotiate efficient contracts stipulating employment and wage variables. In the current context, employers may oppose negotiating efficient job security provisions for fear of raising worker expectations of job security and of undermining their own bargaining position over time. Although consultation requirements are weak in most countries, the principle of managerial prerogative is seriously compromised by this law, and the right to consultation is likely to influence worker expectations of layoff procedure and job security. More generally, the most important consequences of mandatory advance notice, severance payments, and consultation requirements may be distributional. By increasing worker expectations of job security, employment protection laws may affect labor's bargaining power and in turn affect how the costs of economic adjustment are shared by workers and firms.

Thus far, the effects of various employment protection laws have been treated in isolation from other facets of the industrial relations systems in Europe. Labor market institutions and government programs, however, potentially have an important impact on how efficiently job security laws operate in European countries and on who bears the costs of adjustment. For example, to achieve its intended results, a system of notice and consultation requires some form of labor representation in the workplace. Works councils, which were created or reestablished in most continental European countries following World War II, meet this need. Works councils have jurisdiction over working conditions in the establishment and have access to relevant company information. The legislation regarding collective dismissal for economic reasons passed during the 1960s and 1970s involved a natural extension of the works councils' powers.[17] The existing organization, with a group of workers specializing in selected management issues and with established channels of communication, facilitates the administration of dismissal law.

Other aspects of European industrial relations help compensate employers for the costs of providing job security. For example, European employers tend to enjoy wide discretion in determining who is laid off. This differs from the seniority-based layoff system prevailing in the unionized sector of the United States. European employers may use layoffs to shed their least productive workers. Thus while European worker rights in the timing and size of layoffs are relatively strong compared with those of American workers in the unionized sector, their rights to determine the order of layoff are relatively weak (Piore 1986).

Another important feature of an industrial-relations system is the flexibility employers have to reassign workers from one job to another within the enterprise. European countries vary according to the degree of internal flexibility of the work force in this respect. Sengenberger (1986) has characterized Germany as having a high degree of internal flexibility, and France and the United Kingdom (like the unionized sector in the United States) as having a low degree of internal flexibility.

Finally, government programs, like unemployment insurance for short-time work and early retirement measures, shift some of the costs of using alternatives to layoff onto society at large. Such government programs, along with measures that increase the internal flexibility of the work force, are important mechanisms for lowering the costs to employers of restrictions on layoff.

Recent Developments in Western Europe

Opponents of European dismissal law argue that in recent years macroeconomic recessions and the need for structural adjustment have exacerbated the law's negative effects, contributing to economic stagnation. The weakening of employment protection legislation has been viewed by many as a recognition of these problems. Above, it was argued that it is questionable whether these laws have had such large effects and that, in some cases, restrictions may have improved the operation of labor markets.

Certainly it is the case, however, that the macroeconomic recessions and structural changes in Europe in the 1970s and 1980s have increased not only worker dislocation, but also the costs of job security policies to employers. During a period of strong and steady growth, the impact of restrictions on collective dismissals are minimal and the issue of who bears the costs of adjustment is relatively uncontroversial. Associated with the greater economic turbulence of recent years has been tremendous pressure to shift more of these costs onto labor. More generally, high unemployment and slow growth in Europe have placed downward pressure on labor costs, of which the cost of job security is but one component.

Yet, institutions are complex and may adapt in a variety of ways to a new economic environment. Pressures to lower employer costs of job security may be released through several channels: the relaxation of employment protection legislation itself; an increase in the internal flexibility of the work force to reduce the costs of using alternatives to layoff; or a shift of some of these costs onto the government. In practice, European countries have responded with a combination of all of these approaches.

While the relaxation of dismissal law has been significant in certain countries, it has not altered basic notice and consultation requirements. Job security is deeply rooted in European society, and consequently pressures to lower employer costs of job security also have led to changes that serve to protect a system of job security. Below, I review developments in four major areas: employment dismissal law, temporary work and fixed-term contracts, the reduction and reorganization of working time, and government assistance programs.[18] Trends in the first two areas reflect a weakening of job security. However, trends in the last two represent alternative institutional responses to enhance job security by reducing its costs to employers.

Dismissal Law

Despite the rhetoric against dismissal law, there has been no widespread movement in Europe to overhaul this legislation. Certain countries have adopted significant changes to the law, addressing specific employer complaints. For example, Belgium reduced the mandatory notice period for white-collar workers, who receive far greater legal protection against dismissal than blue-collar workers. The Netherlands simplified administrative procedures for laying off workers, while France eliminated government approval of layoffs entirely. West Germany raised the threshold for cases covered by collective dismissal law and provided some regulatory relief for small and new firms. The changes, though important, have been on the margin and in most cases have addressed what were probably inefficiencies specific to those particular countries.

Temporary Work and Fixed-Term Contracts

In addition to regulating dismissals, European countries limit the use of temporary work and fixed-term contracts. More important than the relaxation of dismissal law has been the relaxation of restrictions on the use of temporary workers and fixed-term contracts, which has allowed firms to circumvent legal restrictions on dismissal.

Possibly the most important modifications in this area have occurred in West Germany. The 1985 Employment Promotion Act doubles the permissible length of temporary employment from three to six months and triples the permissible length of fixed-term contracts from six to eighteen months. New firms may conclude a fixed-term contract of up to twenty-four months.

Similarly, in the Netherlands the government effectively doubled the maximum permissible length of a fixed-term contract from six months to one year by allowing firms to renew these contracts. Belgium and France also have weakened restrictions on the use of fixed-term contracts in special circumstances.

The Reduction and Reorganization of Working Time

Other important developments in Europe have concerned the reduction and reorganization of working time. The two types of measures often are linked and have been important mechanisms for increasing job security. Working-time reduction, as an alternative to layoff or a means of stimulating new hiring, most directly increases job security. The quid pro quo for such reductions typically has been greater flexibility on when these hours are worked. Night work, weekend work, and the calculation of overtime hours on a longer basis allow firms to increase plant utilization and labor productivity, while lowering labor costs. Such internal flexibility helps compensate employers for the cost of using alternatives to layoff.[19]

Developments in this area are the outgrowth of both government and private initiative. Since 1982 Belgium has permitted exceptions to a number of regulations concerning overtime and weekend and night work, provided that firms also reduce overall working time and create jobs. In 1985 it passed a law allowing the calculation of working time on a longer basis, subject to union concurrence. The Dutch government introduced the thirty-eight-hour work week in 1985. This measure grew out of a 1982 agreement between employers and unions to freeze real wage levels, reduce working time, and reorganize working time through such measures as weekend work and the calculation of working time on a longer basis. France also reduced the statutory work week in 1982 from forty to thirty-nine hours, and at the same time widened the scope for flexible working time. Specifically, the law allows the transfer of time from one week to another, greater flexibility in the use of overtime, and exceptions to Sunday work restrictions.[20]

In contrast to other Continental countries, the West German government has not introduced any working time reduction or flexibility measures. The major private-sector initiative in this area has been the work-week reduction negotiated in the metal-working industry. Typically, employers in the metal-working industry have reduced working time in a flexible way,[21] and as a result have maintained or increased plant utilization in most cases.

Government Assistance for Job Security

European governments have absorbed some of the costs of restrictions on dismissal by subsidizing alternatives to layoff. Short-time unemployment insurance has already been mentioned. In recent years short-time work has been utilized extensively in sectors undergoing restructuring, like steel. The French government also has assisted firms that have permanently reduced their average work week.

Another alternative to layoff, and a working-time reduction measure of sorts, is early retirement. A number of European countries including France, the Netherlands, Luxembourg, West Germany, and Britain recently have passed legislation that encourages retirement at an earlier age. In France and the Netherlands, the government has lowered the age of early retirement and has guaranteed incomes to older workers who are laid off. As a result, employers in these countries have laid off older workers and thereby used the unemployment insurance system to help finance early retirement schemes. Similar practices have been widespread in West Germany as well, although the government sought to curb this use of unemployment insurance by making companies reimburse the state in these circumstances. In addition, West Germany and Britain have passed special legislation to help finance early retirement if the firm replaces the retiree with a new recruit.

Countries also have developed special programs targeting declining firms or sectors. For example, the Luxembourg steel industry has reduced its work force by almost one-half since the mid-1970s without layoff. Instead of laying off workers, the industry has introduced measures involving the reassignment of workers within the firm, the subcontracting of excess labor to the government or other firms, and early retirement. The government has helped pay the wages of these extra workers and has covered all of the costs of early retirement.

In another innovation to encourage alternatives to layoff, the French government provides special assistance to firms that help place or retrain excess workers. The program is intended to facilitate private-public coordination, improve the delivery of placement and retraining services, and increase employment security.

Striking a Balance in Western Europe

The reforms in labor law, industrial relations experiments, and government assistance programs show the variety of approaches that have been adopted in West European countries to lower the costs to employers of providing job security. Overall, recent developments are consistent with Europe's history of strong worker rights in jobs and private-sector practices of job security.

Changes to employment protection law have helped reduce these costs. However, the relaxation of this law has been limited. Even in West Germany, where some of the most substantial reform of employment protection law occurred, the changes are considered experimental and temporary. In commenting on these developments in Germany, Manfred Weiss writes:

In spite of recent changes labor law as a whole is strongly in favor of [the indefinite] contract. The point has to be stressed that this legal development is connected with a general understanding in German society that employees have to have the possibility to develop a lifetime perspective by having the chance to stay indefinitely in an employment relationship. This attitude, which is very different from the job mentality as for example existing in the USA, certainly is not without influence on the legal development. (Weiss 1987, 55)

German law reflects a consensus between management and labor that is crucial to good industrial relations. Overall, employers and the government have been reluctant to tamper too much with the system for fear of upsetting its delicate balance.

Other developments in Europe have helped lower labor costs and simultaneously strengthen job security. Government programs have been instrumental in absorbing the costs of job security in the short run through unemployment insurance for short-time work, early retirement measures, and a variety of targeted programs.

Depressed macroeconomic conditions and restructuring in major sectors have precipitated important longer-term changes within the workplace. Many countries have enacted legislation removing restrictions on working time, indirectly supporting job security by reducing the costs to employers of using alternatives to layoff. European employers have been particularly interested in the reorganization of working time, and some unions have begun to accept the need for greater flexibility within the workplace.

Yet, serious collective bargaining on internal flexibility measures is in its infancy. The less stable economic environment characterizing the 1980s may well require further innovations to lower the costs of providing job security. If so, the long-term viability of job security practices in Europe will depend critically on collective bargaining in this area.

Lessons for U.S. Policy

West European experiences with employment protection legislation hold potentially valuable lessons for U.S. policy, though one must be careful in drawing parallels across countries. Both the labor law and the broader configuration of industrial relations are quite different in Europe and the United States.

The Worker Adjustment and Retraining Notification Act recently passed in the United States is weak compared to collective dismissal legislation in Europe. The act requires employers to provide notice to workers and government officials prior to mass layoff. However, U.S. law does not have other provisions common in Europe such as severance payment and consultation requirements and government authority to delay layoffs.[22] As emphasized above, there are potential efficiency gains from advance notice and other government regulation of work force adjustment. In addition, as workers gain more formal rights to their jobs, some of the costs of adjustment are likely to be shifted onto employers. The efficiency and distributional impact of U.S. law as currently written, however, is likely to be small compared with the impact of European law.

But U.S. labor has hoped, and U.S. business feared, that the advance-notice provision would be the beginning of a broader expansion of worker rights in jobs. The extension of employment-protection legislation in the United States along the lines of the laws in Europe, however, might have a substantially different impact in this country than abroad. Current collective dismissal law in Europe grew out of a legal and industrial relations tradition of strong job security. Industrial relations in Europe is adapted—and continues to adapt—to this structure of rights. The works council provides the body necessary for promoting the efficient exchange of information and consultation between employers and workers. Greater employer discretion to deploy the work force has helped compensate employers for the costs of strong worker rights in jobs. Government programs also have helped cover some of the costs to employers of providing job security.

In contrast, in the United States, where layoff is the dominant mode of work force adjustment during downturns, government policy and labor relations are oriented toward a weaker configuration of worker rights in jobs. Were worker rights to be expanded, U.S. industrial relations would have to adapt, as have European institutions, in order to reap the potential efficiency gains and limit the costs to employers of stronger job security.

Notes

1. Inappropriate government regulation does not necessarily result in economic inefficiency, however, for parties may undo the effects of regulations in wage negotiations. This argument is developed below.

2. For summaries of the literature, see Azariadis (1981) and Azariadis and Stiglitz (1983).

3. Models vary in what must be negotiated for contracts to be efficient. If worker utility depends only on income, then the negotiation of total compensation—wages and severance payments or wages and employment levels—is sufficient for efficiency. If non-monetary factors, such as attachments to workplace and community, also affect utility, then all three variables must be specified.

4. For surveys on private-sector assistance to dislocated workers see the U.S. General Accounting Office (1986) and Brown (1987). Brown and Ashenfelter (1986) find little evidence of efficient implicit contracts.

5. Hamermesh (1987) studies how age-earnings profiles change prior to layoff and finds some evidence that workers cut back on firm-specific human capital investments.

6. The employers' monopoly on information on the state of demand in the industry may result in either under- or overemployment, depending in part on the nature of preferences, whereas the employee information on alternative employment opportunities will unambiguously lead to underemployment. See Azariadis and Stiglitz (1983) for an overview of the theoretical literature on these points.

7. Rhine (1986) claims this scenario characterizes the plant closure by U.S. Steel at Youngstown. Recently, U.S. courts have allowed some exceptions to employment-at-will based on the concept of implied contracts.

8. For a development of this argument, see Hedlund (1986).

9. There also may be negative externalities arising from the fact that the unemployment insurance systems in the United States and Europe are not perfectly experience rated.

10. This claim assumes that the severance pay or advance notice requirement does not significantly increase the costs of negotiating efficient contracts.

11. See Azariadis (1981) and Azariadis and Stiglitz (1983).

12. See, for example, Blades (1967), Shapiro and Tune (1974), Rhein (1986), Summers (1976), and the Fried (1984) critique of Epstein (1984).

13. The concept of employment-at-will is traced to an 1877 treatise by an American, H.G. Wood, not, as widely believed, to English common law.

14. Background on the historical development of dismissal law in the United States, Britain, and France is found in Meyers (1964) and in Germany in Weiss (1987).

15. Interestingly, West German law, which has the strongest negotiation requirements, has no minimum severance payment.

16. Because in many countries severance pay can be given in lieu of advance notice, mandatory advance notice is similar to mandatory severance pay.

17. Recent labor legislation in the United States encourages employers to consult with workers in the event of mass layoff or plant closure. To deal

with the absence of worker representation in the nonunion setting, a special government service, patterned on a Canadian program, helps firms experiencing economic difficulties set up management-labor teams.

18. The list, while not comprehensive, touches on some of the most important measures designed to increase labor flexibility. Wages are covered only in the context of working time reductions. A more extensive treatment is beyond the scope of this paper.

19. Such internal flexibility is itself a weakening of worker rights and has been highly controversial in some European unions.

20. The details of working-time reorganization must be decided at the plant level. Where unions are present, this requires decentralized collective bargaining. The 1982 Collective Bargaining Act, part of the Auroux Laws, was designed to improve industrial relations and increase flexibility at the work place by fostering dialogue between unions and management at the firm level. A key provision of the act requires firms with unions and at least fifty employees to open pay and working hour negotiations every year, although there is no obligation to bargain in good faith or reach agreement (Eyraud and Tchobanian 1985).

21. A survey of employers shows that three-quarters of the firms have reduced working time in a flexible way: 44 percent give an extra day of leave; 17 percent vary the reduction in working time according to the category of worker involved; and 15 percent average the work week over a two-month period (Maury 1985, 44).

22. The U.S. law also contains clauses that relieve businesses from the obligation to provide workers with advance notice of layoff under a variety of circumstances, including unforeseen business conditions. Therefore technically, the law is only meant to prohibit employers from intentionally withholding information from employees. In practice though, the cost of defending potential lawsuits may inhibit employers from laying off workers without notice, even where the layoff was unforseen.

References

Azariadis, C. 1981. "Implicit Contracts and Related Topics: A Survey," in Z. Hornstein, et al., eds. *The Economics of the Labour Market*. London: HMSO.

Azariadis, C., and Joseph E. Stiglitz. 1983. "Implicit Contracts and Fixed-Price Equilibria," *Quarterly Journal of Economics*, 93 (Supplement), 1–22.

Blades, Lawrence E. 1967. "Employment-at-Will vs. Individual Freedom: On Limiting the Abusive Exercise of Employer Power," *Columbia Law Review* 67 (December), 1404–1435.

Blanpain, R., ed. 1980. "Job Security and Industrial Relations," *Bulletin of Comparative Labor Relations* 11.

Brown, James N., and Orley Ashenfelter. 1986. "Testing the Efficiency of Employment Contracts," *Journal of Political Economy* 94 (June), 540–587.

Brown, Sharon P. 1987. "How Often Do Workers Receive Advance Notice of Layoffs?" *Monthly Labor Review* 110 (June), 13–17.

Despax, Michel, and Jacques Rojot. 1987. "Labour Law and Industrial Relations in France," in R. Blanpain, ed., *International Encyclopedia for Labour Law and Industrial Relations*. Boston: Kluwer Law and Taxation Publishers.

Ehrenberg, Ronald G., and George H. Jakubson. 1988. *Advance Notice Provisions in Plant Closing Legislation*. Kalamazoo, Michigan: W. E. Upjohn Institute.

Epstein, Richard. 1984. "In Defense of the Contract at Will," *University of Chicago Law Review* 51 (Fall), 947–982.

Eyraud, François, and Robert Tehobanian. 1985. "The Auroux Reforms and Company-Level Industrial Relations in France," *British Journal of Industrial Relations* 23 (July), 241–259.

Fried, Charles. 1984. "Individual and Collective Rights in Work Relations: Reflections on the Current State of Labor Law and Its Prospects," *University of Chicago Law Review* 54 (Fall), 1012–1040.

Gennard, John. 1979. *Job Security and Industrial Relations*. Paris: Organization for Economic Cooperation and Development.

Hamermesh, Daniel S. 1987. "The Costs of Worker Displacement," *Quarterly Journal of Economics* 102 (February), 51–75.

Hedlund, Jeffrey. 1986. "An Economic Case for Mandatory Bargaining Over Partial Termination and Relocation Decisions," *Yale Law Journal* 95 (5), 949–968.

Lazear, Edward P. 1988. "Employment-at-Will, Job Security, and Work Incentives," in Robert A. Hart, ed., *Employment, Unemployment and Labor Utilization*. Boston: Unwin Hyman, 39–61.

Leontief, Wassily. 1946. "The Pure Theory of the Guaranteed Annual Wage Contract," *Journal of Political Economy* 54 (February), 76–79.

Maury, Jean-Michel. 1985. *Labour Market Flexibility in the Member States of the Community*. Paris: Centre for Research and Information on Technology, Economics, and the Regions.

Meyers, Frederick. 1964. *Ownership of Jobs: A Comparative Study*. Los Angeles: Institute of Industrial Relations, University of California at Los Angeles.

Piore, Michael J. 1986. "Perspectives on Labor Market Flexibility," *Industrial Relations* 25 (Spring), 146–166.

Rhine, Barbara. 1986. "Business Closings and Their Effects on Employees—Adaptation of the Tort of Wrongful Discharge," *Industrial Relations Law Journal* 8 (3), 362–400.

Riordan, Michael H., and Michael L. Wachter. 1982. "What Do Implicit Contracts Do?" *Proceedings of the Thirty-fifth Annual Meeting of the Industrial Relations Research Association*, 291–298.

Rosen, Sherwin. 1984. "Commentary: In Defense of the Contract at Will," *University of Chicago Law Review* 51 (Fall), 983–987.

Schelling, Thomas C. 1960. *The Strategy of Conflict*. Cambridge, MA: Harvard University Press.

Sengenberger, Werner. 1986. "Revisiting the Legal and Institutional Framework for Employment Security—An International Comparative Perspective." Presented at the International Symposium on Employment Security and Labor Market Flexibility, Yokohama National University, December 9–12.

Shapiro, J. Peter, and James F. Tune. 1974. "Implied Rights to Job Security," *Stanford Law Review* 26 (January), 335–369.

Summers, Clyde W. 1976. "Individual Protection Against Unjust Dismissal: Time for a Statute," *Virginia Law Review* 62 (3), 481–532.

U.S. General Accounting Office. 1986. "Dislocated Workers: Extent of Business Closures, Layoffs, and the Public and Private Response, GAO/HRD-86-116BR.

Vranken, Martin. 1986. "Deregulating the Employment Relationship: Current Trends in Europe," *Comparative Labor Law* 7 (Winter), 143–165.

Weiss, Manfred. 1987. "Labour Law and Industrial Relations in the Federal Republic of Germany," in R. Blanpain, ed., *International Encyclopedia for Labour Law and Industrial Relations*. Boston: Kluwer Law and Taxation Publishers.

Discussion

Michael Wachter (University of Pennsylvania) noted that the existence of market failures attributable to asymmetries in the information available to firms and workers does not imply that current employment security practices are inefficient. If the transactions costs associated with strong employment security practices are high, Wachter reasoned, parties might choose not to adopt them even in the absence of information asymmetries. The fact that union contracts in the United States so seldom have contained even weak job security clauses suggests that the value workers attach to such clauses is not sufficiently high to offset the transactions costs associated with having them. Wachter was also sceptical that the externalities associated with plant closings are as large as has sometimes been claimed.

Werner Sengenberger (ILO) noted that, during the 1950s, the UAW was very interested in the concept of a guaranteed annual wage.

Robert McKersie (MIT) commented that this interest led to the negotiation of Supplemental Unemployment Benefit programs that "top up" automobile workers' unemployment benefits while they are on temporary layoff. While U.S. unions may not have pressed hard for employment security provisions, at least some have been very interested in income security for their members.

Jan Svenjar (University of Pittsburgh) commented that, in talking about the efficiency of contract provisions, one needs to be clear about whose objectives one is trying to maximize. In the United States, union contracts arguably are structured to serve senior workers' interests; in Germany, the institutional structure arguably is intended to serve the interests of a wider group.

8

Continuous-Process Technologies and the Gender Gap in Manufacturing Wages

Susan B. Carter and Peter Philips

The gender gap in manufacturing wages closed by about half during the early stages of industrialization as manufacturing was transferred from homes and artisan shops to factories. But about the time of the transformation of small, idiosyncratically run factories into large, integrated, scientifically managed plants, this improvement came to a halt. Except for variation associated with the business cycle, the gender gap in manufacturing wages remained essentially constant throughout the twentieth century (Goldin 1990). This paper explores the role of the transition from small-scale, batch-process production to large-scale, continuous-process production in bringing about this result. To place our contribution in perspective we begin with some definitions and a brief review of the literature.

The gender gap is derived from the ratio of women's to men's wage rates. The lower is this ratio, the larger the "gap." While the gap is sometimes taken as a measure of discrimination, recent studies emphasize the multitude of factors that influence its size and direction of change over time. A gender gap in wages would exist if

Katharine Abraham, Francine Blau, Michael Carter, Bernard Elbaum, Elizabeth Savoca, William Sundstrom, Richard Sutch, Gavin Wright, and members of the New Directions in Labor Markets and Human Resource Policies Conference, the Stanford-Berkeley Economic History Colloquium, and the University of California Intercampus Group in Economic History offered valuable comments and suggestions on early drafts. The data were made available by the University of California Historical Labor Statistics Project. The processing of the original published data into a computerized format was supervised by Susan Carter, Roger Ransom, and Richard Sutch. Financial support for this work was provided by the National Science Foundation, Smith College, and the University of California. The data are archived at the Laboratory for Historical Research at the University of California, Riverside, California 92521. We gratefully acknowledge the support of the Historical Labor Statistics Project and the financial support of the National Science Foundation and of a Smith College Picker Fellowship. Errors are the responsibility of the authors.

women and men were equally productive but rewarded differently for the same human capital traits. Differences in productive attributes arising from differences in physiology, or choices regarding skill acquisition and/or discrimination in access to skills, could lead to a gender gap in wages even where productive attributes were rewarded equally. Moreover, if differences in attributes exist, shifts in demand across productive traits could cause a change in the gender gap in the absence of any change in the productive the characteristics or in the extent of discrimination. Finally, since the gender gap is computed on the basis of wages of currently employed workers, it is the characteristics of those in the paid labor force rather than the characteristics of the population as a whole that are relevant. Thus a rapid influx of (inexperienced) women into the paid labor force could widen the gap even while the labor market experience of all women was increasing (Smith and Ward 1984; Goldin 1990).

Women's low wages at the beginning of the nineteenth century have been attributed to their relatively small holdings of traits valued in the production processes of that era. Women's productive attributes were relatively meager because production processes required great physical strength and because women faced discrimination in access to craft skills. It is also said that women's expectations of brief labor market careers made them reluctant to invest in skill acquisition. However, these conditions were also present at the end of the nineteenth century (Aldrich and Albelda 1980; Goldin and Sokoloff 1982; Goldin 1984; Eichengreen 1984).

Women's relative wage rose over the course of the nineteenth century, it appears, because shifts in labor demand raised the relative remuneration of traits possessed by women all along. The "adoption of machinery and the replacement of human physical labor with inanimate power" reduced the return to physical strength (Abbott 1924; Baker 1964; Goldin and Sokoloff 1982; Baron and Klepp 1984; Goldin 1987). The reduction in skill requirements and the replacement of on-the-job training with formal education reduced the importance of women's relative lack of skills and increased returns to the type of skills (those acquired in schools) to which women did have access and in which they were likely to invest (Hartmann 1976; Baron 1982; Carter and Prus 1982; Clifford 1982; Stansell 1983, 1987; Goldin 1984, 1987; Kessler-Harris 1984; Cohn 1985; Brown and Philips 1986a; Prus 1990). Working women's relative skill level did not decline, and the shift in demand away from physical strength and toward general education continued through the twentieth century, yet the relative wage of women did not continue to improve. In fact, Goldin argues that the portion of the wage gap not accounted for by gender differences in productivity actually expanded after 1890.[1] A desire to understand the absence of continued improvement in women's relative earnings in the twentieth century led us to look for possible changes in gender-specific employment and wage-setting policies.[2]

Rent-sharing theories of wage determination suggest a possible source of change in such policies. In the rent-sharing view, workers' sense of the "fairness" of their wage affects their productivity. As George Akerlof puts it, "In most jobs keeping busy makes the time go faster. Payment of a fair wage legitimizes for the worker the use of this busyness for the advantage of the firm" (Akerlof 1984, 82). If workers' evaluation of the fairness of their wage depends on the profitability of the firm, then the shift from small to large productive units should enlarge the number of jobs in which above-market wages are paid. The advent of large productive units increases the proportion of jobs that are difficult to supervise while at the same time increasing profits, reducing labor share, increasing the importance of dedicated capital, and shielding firms from competition. These developments encourage the payment of above-market wages and, at the same time, make them less costly since they result in a less than proportional increase in labor costs (Kreuger and Summers 1987, 42).

If workers' concern over fairness extends to the identity of their coworkers, then rent-sharing theories suggest that the appearance of large productive units may have also meant a decline in women's employment opportunities and relative wage. An increase in the proportion of jobs that are costly to supervise would mean that hiring women into positions that male workers felt were properly men's jobs would reduce the productivity of male employees. Moreover, as women were denied the experience necessary for adequate performance in more senior positions, males could be employed exclusively and the relative male wage rise without increasing the user cost of male labor (Wright 1986, 188–189).[3] Finally, the insulation from competition in product markets enjoyed by large productive units would mean a greater ability to accede to those male worker demands that did reduce profitability.

The plausibility of this rent-sharing explanation for the exclusion of women is reinforced by studies of modern labor markets that show that in firms with internal labor markets, women are often excluded from the tall job ladders that eventually result in high pay (Osterman 1979; Cabral, Ferber, and Green 1981; Kelley 1982; Eberts and Stone 1985; Figart 1987; Hartmann 1987). Differential promotion rates implied by the different ladders men and women climb affect both the initial wage level and the growth of wages over time. Craig Olson and Brian Becker calculate that if women had received the same rewards for increases in productive attributes as men, the female/male wage gap would have closed at a fifty percent more rapid rate than that which actually obtained in a firm they studied (Olson and Becker 1983). Together this evidence suggests that a spread of employment policies motivated by rent sharing may have been responsible for stalling improvements in women's relative wage.

We develop this argument by describing the organizational correlates of the shifts in product demand and the batch-production techniques that were dominant in small productive units throughout the nineteenth and early twentieth centuries, emphasizing the mechanisms through which they raised women's relative wage. We suggest that the displacement of small by large firms was the proximate cause of the halt to progress after 1900.

Small Firms, Mechanized Batch-Production Techniques, and the Gender Gap in Manufacturing Wages, 1832–1900

Prior to industrialization, when wage-earning opportunities were largely limited to agricultural labor and domestic-service work, the ratio of women's to men's wages was 0.29. By 1885 it had risen to 0.56 (Goldin 1987, 151). This improvement resulted from the expansion of markets for low-quality, standardized final products that permitted an extension of the division of labor and created new jobs with lower physical strength and skill requirements (Abbott 1924; Baker 1964; Goldin and Sokoloff 1984; David 1987; Goldin 1987). It also derived from the tendency of mechanization to shift the locus of training away from the male craft guilds that had restricted women's access to skills (Hartmann 1976; Baron 1982; Kessler-Harris 1984). In the account that follows we review these influences while emphasizing the contribution of organizational forms characteristic of batch-production technologies and of small productive units in the nineteenth century.

The expansion of markets for low-quality, standardized products in the nineteenth century led to the reorganization of production along several different lines. In the production of shoes, hats, flowers, and garments, outwork systems appeared. These outwork systems offered new income-earning opportunities to men as well as to women. Decentralized, with little fixed capital investment or technical integration, outwork systems permitted the easy separation of workers with different backgrounds and the monitoring of worker effort. Male workers had little opportunity to resist the employment of women in this sphere. The proliferation of this outwork increased women's relative employment opportunities and wages since women's prior income-earning opportunities had been comparatively more limited (Dublin 1985).

The transition from outwork to the factory system, both in its workshop and true factory forms, further increased women's relative wages by increasing their relative employment opportunities. Women were able to obtain employment in early factories because quality of workmanship was not significant and the productivity of individual workers could be easily monitored (Goldin 1983; Prude 1983; Brown and Philips 1986b).

In workshops in the needle trades, cigars, and in canning preparation, only small amounts of capital equipment were used. Material flow-through per worker was relatively low. Workers were paid piece rates. In these workshops masses of workers performed the same hand task such as buttonholing garments, leaf stripping for cigars, or peach pitting for canning. Each hand laborer finished one small batch of material at a time. These conditions meant that unit costs were not affected by worker slowness. Workers could develop considerable speed and skill in many jobs in these workshops and factories. Very fast workers performing activities like packing, packaging, and labeling in industries such as confections, novelties, and canning were considered quite skilled by their coworkers. But because these operations were carried out with batch-process methods and paid by the piece, the employer did not require that all workers work fast and did not have to motivate workers to maintain speed. Two slow workers were just as effective as one fast worker. Moreover, making places for slow, inexperienced workers was good insurance against the scarcity of an effective labor supply (Gordon, Edwards, and Reich 1982). These conditions meant that monitoring costs were low.

The major risk posed by new workers was the destruction of small amounts of the employer's raw materials or semi-finished products. However, a beginner's rate could be paid so that the risks associated with the unproven skills of a new hire were transferred to the worker (Kansas Bureau of Labor and Industrial Statistics 1890, 311–326). Under these conditions employers were willing to offer jobs to all applicants, women included. These conditions permitted even women with family responsibilities to work since they could often bring their children with them.

This is not to say that women were necessarily offered equal pay for their work. An investigation by the California Bureau of Labor Statistics revealed that as late as 1887, "instances are frequent where a young man and woman standing side by side in the same department, the former receives double the salary the latter is paid." Yet such situations were becoming less common. The bureau went on to say, "the result of such competition is generally the lowering down of the men instead of the leveling up of the women. Men are by such a process often forced to quit the field and seek new pastures" (California Bureau of Labor Statistics 1888, 80).

Few women found employment in crafts where skills were highly valued secrets. Male relatives were most likely to be taught. Blacks, the foreign born, and women were universally excluded (Hartmann 1976). The custom-work branches of the clothing and hatmaking industries were the only sectors that offered craft employment to women. Significantly, many of the skilled women workers in these fields seem to have been self-taught and self-employed (Jensen 1984, 11). Thus, the expansion of markets for low-quality, standardized final products shifted demand toward the productive traits possessed by women. In an environment of batch-production technologies and small firms, the operation of market forces led to an expansion of employment opportunities and to a rise in the relative wage of women.

Large Firms, Continuous-Process Technologies, and the Gender Gap in Manufacturing Wages, 1900–1980

While the de-skilling of craft occupations and the lightening of the physical demands of work were continued with the introduction of high throughput, continuous-process technologies in the last decades of the nineteenth century, they ceased to have the same positive effects on women's employment opportunities and relative wages. We hypothesize that the different effects of these technologies on the gender gap in manufacturing wages resulted from their different implications for the operation of competitive forces. The greater capital intensity and integration of production processes associated with continuous processing expanded opportunities for the exercise of male worker power while simultaneously insulating firms from product market competition. These developments lowered the relative wage of women by limiting their employment opportunities in high-wage industries.

Hiring and Training Costs

Hiring costs increased with the adoption of capital-intensive, high throughput, continuous-process, mechanized line production. More equipment and raw material raised the potential damage of an inept worker directly. Examples are given in the testimony of Armour McLaughlin, partner in a (capital-intensive) brewery, to the California Bureau of Labor Statistics in 1888.

Green men cause us a good deal of trouble. . . . I had one green man that washed down the sediment off the cooler into the beer, which was pretty near a dead loss to the institution. Have had a great deal of beer spoilt by green men burning the wrong kind of coal.

Careful men and competent men of our own selection would not have done that. Once a customer came to me and told me the yeast was very bad, and I learned that a green man had kept the yeast in the cellar for two weeks. . . . Another man was on the night watch in the malt house, and he put his candle in the elevator, and it created a fire which caused an explosion in the malt house, and caused a great deal of damage. We did not discover all the damage at once, which caused additional expense (California Bureau of Labor Statistics 1888, 116)

The switch from batch production based on a mass of workers doing the same task to flow production based on a line of workers doing marginally differentiated tasks also meant that a higher percentage of total materials passed through each individual's hands. Because this made the productivity of each worker down the line technically more dependent upon the productivity of individual workers up the line, slow workers, especially those in strategic positions, could slow the pace of entire work teams and their equipment (Brown and Nuwer 1987).

Second, while continuous-process technologies typically de-skilled craft workers by disaggregating the bundle of skills and knowledge that had previously been concentrated under the ownership of a craft community, it created a new skill acquisition system that raised hiring costs. Under continuous-process technologies the skills embodied in a single craft were distributed across many semi-craft workers who gradually accumulated skills and knowledge through incremental on-the-job training (Elbaum 1984). While many of the skills acquired in this training process were general to an entire industry, the knowledge that a particular worker had completed a certain level of training was detectable only through the direct observation of coworkers and immediate supervisors. It may also have been true that with increasing technical interdependence in production the layout of the line and the particular constellation of machinery created more firm-specific skills than existed in the earlier technology. Such a mingling of firm-specific skills with industry-general skills would have made it increasingly difficult for other firms to assess the skills acquired by a worker in another company in the same industry, again increasing hiring costs.

Yet it seems unlikely that this increase in hiring costs would narrow women's employment opportunities. Women workers had been employed in the most capital-intensive industries of the nineteenth century, textile manufacturing and, after 1870, shoe manufacturing. Firms in these industries initially hired women because men were unavailable. Firms then adopted a variety of methods designed to reduce labor turnover such as offering opportunities for promotion, the hiring of relatives, the use of contracts requiring a year's service and two weeks notice as a condition of earning an honorable discharge (Dublin 1979, 49, 59, 196). These policies were effective in creating a stable female labor force. Although female cotton textile operatives have been described as "at best a very impermanent working group" (Ware 1931, 224) the job tenure of these women averaged about seven and a half years (Carter and Savoca, 1990). Since the expected tenure of male workers was not much greater, gender differences in turnover costs do not appear large enough to have deterred the employment of women (Carter and Savoca 1989).[4]

Monitoring Costs

Continuous-process technologies appear to have made it more difficult to monitor the quality and intensity of work. Piece rates were impractical in technically integrated production processes in which an individual worker's speed was limited by the volume of work coming his/her way, and in which output quality was difficult to link to a particular worker. Time-rate wages set at workers' opportunity cost of time did not provide an incentive to avoid shirking as long as detection of shirking was uncertain. These are precisely the circumstances in which above-market wages would be expected to stimulate worker productivity. These circumstances might also motivate employers to honor other worker demands. In particular, if male workers resented the employment of women, then the improvement in male productivity following an employment ban on women might offset the increase in the wage bill.

Moreover, continuous-process technologies provided other opportunities for male workers to oppose the introduction of female help. The new technology required the cooperation of in-place workers in training both new hires and more seasoned workers moving up newly established learning ladders. Continuous-process technologies also made employers vulnerable to the intentions and demands of strategically placed workers in key positions along the production line. Thus, despite the craft-deskilling elements of continuous processing, the new technology required that the employer be sensitive to the demands of the current work force (Edwards 1979; Gordon, Edwards, and Reich 1982; Jacoby 1985; Brown and Nuwer 1987).

Testing for the Effects of Continuous-Process Technologies and Large Firm Size

Since continuous-process technologies and large firm size did not diffuse evenly across industries, it is possible to test our hypotheses with cross-sectional data. In particular, our argument implies that industries employing large-scale, continuous-process production technologies hired fewer women and paid higher wages. Thus we expect a negative correlation between the percentage of an industry's work force that is female and the male wage. Also, to the extent that horizontal equity constraints lead employers paying efficiency wages for some jobs to pay higher wages to workers in all jobs, we expect women in (largely male) efficiency wage-paying industries to receive wage premiums as well (Akerlof 1984; Krueger and Summers 1987, 41). Moreover, if most women were crowded into industries in which efficiency wage considerations were unimportant, the differential for

Table 8.1
Continuous-process technology and female employment by industry, 1889
and 1899 (t-statistics in parentheses)

	1889	1899
Machinery-labor ratio (in thousands)	−1.013*	−0.583*
	(4.284)	(4.851)
Constant	−2.045	−2.312*
	(12.659)	(15.209)
R^2	0.051	0.063
Number	326	351

Note: The dependent variable is the log of the odds ratio, $P/(1-P)$ where
P is the percentage of wage earners who are female.
*Significant at 0.05 level.
Sources: U.S. Census Office. *Report on Manufacturing Industries at the
Eleventh Census: 1890. Vol. VI, Pt. 1.* Washington, D.C.: Government
Printing Office, 1895, Table 4 and U.S. Census Office. *Twelfth Census of the
United States, 1900. Manufactures. Volume VII, Pt. I.* Washington, D.C.:
United States Census Office, 1902, Table 2.

women in efficiency wage-paying industries is expected to be greater
than for men.

Table 8.1 provides evidence on the effect of continuous-process
technologies on the employment of women in a cross-section of 326
and 351 industries in 1889 and in 1899 respectively. Our proxy for
continuous-process technologies is the machinery-labor ratio, the
value of machinery, tools, and implements divided by the average
number of wage earners. The dependent variable is the log of the
odds ratio, $P/(1-P)$ where P is the proportion of the industry work
force that is female. The regression results are consistent with the
hypothesis that continuous-process technologies reduce the employment of women. Moreover, the magnitude of the coefficients suggests that the effect is large. The coefficients from the regression
using 1899 data imply that at the mean value of the machinery-labor
ratio the proportion of women is 7.2 percent. At a value of the
machinery-labor ratio one standard deviation above the mean, the
predicted share of the work force that is female is only 3.8 percent.
The coefficients from the equation using 1889 data imply an even
larger effect.[5]

An apparent difficulty with our second hypothesis is that it seems
to be contradicted by evidence developed by Goldin showing that
the male and the female wage were uncorrelated with the proportion

Table 8.2
Determinants of the average industry wage, by gender, 1889 and 1899

	1889		1899	
	Men	Women	Men	Women
Percent female	−0.218	−0.0259	0.011	0.022
	(−1.611)	(−0.178)	(0.114)	(0.235)
Constant	6.228*	5.552*	6.117*	5.570*
	(122.940)	(99.841)	(166.460)	(165.154)
R^2	0.048	0.0006	0.0003	0.001
Number	54	53	54	53

Notes: Industries are those in which total employment in 1899 was 25,000 or more. The dependent variable is the natural log of the average industry wage (t-statistics in parentheses).
*Significant at 0.05 level.
Sources: U.S. Census Office. *Report on Manufacturing Industries at the Eleventh Census: 1890. Vol. VI, Pt. 1.* Washington, D.C.: Government Printing Office, 1895, Table 4 and U.S. Census Office. *Twelfth Census of the United States, 1900. Manufactures. Volume VII, Pt. I.* Washington, D.C.: United States Census Office, 1902, Table 2.

of the industry's work force that is female (Goldin 1987). "Women earned less than men in manufacturing not because males constituted 99 percent of the labor force in iron and steel, agricultural implements, shipbuilding, and masonry," Goldin writes. "Women earned proportionately less even in the industries in which they were very numerous, such as boots and shoes, cotton, woolens, boxes, and clothing" (Goldin 1987, 149). Because our hypothesis implies that industry affiliation *does* affect the gender gap in manufacturing wages we first show why her evidence does not lead us to reject our hypothesis.

In Table 8.2 we reproduce Goldin's results using the average industry wage of males and females in the fifty-four industries with total employment of 25,000 or more in 1899. We too find that "percent female" is not a statistically significant determinant either of the male wage or of the female wage in 1889 and in 1899. Table 8.3 shows why. It ranks the fifty-four industries according to their average male wage in 1889 and in 1899. The proportion of the industry work force female in each year is also presented. In 1889, as one would expect, the virtually all-male marble, malt liquor, carpentering, painting, masonry, and plumbing industries account for six of the top seven

Table 8.3
Rank order of industries by average male wage with percent female, 1889
and 1899

Industry	Ranking 1889	Percent Female 1889	Ranking 1899	Percent Female 1899
Marble	1	0	22	0
Liquors, malt	2	1	2	1
Printing, newspapers	3	12	3	17
Carpentering	4	0	8	0
Painting	5	0	5	0
Masonry	6	0	11	0
Plumbing	7	0	6	0
Printing, books	8	19	12	21
Clothing, men's custom	9	28	9	29
Shipbuilding	10	0	17	0
Clothing, women's dressmaking	11	98	1	90
Clothing, women's factory	12	67	4	69
Cars, railroad	13	0	13	0
Foundry	14	1	19	1
Electrical apparatus	15	17	16	15
Meat packing	16	3	25	5
Glass	17	5	7	8
Planing mills	18	0	39	0
Iron and steel	19	0	15	0
Bread	20	12	18	18
Silk	21	62	40	59
Tin	22	4	21	6
Cars, not railroad	23	1	23	0
Furniture	24	2	45	3
Wagons	25	1	30	1
Boots and shoes	26	30	32	34
Blacksmithing	27	0	24	0
Pottery	28	11	43	11
Clothing, men's factory	29	53	10	59
Hardware	30	9	35	10
Saddles	31	4	34	4
Dyeing	32	12	33	15
Leather	33	0	42	2
Paper	34	24	38	16
Cigars	35	29	28	38
Carpets	36	49	31	47
Candy	37	44	37	50
Shirts	38	82	26	82
Boxes, wooden	39	8	48	6

Table 8.3 (continued)

Industry	Ranking 1889	Percent Female 1889	Ranking 1899	Percent Female 1899
Agricultural implements	40	1	27	0
Furnishing goods	41	80	20	85
Boxes, fancy and paper	42	70	36	70
Worsted	43	51	41	50
Paving	44	0	44	0
Hosiery	45	73	46	72
Wool	46	42	47	38
Flouring	47	1	29	1
Millinery	48	99	14	99
Cotton	49	55	51	48
Tobacco	50	41	52	45
Brick	51	0	50	0
Lumber	52	1	49	1
Turpentine and rosin	53	0	54	0
Fruit	54	58	53	59

Sources: U.S. Census Office. *Report on Manufacturing Industries at the Eleventh Census: 1890. Vol. VI, Pt. 1.* Washington, D.C.: Government Printing Office, 1895, table 4, and U.S. Census Office. *Twelfth Census of the United States, 1900. Manufactures. Volume VII, Pt. I.* Washington, D.C.: United States Census Office, 1902, Table 2.

high-paying male industries. Somewhat surprisingly, the all-male turpentine and rosin, lumber, and brick industries are at the bottom of the list.[6] The existence of low-paying, all-male industries reflects the continued importance of physical strength requirements in manufacturing into the twentieth century. Requiring little more than brute strength, labor demand characteristics in these latter industries excluded women but did not lead to high wages for the men who found employment there. These findings suggest that industry demand characteristics as well as the personal productive characteristics of workers were important determinants of the gender gap in manufacturing wages at the end of the nineteenth century. We test this hypothesis by asking whether industry affiliation helps explain wage variation after the effect of personal productive characteristics of workers has been assessed. We follow William Dickens and Lawrence Katz (1987) who use analysis of covariance to test a similar hypothesis for the modern work force.

This test involves first postulating an earnings function in which wages depend upon human capital factors, personal characteristics, and industry,

$$\log W_{ij} = a + X_i B + Z_j C + e_{ij}, \tag{1}$$

where:
W_{ij} = weekly wage of individual i in industry j;
X_i = vector of individual characteristics for individual i;
Z_j = vector of dummy variables indicating industry affiliation;
e_{ij} = random disturbance term;

a is the intercept; and B and C are parameter vectors. The total proportion of wage variation (share of total sum of squares) explained by the covariates (the variables in X) and industry affiliation is given by the R^2 of equation (1).

A test of the adequacy of personal productive characteristics for explaining wage differences is whether the addition of the industry dummies results in a statistically significant increase in the total proportion of wage variation explained. Moreover, this is a stringent test. We expect productivity measures such as experience and schooling to be correlated with industry affiliation. This correlation reduces the independent explanatory power of the industry dummies. We follow Dickens and Katz in adopting this conservative approach of crediting the industry effects only with the increase in explanatory power arising from adding industry dummies to a log wage regression already including personal productive characteristics (Dickens and Katz 1987, 51). We estimate separate equations for women and for men since we hypothesize that industry affiliation affects them differently.

Data

Data for this test come from a survey of 3,493 workers conducted by the California Bureau of Labor Statistics in San Francisco in 1892 (California Bureau of Labor Statistics 1893; Carter, Ransom, and Sutch 1990). Information on a range of personal characteristics including gender, age, nationality, union membership, industry and occupation, work experience, and wage were reported. While the actual observations are limited to one urban labor market, the sample appears to be fairly representative of the 1890s manufacturing labor force in the United States as a whole. It was drawn largely from the manufacturing sector of the San Francisco economy despite the fact that, as chief entrepôt for the Pacific Coast and as the center for the coastal trade from Alaska to Panama, over one-fourth of the San Francisco labor force was in trade and transportation and over one-third was in the professional, domestic, and service sector (Issel and Cherny 1986, 54). Because the emergence of firm-based career jobs and job ladders was driven by mechanization and was therefore concentrated in manufacturing, this survey's focus on manufacturing workers is appropriate for our purposes.

Manufacturing employment in the sample is concentrated in construction and light manufacturing. Unfortunately, the sugar-refining industry, which had the highest value-added of any industry in the city, is absent, as is the emerging canning industry. The most widely represented factory producers in the sample are breweries, iron-works, and shoe factories.

In two respects, however, the survey is not representative of the manufacturing labor force as a whole. First, while half the men in the sample were foreign-born, they were not members of ethnic groups likely to be experiencing the worst discrimination. No Chinese and only twenty-one Italians were surveyed. Over one-fourth of the foreign-born males were Germans and almost one-fifth were Irish, who did very well in San Francisco (Burchell 1980, 2–14). English, Swedish, and other northern European workers account for another third of the foreign-born sample. Thus evidence in this survey can provide only limited insight into the experiences of the most disadvantaged workers. Second, the San Francisco labor force was one of the most highly unionized in the country in the 1890s. Whereas economy-wide less than 5 percent of the work force was unionized, in San Francisco almost one-third of the men and over 5 percent of the women were union members (Friedman 1986).

The Effects of Industry Affiliation

Means and standard deviations of the personal characteristics used in our analysis are shown in table 8.4. Table 8.5 reports the results of wage equations with these variables alone. The results are comparable to those obtained by other researchers (Eichengreen 1984; Goldin 1984). Experience has a significant positive effect on earnings.

Table 8.4
Means and standard deviations of variables by gender, San Francisco
workers, 1892

	Men	Women
Weekly wage	14.791	6.025
	(6.458)	(2.977)
Experience	16.077	4.842
	(11.647)	(5.517)
Schooling	8.880	9.651
	(2.751)	(3.048)
Single (yes=1)	0.589	0.975
	(0.492)	(0.155)
Foreign-born (yes=1)	0.454	0.166
	(0.498)	(0.373)
Number	2094	487

Note: Standard deviations are given in parentheses.
Source: California Bureau of Labor Statistics, *Fifth Biennial Report*,
Sacramento, 1893.

Its effects diminish with time. Earnings rise more rapidly for women
than for men, although women's earnings peak earlier. Schooling,
defined as age at labor market entry minus six, has a positive significant effect on the earnings of both women and men. Single men
earn less than married men, whereas marriage does not enhance the
wage-earning abilities of women. While foreign-born women suffer
a wage disadvantage in this labor market, there is no apparent pen-
alty for being a foreign-born male. The absence of Chinese and Italian
men from the sample undoubtedly explains this result.

Table 8.6 reports the results of our test of the role of industry
affiliation on wage determination. Results are presented separately
by gender. Line 1 of table 8.6 shows the proportion of total variation
in the log of weekly wages accounted for by the five personal characteristics shown in table 8.5—experience, experience squared,
schooling, marital status, and nationality—and a set of industry dummies. Because no women are employed in some industries and no
men in others, there are different numbers of industry categories for
males and for females.

Line 2 shows the proportion of total variation in the log of weekly
wages accounted for by the five personal characteristics alone. (They
are the R^2 from the equations reported in table 8.5.) The difference

Table 8.5
Personal characteristics and wage determination by gender, San
Francisco, 1892

	Men	Women
Experience	0.063*	0.100*
	(25.558)	(13.355)
Experience squared	−0.001*	−0.002*
	(−21.042)	(−9.322)
Schooling	0.021*	0.019*
	(6.684)	(3.139)
Single (yes=1)	−0.101*	−0.200
	(−5.004)	(−1.568)
Foreign-born (yes=1)	−0.001	−0.242*
	(0.066)	(−4.629)
Constant	1.857*	1.371*
	(42.464)	(9.193)
R^2	.368	.320
Number	2094	487

Note: t-statistics are given in parentheses.
*Significant at 0.05 level.
Source: California Bureau of Labor Statistics, *Fifth Biennial Report*,
Sacramento, 1893.

between lines 1 and 2, shown in line 3, is a lower-bound estimate of
the share of total wage variation accounted for by industry affiliation.
Unless the unmeasured aspects of labor quality are only weakly
correlated with the measured aspects, industry would not pick up
these worker quality differences.[7]

An upper-bound estimate of the importance of industry affiliation
in accounting for wage variation is given in line 4, which shows the
share of total wage variation accounted for by industry dummies
alone. This is an upper bound since it attributes to industry the effects
of personal characteristics that are correlated with industry. Taken
together, lines 3 and 4 imply that industry effects account for from
11 to 20 percent of male wage variation and from 22 to 27 percent of
female wage variation.

F-statistics for the hypothesis that the industry effects are all zero
are 5.86 and 11.89 for males and females respectively. These statistics
lead us to reject the hypothesis that industry effects are irrelevant at
all conventional levels of significance testing. Moreover, the fact that

Table 8.6
Analysis of sources of wage variation by gender, San Francisco, 1892

	Share of Total Sum of Squares	
Source of Variation	Men	Women
1. Personal characteristics and industry (RA)	.481	.542
2. Personal characteristics only (RB)	.368	.320
3. Industry effects (RA − RB)	.113	.222
4. Industry only (RC)	.199	.272
5. Personal characteristics effects (RA − RC)	.282	.270
Total sum of squares	512.05	109.87
Variance of log (wage)	.245	.226
Standard deviation of log (wage)	.495	.475
Mean of log (wage)	2.588	1.686
Total number of observations	2094	487
Number of industry cells	42	20
Number of personal characteristics	5	5

Source: California Bureau of Labor Statistics, *Fifth Biennial Report*, Sacramento, 1893.

industry effects are larger for females than for males is consistent with our hypothesis that horizontal equity considerations result in proportionately larger wage premia to the few women finding employment in the high-wage male industries.

Next we test whether it is industries employing continuous-process technologies that pay high wages. As in table 8.1, we measure the continuous-process technologies by the machinery-labor ratio, the value of machinery, tools, and implements in an industry divided by the average number of wage earners. We add this to the measures of personal productive characteristics included in the wage regressions in table 8.5. The results are reported in table 8.7. For both male and female workers, the machinery-labor ratio has a positive, statistically significant effect on the wage. Moreover, the effect is larger for women than for men. The relative magnitudes of the coefficients on the machinery-labor ratio suggest that, had women been hired in industries that were as machinery-intensive as men's, their wages would have been 14 percent higher than was actually the case.

Table 8.7
Continuous-process technology and wage determination by gender, San Francisco, 1892

	Males	Females
Machinery-labor ratio	0.046*	0.293*
	(4.633)	(3.639)
Experience	0.063*	0.102*
	(25.564)	(13.783)
Experience squared	−0.001*	−0.002*
	(20.974)	(9.602)
School	0.019*	0.019*
	(5.898)	(3.151)
Single (yes=1)	−0.105*	−0.195
	(5.213)	(1.543)
Foreign-born (yes=1)	−0.021	−0.224*
	(1.153)	(4.317)
R^2	0.375	0.374
Number	2094	487

Note: t statistics are given in parentheses.
*Significant at 0.05 level.
Source: California Bureau of Labor Statistics, *Fifth Biennial Report*, Sacramento, 1893.

Implications

We have argued that the small-scale manufacturing firms of the nineteenth century provided an environment in which competitive forces worked to erode gender-based discrimination in access and rewards to productive traits. This environment, along with shifts in demand away from physical strength and skill, caused the gender gap in manufacturing wages to fall. The advent of large-scale, capital-intensive, continuous-process technologies in the late nineteenth and early twentieth centuries created a new environment with more opportunities for the exercise of male worker power. This power was used to limit women's access to the firm-specific skills valued in the production process, bringing an end to improvements in their relative wage. Since large, technically integrated firms employed the majority of American manufacturing workers over most of the twentieth century, their effects on labor market competition had important consequences for women's employment in manufacturing as a whole.

Since the 1970s, however, the employment share of large manufacturing firms has been falling (see chapter 5 of this volume). This might seem to presage a return to labor market competition and to improvements in women's relative wage.

Our study suggests caution in accepting this view. The likelihood that these new small firms will enhance employment and wage-earning opportunities for women will depend upon their requirements for skills and for interdependencies among workers. The small manufacturing firms of the nineteenth century facilitated the workings of competition because of their low skill requirements and the relative absence of integration among the activities of individual workers. The batch production method, the small amounts of capital involved, the ease of measuring workers' output, the absence of training, and the learning-by-doing nature of skill acquisition limited the importance of employee interactions and thus opportunities for the exercise of male worker power.

Small manufacturing firms of the late twentieth century, organized according to the principle of flexible specialization, appear to differ from those of the late nineteenth century in almost all of these dimensions. They require a skilled labor force, where skill includes ongoing practical training and production experience as well as formal general education, in order to compete in the sophisticated, rapidly changing, technologically advanced markets where small firms have an advantage. They require cooperation, trust, and mutual respect among their workers to achieve the flexibility necessary to survive in such markets. These conditions provide the same possibilities for excluding women as do the capital-intensive, continuous-process production methods of large firms. We may see a renewal of improvements in wage-earning opportunities for women despite these structures, of course. But that would be because political struggles and increases in women's education and labor-force attachment over the past quarter-century have changed social norms regarding the exclusion of women.

Notes

1. For the twentieth century Paul McGouldrick and Michael Tannen speculate that the *increase* in the productivity-standardized gender gap in textile and clothing wages between 1909 and 1969 may have been due to a "growing intermittency of work experience for women" (McGouldrick and Tannen

1980, 813. See also Niemi 1982; and Thorton and Hyclak 1982). But James Smith and Michael Ward's evidence rules out this explanation (Smith and Ward 1984).

2. In her most recent work Goldin also explains the growth of the unexplained portion of the gender gap in terms of the appearance of internal labor markets (Goldin 1990).

3. Gavin Wright explains the growth of a racial wage gap in terms of a shift in the locus of skill acquisition to the firm, permitting in-place white workers to limit blacks' access to these skills. "Since most of the important skills were learned on the job, and there were few true individual differences in aptitude, there was no great loss of efficiency in passing over blacks for promotion indefinitely, so long as a substantial representation of whites persisted on the lower rungs. Why should we believe there are any great costs to following an arbitrary racial advancement rule, when even sophisticated modern tests have little objective value in predicting job performance? Furthermore, any such rule consistently followed will tend to be self-confirming, as blacks had little reason to acquire skills that they would never be able to use. Thus, on reflection, there is little reason to think that industrialization should always tend to undermine racial inequities or promote relative minority advancement" (Wright 1986, 193–194).

4. Women's share of employment in these industries later fell with the appearance of foreign-born men willing to work in the mills. But Gavin Wright suggests that the declining importance of women in cotton textiles is best understood as the outcome of a shift to a *family* labor system. Because female employees quit or moved to an intermittent work status as they married and had children while male employees continued in full-time wage work, firms found themselves with an increasing proportion of male workers. Firms' commitment to make use of all family members then led them to redesign jobs to make use of these men (Wright 1986, 142–145). Since the large firms outside of the textile industry that appeared at the turn of the century did not rely on family labor systems, there is no obvious implication for the changes we are attempting to explain.

5. Differences in coverage and in disaggregation within industry make it hazardous to draw any inferences about temporal changes in the effect of continuous-process technologies on the employment of women from differences in the coefficients on the machinery-labor ratio in 1889 and 1899.

6. The rise in the relative earnings of males in the clothing trades between 1889 and 1899 results in part from the decline in wages in the (all-male) building trades in the 1890s (Jackson 1984; Kazin 1987), but is probably also due to a change in the census' method of defining "Average Number of Wage Earners" (U.S. Department of the Interior 1903, xiv). The definitional change appears to have reduced reported employment in female-dominated industries more than in male-dominated industries. Since the wage is computed by dividing total wages by the average number of wage earners, this bias would be expected to raise measured wages more in female- than in male-dominated industries.

7. The Spearman rank order correlation coefficients between average industry wage and average industry wage estimated on the basis of personal characteristics of workers in the industry are 0.387 for union males, 0.576 for non-union males, 0.714 for union females, and 0.544 for non-union females. Across all groups the Spearman rank order correlation coefficient is 0.859. All of these coefficients are significant at all standard levels of significance. The correlation coefficient across all groups is similar to the magnitude of the rank order correlation coefficient between industry wage differentials, estimated with and without controls for labor quality, computed by Alan Krueger and Lawrence Summers using 1984 Current Population Survey data, which is 0.95 (Krueger and Summers 1987, 19).

References

Abbott, Edith. 1924. *Women in Industry*. New York: D. Appleton.

Akerlof, George A. 1984. "Gift Exchange and Efficiency Wages: Four Views," *American Economic Review* 74 (May), 79–83.

Aldrich, Mark, and Albelda, Randy. 1980. "Determinants of Working Women's Wages during the Progressive Era," *Explorations in Economic History* 17 (October), 323–341.

Baker, Elizabeth F. 1964. *Technology and Women's Work*. New York: Columbia University Press.

Baron, Ava. 1982. "Women and the Making of the American Working Class: A Study of the Proletarianization of Printers," *Review of Radical Political Economy* 14 (Fall), 23–42.

Baron, Ava, and Klepp, Susan E. 1984. "'If I Didn't Have My Sewing Machine . . .': Women and Sewing Machine Technology," in Joan M. Jensen and Sue Davidson, eds., *A Needle, A Bobbin, A Strike: Women Needleworkers in America*. Philadelphia: Temple University Press.

Bielby, William T., and Baron, James N. 1984. "A Woman's Place is with Other Women: Sex Segregation within Organizations," in Barbara F. Reskin, ed., *Sex Segregation in the Workplace: Trends, Explanations, Remedies*, Washington, D.C.: National Academy Press.

Brown, Martin, and Nuwer, Michael. 1987. "Technical Change, Strategic Labor, and Wage Structure in the U. S. Steel Industry, 1910–1930," *Industrial Relations* 26 (Fall), 253–266.

Brown, Martin, and Philips, Peter. 1986a. "The Historical Origin of Job Ladders in the U.S. Canning Industry and their Effects on the Gender Division of Labour," *Cambridge Journal of Economics* 10 (June), 129–145.

Brown, Martin, and Philips, Peter. 1986b. "Craft Labor and Mechanization in Nineteenth Century American Canning," *The Journal of Economic History* 46 (September), 743–756.

Brown, Martin, and Philips, Peter. 1986c. "Competition, Racism, and Hiring Practices among California Manufacturers, 1860–1882," *Industrial and Labor Relations Review* 40 (October), 61–74.

Brown, Martin, and Philips, Peter. 1986d. "The Decline of Piece Rates in California Canneries: 1890–1960," *Industrial Relations* 25 (Winter), 81–91.

Brown, Martin, and Philips, Peter. 1986e. "The Decline of the Piece-Rate System in California Canning: Technological Innovation, Labor Management, and Union Pressure, 1890–1947," *Business History Review* 60 (Winter), 564–601.

Burchell, R.A. 1980. *The San Francisco Irish 1848–1880*. Berkeley: University of California Press.

Cabral, Robert, Ferber, Marianne A., and Green, Carole A. 1981. "Men and Women in Fiduciary Institutions: A Study of Sex Differences in Career Development," *Review of Economics and Statistics* 63 (November), 573–589.

California Bureau of Labor Statistics. 1888. *Third Biennial Report*. Sacramento, California.

California Bureau of Labor Statistics. 1893. *Fifth Biennial Report*. Sacramento, California.

Carter, Susan B., and Prus, Mark. 1982. "The Labor Market and the American High School Girl: 1890–1928," *The Journal of Economic History* 42 (March), 163–171.

Carter, Susan B., Ransom, Roger L., and Sutch, Richard. 1990. *Codebook and User's Manual: A Survey of 3,493 Wage Earners in California, 1892 Reported in the Fifth Biennial Report of the California Bureau of Labor Statistics*. Berkeley: University of California Institute of Business and Economic Research.

Carter, Susan B., and Savoca, Elizabeth. 1989. "Gender Differences in Learning and Earning in Nineteenth Century America," Northampton, Massachusetts: Smith College Economics Department Working Paper.

Carter, Susan B., and Savoca, Elizabeth. 1990. "Labor Turnover and Lengthy Jobs in Nineteenth Century America," *The Journal of Economic History*, 50 (March), 1–16.

Clifford, Geraldine Joncich. 1982. "'Marry, Stitch, Die, or Do Worse': Educating Women for Work," in Harvey Kantor and David B. Tyack, eds., *Work, Youth, and Schooling: Historical Perspectives on Vocationalism in American Education*. Stanford: Stanford University Press.

Cohn, Samuel. 1985. *The Process of Occupational Sex-Typing: The Feminization of Clerical Labor in Great Britain*. Philadelphia: Temple University Press.

David, Paul A. 1987. "Industrial Labor Market Adjustments in a Region of Recent Settlement: Chicago, 1848–1868," in Peter Kilby, ed., *Quantity and Quiddity: Essays in U.S. Economic History*. Middletown, Connecticut: Wesleyan University Press.

Dickens, William T., and Katz, Lawrence F. 1987. "Inter-Industry Wage Differences and Industry Characteristics," in Kevin Lang and Jonathan S. Leonard, eds., *Unemployment and the Structure of Labor Markets*. New York: Basil Blackwell.

Doeringer, Peter, and Piore, Michael. 1971. *Internal Labor Markets and Manpower Analysis*. Lexington, Massachusetts: Lexington Books.

Dublin, Thomas. 1979. *Women at Work: The Transformation of Work and Community in Lowell, Massachusetts, 1826–1860*. New York: Columbia University Press.

Dublin, Thomas. 1985. "Women and Outwork in a Nineteenth Century New England Town: Fitzwilliam, New Hampshire, 1830–1850," in Steven Hahn and Jonathan Prude, eds., *The Countryside in the Age of Capitalist Transformation*. Chapel Hill: University of North Carolina Press.

Eberts, Randall W., and Stone, Joe A. 1985. "Male-Female Differences in Promotions: EEO in Public Education," *Journal of Human Resources* 20 (Fall), 504–521.

Edwards, Richard. 1979. *Contested Terrain: The Transformation of the Workplace in the Twentieth Century*. New York: Basic Books.

Eichengreen, Barry. 1984. "Experience and the Male-Female Earnings Gap in the 1890s," *The Journal of Economic History* 44 (September), 822–834.

Elbaum, Bernard. 1984. "The Making and Shaping of Job and Pay Structures in the Iron and Steel Industry," in Paul Osterman, ed., *Internal Labor Markets*. Cambridge, Massachusetts: The MIT Press.

Figart, Deborah M. 1987. "Gender, Unions, and Internal Labor Markets: Evidence from the Public Sector in Two States," *American Economic Review* 77 (May), 252–256.

Friedman, Gerald. 1986. "Politics and Union Growth: Unions and the Labor Movement in France and the United States," Doctoral dissertation., Harvard University.

Goldin, Claudia. 1983. "The Changing Economic Role of Women: A Quantitative Approach," *Journal of Interdisciplinary History* 13 (Spring), 707–733.

Goldin, Claudia. 1984. "The Historical Evolution of Female Earnings Functions and Occupations," *Explorations in Economic History* 21 (January), 1–27.

Goldin, Claudia. 1986. "Monitoring Costs and Occupational Segregation by Sex: A Historical Analysis," *Journal of Labor Economics* 4 (January), 1–27.

Goldin, Claudia. 1987. "The Earnings Gap in Historical Perspective," in Peter Kilby, ed., *Quantity and Quiddity: Essays in U.S. Economic History*. Middletown, Connecticut: Wesleyan University Press.

Goldin, Claudia. 1990. *Understanding the Gender Gap: An Economic History of American Women*. New York: Oxford University Press.

Goldin, Claudia, and Sokoloff, Kenneth. 1982. "Women, Children, and Industrialization in the Early Republic: Evidence from the Manufacturing Censuses," *The Journal of Economic History* 42 (December) 741–774.

Gordon, David, Edwards, Richard, and Reich, Michael. 1982. *Segmented Work, Divided Workers*. New York: Cambridge University Press.

Hartmann, Heidi I. 1976. "Capitalism, Patriarchy, and Job Segregation by Sex," in Martha Blaxall and Barbara Reagan, eds., *Women and the Workplace: The Implications of Occupational Segregation*. Chicago: University of Chicago Press.

Hartmann, Heidi. 1987. "Internal Labor Markets and Gender: A Case Study of Promotion," in Clair Brown and Joseph Pechman, eds., *Gender in the Workplace*. Washington, D.C.: Brookings Institution.

Issel, William, and Cherny, Robert W. 1986. *San Francisco, 1865–1932: Politics, Power, and Urban Development*. Berkeley: University of California Press.

Jackson, Robert Max. 1984. *The Formation of Craft Labor Markets*. New York: Academic Press.

Jacoby, Sanford. 1983. "Industrial Labor Mobility in Historical Perspective," *Industrial Relations* 22 (Spring), 261–282.

Jacoby, Sanford. 1985. *Employing Bureaucracy: Managers, Unions, and the Transformation of Work in American Industry, 1900–1945*. New York: Columbia University Press.

Jensen, Joan M. 1984. "Needlework as Art, Craft, and Livelihood before 1900," in Joan M. Jensen and Sue Davidson, eds., *A Needle, A Bobbin, A Strike: Women Needleworkers in America*. Philadelphia: Temple University Press.

Kansas Bureau of Labor and Industrial Statistics. 1890. *Fifth Annual Report*. Topeka, Kansas: Kansas Publishing House.

Kazin, Michael. 1987. *Barons of Labor: The San Francisco Building Trades and Union Power in the Progressive Era*. Urbana: University of Illinois Press.

Kelley, Maryellen R. 1982. "Discrimination in Seniority Systems: A Case Study," *Industrial and Labor Relations Review* 36 (October), 40–54.

Kessler-Harris, Alice. 1984. *Out To Work: A History of Wage-Earning Women in the United States*. New York: Oxford University Press.

Krueger, Alan B., and Summers, Lawrence H. 1987. "Reflections on the Inter-industry Wage Structure," in Kevin Lang and Jonathan S. Leonard, eds., *Unemployment and the Structure of Labor Markets*. New York: Basil Blackwell.

Loveman, Gary, Piore, Michael, and Sengenberger, Werner. 1990. "The Evolving Role of Small Business and Some Implications for Employment and Training Policy," chapter 5 in this volume.

McGouldrick, Paul, and Tannen, Michael. 1980. "The Increasing Pay Gap for Women in the Textile and Clothing Industries, 1910 to 1970," *Journal of Economic History* 39 (December), 799–814.

Nelson, Daniel. 1975. *Managers and Workers: Origins of the New Factory System in the United States, 1880–1920.* Madison: University of Wisconsin Press.

Niemi, Albert W., Jr. 1982. "The Increasing Pay Gap for Women in Textile and Clothing Industries: A Reexamination," *Journal of Economic History* 42 (June), 423–426.

Olson, Craig A., and Becker, Brian E. 1983. "Sex Discrimination in the Promotion Process," *Industrial and Labor Relations Review* 36 (July), 624–641.

O'Neill, June. 1986. "The Trend in the Male-Female Wage Gap in the United States," *The Journal of Labor Economics* 3 (January), S91–S116.

Osterman, Paul. 1979. "Sex Discrimination in Professional Employment: A Case Study," *Industrial and Labor Relations Review* 32 (July), 451–464.

Philips, Peter. 1982. "Gender-Based Wage Differentials in Pennsylvania and New Jersey Manufacturing, 1900–1950," *The Journal of Economic History* 42 (March), 181–186.

Prude, Jonathan. 1983. *The Coming of Industrial Order: Town and Factory Life in Rural Massachusetts, 1810–1860.* Cambridge, England: Cambridge University Press.

Prus, Mark. 1990. "Mechanization and the Gender-Based Division of Labor in the U.S. Cigar Industry," *Cambridge Journal of Economics* 14 (March), 63–80.

Raff, Daniel M. G. 1988. "Wage Determination Theory and the Five-Dollar Day at Ford," *The Journal of Economic History* 48 (June), 387–399.

Smith, James P., and Ward, Michael P. 1984. *Women's Wages and Work in the Twentieth Century,* Santa Monica: Rand Corporation.

Stansell, Christine. 1983. "The Origins of the Sweatshop: Women and Early Industrialization in New York City," in Michael H. Frisch and Daniel J. Walkowitz, eds., *Working-Class America: Essays in Labor, Community, and American Society.* Urbana: University of Illinois Press.

Stansell, Christine. 1987. *City of Women: Sex and Class in New York, 1789–1860.* Urbana: University of Illinois Press.

Thorton, Robert J., and Hyclak, Thomas. 1982. "The Increasing Pay Gap for Women in the Textile and Clothing Industries, 1910 to 1970: An Alternative Explanation," *Journal of Economic History* 42 (June), 427–431.

U.S. Department of the Interior, Census Office. 1895. *Report on Manufacturing Industries in the United States at the Eleventh Census: 1890.* Vol. 6., Pt. 1. Washington, D.C.: Government Printing Office.

U.S. Department of the Interior, Census Office. 1902. *Twelfth Census of the United States, 1900*, Census Reports Vol. 7, Manufactures, Pt. 1. Washington, D.C.: Government Printing Office.

U.S. Department of the Interior, Census Office. 1903. *Special Reports, Employees and Wages*, by Davis R. Dewey. Washington, D.C.: United States Census Office.

Ware, Caroline. 1931. *The Early New England Cotton Manufacture: Study of Industrial Beginnings*. Boston: Houghton Mifflin.

Wright, Gavin. 1986. *Old South, New South: Revolutions in the Southern Economy Since the Civil War*. New York: Basic Books.

Discussion

Francine Blau (University of Illinois) commented that, even if the female-to-male wage ratio rose during the nineteenth century but stagnated for much of the twentieth, female labor force participation rates rose more during the twentieth century than during the nineteenth. The labor force participation rates of women with small children have increased especially dramatically since 1960; today, for example, over 50 percent of women with children under the age of one year are in the labor force. These facts imply that one cannot say that either period was unambiguously better for working women.

Keven Lang (Boston University) agreed with the authors that male-female differences in job attachment do not offer an especially appealing explanation for male-female wage differences. Although there is reason to believe that women are less attached to the labor force than men, lower labor force attachment does not imply lower job attachment. Blau concurred, noting that male-female differences in average job tenure have always been relatively small. Still, Lang speculated, employer beliefs concerning women's weak job attachment, even if erroneous, might reduce their willingness to hire women.

9 Reducing Gender and Racial Inequality—the Role of Public Policy

Peter Gottschalk

In this chapter I review the growing literature on changes in the relative economic status of minorities and women and ask why we have been so much more successful in reducing earnings inequality between race/sex groups than in reducing inequality within groups. The paper focuses on two sets of questions. The first set is factual. What has happened to the earnings gap between whites and non-whites and between men and women? Have the inequalities within groups shown similar patterns? The second set of questions is causal. What impact have public programs had on these outcomes? Specifically, how effective have affirmative action and human capital programs been in eliminating differences in earnings between groups and within groups?

I argue that the answer to the factual questions depends crucially on whether one is interested in the average experiences of minorities and women or in the experiences of minorities and women at the bottom of the earnings distribution. The gaps between blacks and whites and between females and males are substantially smaller today than in the 1960s. While progress in recent years for blacks has not been as swift as in the past, there has been a long-run convergence in average earnings of blacks and whites—the average earnings of blacks relative to whites rose most rapidly during the 1940s and 1960s and rose very little in the late 1980s. The timing of changes in the gender gap is different, but again the gap today is historically low—prior to 1980 there was little systematic change in the gender gap, but after 1980 the average earnings of women started to catch up with the average earnings of men.

The picture is considerably bleaker when one focuses on minorities and women in the lower tail of their earnings distributions. Starting in the mid-1970s within-group inequality of earnings started to increase for all race/gender groups. This increase in inequality implies that the earnings of persons in the lower tail of the earnings distribution started to fall further behind the earnings of the average person of the same gender and race.

How did these patterns emerge? I argue that the belief, widely held during the 1960s, that antidiscrimination efforts and increased human capital investment could overcome the effects of prior discrimination turned out to be largely right. The integration of the workplace and improvements in educational attainment did raise the average earnings of minorities and women. However, the policies met with much less success when these same antidiscrimination and human capital approaches were used to raise the earning of those at the bottom of the earnings distribution.

The puzzle is why a set of policies that could be so successful for the average minority group member and the average woman have been so much less successful for those at the bottom of the distribution. We now know a considerable amount about the effectiveness of programs designed to improve the labor market position of low-income people but very little about why these programs have had limited success. I argue that we are a long way from unraveling this puzzle. The solution will require going beyond the aggregate data to look at the institutional factors affecting how firms choose among job applicants.

Trends in Earnings by Race and Gender

In this section I present data on the relative earnings of whites and blacks and of males and females. Decennial census data is used to track the long-term changes through 1979. More recent data from the March Current Population Surveys are used to document the year-to-year changes through 1987. I first examine changes in between-group inequality using data on the means of the earnings distributions for nonwhite men, white men, nonwhite women and white women. I then examine the inequality in earnings within each of these groups, using the Gini coefficient as a metric.

Between-Group Inequality

Unconditional Means
Recent tabulations of the 1940 to 1980 censuses prepared by Reynolds Farley and Lisa Neidert give the longest consistent series on average

weekly earnings by race/sex group.[1] These data are used to track the broad sweep of changes over a forty-year period. For changes between 1979 and 1987 I use data on the average annual earnings of full-time, year-round workers classified by sex and race compiled from the March Current Population Survey (CPS) tapes by Lynn Karoly. While the two data sets differ in the population covered and the rate of pay measure used, together they give the most comprehensive picture of changes in between-group earnings inequality over the last half-century.

The two data sets measure the mean earnings of all persons in the relevant working population who worked at some point during the survey week or who worked full-time year-round, respectively. Changes in these averages reflect changes in who works and changes in workers' characteristics, as well as changes in rates of pay, holding characteristics fixed. Whether one should condition on workers' characteristics when making earnings comparisons, and whether selection on unobservables is an important explanation for changes in average earnings, are questions that I will turn to in the next section. For the time being, these data serve as a useful starting point.

Table 9.1 presents the decennial census data. The first four columns present the ratio of black to white average weekly earnings for persons broken down by sex and age. The next four columns show the ratio of female to male average earnings for persons classified by race and age.

The convergence in weekly earnings between blacks and whites is clear in table 9.1. While young black males were still earning only 86.2 percent as much as their white counterparts in 1979, this was substantially higher than the ratio of 56.0 percent in 1939. Older black males experienced a similar 50 percent increase in the ratio of their earnings to older white males' earnings over this forty-year period. The closing of the gap for black females is even more impressive. While black females earned only about 40 percent as much as white women in 1939, they had gained parity by 1979.

The gender gaps show a less consistent pattern. The rapid rise in the earnings of black women, already noted, causes the ratio of black women's to black men's earnings to increase from 62.0 percent to 85.5 percent for young blacks and from 58.4 percent to 67.2 percent for older blacks between 1939 and 1979. White women, however, lost ground relative to white men. By 1979 the earnings of young white women were only 70.4 percent of their male counterparts' earnings,

Table 9.1
Ratios of weekly earnings 1939–1979

| | Black/White Earnings Ratios | | | | Female/Male Earnings Ratios | | | |
| | Persons 20 to 24 | | Persons 45 to 54 | | Persons 20 to 24 | | Persons 45 to 54 | |
	Male	Female	Male	Female	White	Black	White	Black
1939	.560	.419	.442	.394	.830	.620	.655	.584
1949	.740	.709	.514	.521	.793	.760	.568	.576
1959	.694	.625	.542	.558	.827	.746	.531	.546
1969	.889	.925	.578	.772	.804	.836	.466	.622
1979	.862	1.047	.664	1.010	.704	.855	.441	.672
1979 ratio / 1939 ratio	1.54	2.50	1.50	2.56	.85	1.38	.67	1.15

Source: Reynolds Farley and Lisa Neidert, "A Comparison of Racial Differences in Labor Force Participation, Unemployment, Earnings and Income: 1940–1985." Report no. 10 to the National Research Council, Committee on the Status of Black Americans (mimeo), November 1986.

Table 9.2
Ratios of mean earnings of full-time, year-round persons, aged 20 to 64—
1969–1986

	Nonwhite/White Earnings Ratios		Female/Male Earnings Ratios	
	Male	Female	White	Black
1969	.652	.825	.552	.699
1979	.756	.959	.571	.725
1980	.765	.926	.592	.715
1981	.740	.921	.582	.723
1982	.764	.931	.599	.730
1983	.770	.938	.611	.743
1984	.768	.946	.607	.747
1985	.765	.913	.620	.738
1986	.773	.930	.623	.750
$\frac{1979}{1969}$	1.16	1.16	1.03	1.04
$\frac{1986}{1979}$	1.01	.97	1.09	1.03

Source: Tabulations of Current Population Reports by Lynn Karoly, Rand
Corporation.

a substantial drop from the 1939 ratio of 83.0 percent. Similarly, the
ratio of older white women's to older white men's earnings dropped
from 65.5 percent to 44.1 percent over the forty-year period.

Table 9.2 shows earnings ratios tabulated from the 1970 to 1987
March CPS tapes by Karoly. The data in this table differ from the
Farley and Neidert data in table 9.1 in two important respects. First,
the race categories are white and nonwhite, rather than white and
black. Second, annual earnings of full-time, year-round workers are
reported, rather than weekly earnings of all persons with earnings
during the survey week. These differences will affect the earnings
ratios in any one year, but are likely to have less impact on the
changes in the earnings ratios over time.

In order to see whether the two data sources show roughly the
same patterns, the first two rows of table 9.2 show data for 1969 and
1979. Again, the rate of convergence in the racial gap is large, especially when compared to the change in the gender gap. Like the
census data, the CPS data show little change in the gender gap over
the ten-year period.

The pattern between 1979, a cyclical peak, and 1987, the fifth year of an economic recovery, looks quite different. Over that period the nonwhite to white gap remained roughly constant. The ratio of nonwhite to white earnings increased by only 1 percent for males and actually fell for females, after having increased by 16 percent for both groups over the previous decade. In contrast, the ratio of white female to white male earnings increased by 9 percent over this seven-year period, after having risen by only 3 percent over the previous decade.

The picture that emerges from these data shows substantial convergence in earnings between blacks and whites of both sexes both before and after the civil rights movement, but a marked slowdown in that convergence during the 1980s. The earnings of black women have been catching up to those of black men throughout the period, but white women have shown progress relative to white men only recently.

Effects of Changes in Characteristics
So far I have presented comparisons of average earnings not conditioned on workers' characteristics. Average earnings may change either because of changes in income-producing characteristics, such as education, or because of changes in the returns to those characteristics. In this section I first explore the normative basis for deciding whether the policy-relevant earnings series should hold characteristics constant. I then turn to some recent decompositions that measure how much of the convergence in the unconditional mean of earnings across race/sex groups is attributable to changes in income-producing characteristics versus changes in the returns to those characteristics.

If all differences between the income-producing characteristics of minorities and women and those of white men reflected differences in tastes, or other factors not affected by discrimination, then cross-group comparisons that held characteristics constant (i.e., conditional means) would provide a better measure of discrimination than the cross-group comparisons of unconditional means presented thus far. Any wage differentials arising out of differences in characteristics would be irrelevant to measuring the extent of discrimination if those characteristics were freely chosen. For example, if women's decisions to take time off to have children solely reflected their tastes, then one would want to net out the effects of labor market experience on earnings in assessing the effects of discriminatory practices on women's relative earnings.

If, however, discrimination affects workers' characteristics, the choice between conditional and unconditional means is not nearly as clear. Consider three types of discrimination: (1) pure wage discrimination, in which workers with equal attributes receive different wages; (2) discrimination in access to attributes, such as unequal access to education; and (3) employment discrimination, in which employers use a different set of rules in deciding whom to hire from different groups, such as placing higher educational requirements on black applicants than on white applicants.

If the only form of discrimination were pure wage discrimination and if workers' characteristics were the same as they would have been in the absence of discrimination, then the proper comparison would be between workers with equal attributes, i.e., a comparison of conditional means. There are, however, good reasons to suspect that characteristics are not exogenous. First, wage discrimination may affect human capital investment. Any attribute that can be varied by the individual is likely to be responsive to differences in the return to that attribute arising out of wage discrimination, thus making the characteristic endogenous. For example, if low educational attainment of young blacks reflects low returns to education arising out of wage discrimination, then it would be inappropriate to compare blacks and whites within educational groups. The latter comparison would miss the impact of discrimination on the distribution of education. Moreover, one must ask why two groups who freely chose their attributes should end up with such different distributions of characteristics as in fact exist. This is particularly troublesome in comparing blacks and whites. It is difficult to think of a reason why, in a world of equal opportunity, skin color should lead to any differences in attributes, such as education, much less to the sizable differences we observe. While one can make an argument that small biological differences lead to large gender differences in attributes (Becker 1985), an equally plausible explanation for differences between women's and men's labor market attributes is that they reflect discrimination in the home.

Moving beyond the possible incentive effects associated with wage discrimination, there are at least two additional channels whereby discrimination may affect individuals' characteristics. The first of these is discrimination in access to human capital. Insofar as schooling or location are affected by discriminatory practices, minorities and women will have different characteristics that reflect discrimination. In this case, even if equally educated blacks and whites (or men and women) received the same wage, it would be inappropriate to conclude that outcomes were equal across groups. An extreme form of this line of reasoning is that one should condition only on age and other variables that are unambiguously exogenous in assessing the extent of discrimination.

The possible existence of employment discrimination, which also makes characteristics endogenous, raises questions about whether it is appropriate even to condition on age. Employment discrimination results in men and women (or whites and blacks) with equal attributes not having the same probability of being hired and, thereby, creates a selection problem. In the presence of employment discrimination, all attributes that affect hiring probabilities also affect the distribution of attributes in the work force, even if there is equal access to human capital.[2] The key distinction between the effects of discrimination in access to attributes and the effects of employment discrimination is that the former determines the distribution of attributes of all persons (workers and nonworkers), while the latter introduces the effects of discrimination in selecting workers from the original distribution.

To see this important distinction, consider a situation in which there is no discrimination in access to attributes across the population, and the joint distribution of characteristics like age and education is the same within all groups. Suppose further that employers hire the same proportion of, for example, blacks and whites, so that unconditional employment probabilities are the same across the two races, but that employers are relatively more likely to hire young blacks over their older counterparts.[3] The result would be that the age distributions of black and white workers would be different, even though the initial age distributions were identical for the two groups. The lower mean age of black workers would, in turn, translate into lower mean earnings for blacks.

The question is whether one should exclude or include these endogenous compositional effects in measuring the degree of between-group inequality. By conditioning on age (or education or other characteristics) one may miss the effect of employers' differential hiring practices.[4] However, by not conditioning one mixes the effects of this form of discrimination with the effects of the other two types, which have quite different normative implications. For example, the fact that blacks earn less because employers favor younger blacks has a different interpretation than the fact that blacks earn less because they receive lower pay for the same attributes or are not offered equal access to education.

In summary, the convergence in the unconditional means presented thus far overstates the reduction in discriminatory practices if it partially reflects changes in characteristics unrelated to changes in discrimination. On the other hand, the convergence in conditional means would understate the effect of reductions in discrimination if changes in characteristics reflect changes in discrimination. Changes in unconditional and conditional means, however, provide useful bounds on what we would ideally like to measure.

The standard approach to separating the effects of changes in characteristics from changes in returns to those characteristics has been to estimate earnings functions for different time periods and then to decompose changes in average earnings into changes in coefficients and changes in average characteristics. Changes in coefficients are interpreted as reflecting changes in wage discrimination (changes in earnings conditional on characteristics). Changes in attributes reflect the effects of changes in access to human capital and changes in employer selection, as well as exogenous changes in characteristics.

Blau and Beller (1988) examine changes in gender differentials in earnings between 1971 and 1981. They conclude that changes in coefficients and changes in attributes made roughly equal contributions to narrowing the gap between white women and white men over this period. For blacks, convergence in characteristics between men and women was more than twice as important as convergence in returns to those attributes (Blau and Beller 1988, table 7). Gottschalk, Danziger, and Engberg (1989) examine changes between 1969 and 1979 in the black/white earnings gap for male workers. They decompose the change into three parts: changes in coefficients; changes in attributes; and changes in who is hired. They conclude that changes in returns to attributes and changes in the selection of who was working were roughly equally important. Narrowing differentials in the characteristics of blacks and whites were, however, twice as important as either of the other two factors.

The conclusion of these and other studies that have tried to decompose changes in race and gender differentials in earnings is that the rate of convergence across groups is considerably smaller if characteristics are held constant. These studies, however, serve only as lower bounds since the convergence in characteristics may also be the result of reductions in discrimination.

Within-Group Inequality

Increases in the mean earnings of minorities and women need not necessarily translate into improvements in the well-being of those at the bottom of the distribution. If inequality within a group increases sufficiently, the proportion of that group falling below some fixed threshold may actually increase, even though average earnings are rising.[5] Therefore, a full picture of the relative status of disadvantaged minorities and women must take account of changes in the shape of the distribution as well as its mean.

In this section I present evidence on inequality among blacks and women as measured by the Gini coefficient of earnings both from the census and the CPS. Unfortunately, measures of inequality for the census data presented in table 9.1 are not available. However, Danziger and Gottschalk (1987) present data on the annual earnings of males, broken down by race for 1939 and 1979. Like the data in table 9.1, their data show a sharp rise in the ratio of mean black earnings to mean white earnings over this period, from 0.43 to 0.60. Their data also reveal a substantial increase in inequality among blacks. This increase in inequality suggests that the average gains of blacks during this forty-year period were not equally shared. This is confirmed by Danziger and Gottschalk's finding that the share of black male earnings received by the lowest quintile of black males declined from 4.5 percent in 1939 to 3.6 percent in 1979. This 20 percent decline in the share of the lowest quintile offset part of the effect of the growth in mean earnings for this group.

Table 9.3 presents the longest consistent time series available on inequality of earnings for persons classified by sex and race. The sample composition and earnings definition are the same as in table 9.2. Prior to 1980 the data show no trend except for black females, who experienced substantial declines in inequality between 1967 and 1974. Starting in 1980 all groups show substantial increases in within-group inequality.[6] By 1987 the Gini coefficients for white and black males were 15.4 and 12.8 percent higher than in 1980. The com-

Table 9.3
Gini coefficients for earnings of full-time, full-year persons 20 to 64, by sex and race

	Male		Female	
	White	Black	White	Black
1967	.287	.267	.297	.335
1968	.286	.258	.285	.323
1969	.284	.249	.271	.292
1970	.286	.257	.278	.299
1971	.288	.255	.279	.283
1972	.294	.253	.279	.300
1973	.289	.257	.284	.281
1974	.291	.260	.297	.286
1975	.285	.251	.269	.253
1976	.284	.250	.283	.255
1977	.285	.251	.295	.265
1978	.288	.249	.282	.261
1979	.284	.254	.290	.264
1980	.279	.256	.293	.258
1981	.297	.259	.290	.255
1982	.306	.270	.305	.262
1983	.308	.273	.315	.266
1984	.317	.279	.320	.280
1985	.319	.282	.314	.279
1986	.322	.289	.324	.300
$\frac{1986}{1980}$	1.154	1.128	1.105	1.163

Note: The data reported are tabulations of Current Population Reports by Lynn Karoly, Rand Corporation.

parable increases in inequality among white and black females were 10.5 and 16.3 percent.

Descriptive regressions were fit to the data in table 9.3 in order to control for changes in unemployment rates and to test whether the increases in inequality during the 1980s are statistically significant. The fact that the post-1980 increase in inequality is statistically significant even for white males shows that the distributional changes among minorities and women were taking place in an environment in which labor market outcomes were becoming less equal for most groups.[7]

While nonwhites and females experienced growth in within-group inequality, the explanation for this change is, at least partially, related to forces that have little to do with gender or race. Unfortunately, the causes of the change are not well understood.[8] The baby boom certainly had some impact on inequality during the 1970s but demographic stories cannot explain the increase during the 1980s.[9] Likewise, changes in industrial structure are part of the explanation, but they account for only a small part of the observed increase. At this point we can only say that the changes in the distribution of wages have been large and that no simple story explains these changes.

Since the relative economic position of disadvantaged minorities and women reflects both the effects of above-average growth in average wages (as reflected in the changes in between-group inequality) and the effects of the increase in within-group inequality, the convergence in means overstates the improvement in earnings at the bottom of the distribution.[10] While blacks were catching up with whites and women were catching up with men, these average experiences were being offset by blacks and women in the lower tail of their earnings distributions who were falling behind the average experience. Disadvantaged minorities and women were simply not keeping up with their more fortunate counterparts.

The changes in within-group inequality are too widespread and too large to be explained by changes in public policy. However, it is possible that changes in these policies helped reduce between-group inequality and protected some minorities and women from the effects of increases in within-group inequality prior to 1980.

Effectiveness of Policy

How effective have public policies been in reducing the black/white and the female/male wage gap? If public policies have been effective in raising the average wages of minorities and women, why have they not been as successful in countering the effect of increasing inequality within these demographic groups? In this section I review the evidence on the two policy instruments that have been cited as major factors in reducing inequality: antidiscrimination laws and regulations, and educational initiatives.

Effectiveness of Equal Employment Legislation and Regulations

Two major steps were taken during the 1960s to counter discrimination in the labor market. The first was the passage of Title VII of the Civil Rights Act of 1964, which forbids discrimination on the basis of race and sex in employment. The act requires that private establishments not discriminate, but does not require that employers take any affirmative steps to increase the representation of minorities or women on their payrolls. The Equal Employment Opportunity Commission (EEOC), which is charged with administering the law, monitors the employment patterns of private firms with over one hundred employees and federal contractors with 50 or more employees by requiring that these firms file EEO-1 reports with the commission. These reports are a principal source of information used by researchers to evaluate the effectiveness of antidiscrimination efforts.

The second major legal initiative consists of executive orders that apply only to federal contractors. These executive orders not only forbid discrimination by federal contractors on the basis of race (Executive Order 11246, issued in 1965) and gender (Executive Order 11375, issued in 1967), but also require that federal contractors take affirmative action to find qualified minorities and women. An Affirmative Action Plan, with goals and timetables for achieving those goals, must be filed with the Office of Federal Contract Compliance by all federal contractors.

Three types of data have been used to evaluate the effectiveness of these two antidiscrimination efforts. Early studies used time-series data to see whether the employment of minorities and women increased after the introduction of antidiscrimination policy. More recent studies have used cross-sectional data compiled from EEO-1 forms to see whether firms covered by affirmative action regulations increased their employment of minorities and women more rapidly than uncovered firms. Finally, several authors have used institutional information to examine employers' reactions to antidiscrimination policy.

Time Series Evidence

The early work testing the effectiveness of antidiscrimination policy used time-series data to see whether changes in the black/white earnings gap were associated with either major legal changes or EEOC expenditures. Rough proxies for cyclical conditions, such as the level and change in real disposable income, and average employee characteristics were entered as control variables.

These studies have two major drawbacks. First, they are inherently limited, since the number of explanations for changes in labor market outcomes could easily exceed the number of yearly observations. With few degrees of freedom, many competing hypotheses could be found to be consistent with the data. Second, the date when one would expect to see effects of the changes in the law and regulations is unclear. As Smith and Welch (1984) argue, the enforcement of rules and regulations changed as greater powers were granted to the enforcement agencies and as budgets grew. For example, the budget of the EEOC went up fourfold between 1966 and 1970, then quadrupled again by 1975. With this dramatic growth spread out over a ten-year period, one would not expect to see an abrupt change in employment patterns immediately after the passage of the initial legislation and the signing of the executive orders.

Freeman (1973) used annual observations on the relative incomes of blacks and whites between 1947 and 1971 to test for the effectiveness of EEOC policy. He concluded that cumulative EEOC expenditures accounted for a 15 percent increase in the black/white earnings ratio for males and a 27 percent increase for females. This led Freeman to "conclude tentatively that federal policy and civil rights activities underlie the increase in black incomes" in the period 1965 to 1971 (p. 105).

Flanagan (1976) criticized Freeman's study for not properly conditioning on changes in education and cyclical conditions. Since the EEOC effort was conducted during a period of rapidly increasing educational attainment among blacks and sustained low rates of unemployment, either could be proxied by EEOC expenditures. While Butler and Heckman (1977) find that Freeman's results hold up when relative education is added as a regressor and the estimation period is expanded to include years of higher unemployment, any time series evidence is subject to the criticism of inadequate controls. It is simply impossible to condition on enough factors when using annual time-series data covering a short period to isolate the impact of EEOC policy.

Butler and Heckman (1977) developed an ingenious alternative explanation for the improvement in the relative position of blacks. They reasoned that increases in the generosity of transfer programs could have induced persons at the bottom of the earnings distribution to leave the labor market. With fewer low-wage workers to drag down the average, the mean earnings of persons remaining in the labor market would rise. The observed improvement could, therefore, be purely a statistical artifact. Butler and Heckman argue that since the labor force participation rates of blacks dropped relative to those of whites during the period of interest, selection could have had a greater impact on the mean earnings of black workers than of white workers.

The latest salvo in the time-series literature on the impact of selection, however, reinforces Freeman's original optimistic appraisal. Brown (1984) corrects the original data for selection using the extreme assumption that all changes in labor force participation reflect exit or entry of those at the bottom of the unconditional distribution of earnings. Even under this extreme assumption, he finds that 60 percent of the increase in the post-1964 trend toward greater equality remains after correcting for selection. While one can still argue that these studies confound the effects of legal change and the effects of other changes that occurred over the same period, and that the legal change variables used are misspecified, the consensus is that selection is not the major explanation of the increase over time in the mean earnings of blacks relative to whites.

Cross-Sectional Evidence
The availability of data from the EEO-1 forms has allowed in-depth evaluation of differences between the employment patterns of firms covered by affirmative action regulations and uncovered firms. One of the earliest such studies, Ashenfelter and Heckman (1976), used EEO-1 reports covering the period 1966 to 1970. It concluded that the relative employment of blacks in covered firms had indeed grown faster than in uncovered firms, but that there was no evidence that the program had raised the relative occupational position of blacks.

Extensive research by Leonard (1984a, 1984b, 1985, and 1986) with more recent data has come to much more positive conclusions. Leonard finds that between 1974 and 1980 the growth in minority and female employment and the extent of occupational upgrading was significantly higher in firms covered by affirmative action regulations than in uncovered firms. While these findings could simply be the result of reshuffling minorities and women between covered and uncovered employment, the evidence at least confirms the view that firms respond to the pressure of affirmative action.

Moreover, Leonard (1985) presents evidence that enforcement has not been targeted at firms with the worst records. Compliance reviews have tended not to concentrate on firms hiring relatively few minorities and women, but rather on firms with a high proportion of employment in white-collar occupations. Leonard hypothesizes that this is a conscious choice on the part of decision makers. By focusing on firms with relatively inelastic demand, he argues, the enforcement agency hopes to increase both the wages and the employment of minorities and women.

The finding that compliance reviews have been concentrated on firms with a large proportion of skilled white-collar occupations suggests that affirmative action may have played some role in increasing within-group inequality as well as reducing between-group inequality. By focusing on firms that were more likely to raise the wages and employment prospects of blacks with already above-average wages, these policies may have inadvertently been responsible for some of the growing inequality among blacks.[11]

Smith and Welch (1984) also find large differences between the employment patterns of contracting firms and firms outside the purview of affirmative action, though they remain considerably more skeptical than Leonard about the effectiveness of affirmative action. They question both the timing of the change in employment and the accuracy of the information obtained from the EEO-1 forms. They argue that the largest increases in black employment and wages came prior to 1972, the period during which EEOC had the least enforcement powers. Furthermore, where improvement did occur, the changes were so large as to raise questions about the accuracy of the data. However, they conclude that "one can believe that affirmative action shifted black employment toward monitored firms and still register some skepticism about the magnitude of changes suggested by the EEO-1 reports" (p. 289).

Institutional Evidence

Specific employer behavior has also been studied to gain information about the effectiveness of antidiscrimination policy. On the basis of a detailed study of manufacturing employment in South Carolina, Heckman and Payner (1989) conclude that antidiscrimination activity had a major impact on black employment. They show that the proportion of blacks working in the textile industry in South Carolina had been constant for decades prior to 1965. Black employment then jumped substantially above its historic levels just as the executive orders were starting to be enforced. They argue that since much of the output of the textile industry was sold to the U.S. government, this industry was particularly susceptible to changes in federal policies. They explore alternative explanations for the breakthrough in black employment and conclude that the key factor was the change in the legal and administrative environment.

Freeman (1981) examines the behavior of personnel departments and finds that antidiscrimination policy was reflected in personnel practices. A survey of personnel executives shows far-reaching effects. Firms not only instituted new minority recruitment programs but also incorporated affirmative action goals into their performance appraisals to induce managers to hire qualified minority job candidates. While it is always possible that these procedures were pure window dressing, this evidence strongly suggests that the changes shifted the demand for minorities.

In summary, the evidence that antidiscrimination policy affects employment opportunities is considerably stronger now than in the 1970s.[12] The time-series evidence is weaker than originally thought, but the most recent study still shows positive effects. The cross-sectional and institutional evidence further buttress the case for the effectiveness of policy changes.

Increased Human Capital

Many of the policies of the 1960s were predicated on the belief that insidious differences between the races or sexes could be eradicated by opening opportunities and raising the skill levels of minorities and women. While estimates of the rate of return to education were still crude, policy makers could look at the increase in average earnings that had accompanied the increase in average education over time or at the earnings of persons who differed in education in a cross section to conclude that education and training were likely to be effective ways of raising the earnings of disadvantaged groups.

Education and training were viewed not only as a way of eliminating between-group differentials but, even more important, as a way of raising the incomes of those at the bottom of the earnings distribution. As stated by President Johnson,

> The majority of the Nation could simply tax themselves enough to provide the necessary income supplements to their less fortunate citizens . . . . But this "solution" would leave untouched most of the root causes of poverty. Americans want to earn the American standard of living by their own efforts and contributions. It will be far better, even if more difficult, to equip and to permit the poor of the Nation to produce and earn the additional $11 billion and more (Sawhill 1988, 1092).

In this section I review the consensus that has emerged about the role human capital has played in reducing inequality between groups and bringing up the earnings of the least advantaged. I will argue that the hopes of the mid-1960s for the effectiveness of human capital programs turned out to be well founded in the case of reducing between-group differences, but that attempts to transfer these strategies to aiding the least advantaged have been disappointing.

Impact of Education on Between-Group Inequality
There is a broad consensus that changes in educational attainment have been an important factor, maybe even the most important factor, in explaining the convergence in earnings of blacks and whites. The slower rate of progress in reducing the gender-earnings gap prior to 1979 and the accelerated closing of that gap in the more recent period are also consistent with the importance of education.

Smith and Welch (1986) offer the most detailed case for the role of education in reducing the earnings gap between blacks and whites. They argue that convergence both in the quantity of education and in the returns to education were the "the key factor elevating the long-run economic status of black men" (p. 66).

Between 1939 and 1979 the disparity in educational attainment between young blacks and young whites declined by over four years. The decline for older workers was smaller but still substantial. While the quantity of schooling received by blacks was increasing, the returns to schooling were also rising.[13] Though it is impossible to determine whether the increase in relative returns to education was a result of improved quality of education or of changes in discriminatory patterns that allowed educated blacks into higher-paying jobs, the net result was that not only were blacks gaining education faster than whites, but the payoff to education for blacks was increasing relative to that for whites.

Smith and Welch do not distinguish between increases in educational attainment among workers resulting from more schooling in the population as a whole and increases caused by the selective withdrawal from the labor force of black males with below-average education. The effect of selective withdrawal is potentially important, given the large decline in relative labor force participation rates of blacks over the last two decades. The Gottschalk, Danziger, and Engberg (1989) study cited earlier sheds some light on the effect of selection on education on the black/white earnings gap. While they find that selective withdrawal contributed to the increase in educational attainment among black male workers, their findings do not alter Smith and Welch's qualitative conclusions.

Changes in educational attainment are also important in explaining the slow change in the gender ratio prior to 1980 and the subsequent rapid improvement. O'Neill (1985) shows that the educational attainment of working women actually fell relative to that of working men through the 1970s. In 1952 working women had 1.6 more years of education than working men, but by 1969 women had lost this advantage. Smith and Ward (1984) present evidence that this decline in the relative education of female workers was the result of two reinforcing trends. First, the educational attainment of all females (whether working or not) grew less rapidly than that of males. Second, new labor market entrants had less education than the women who preceded them. This selection of less educated women into the labor market further reduced the growth in educational attainment among working women. O'Neill estimates that this widening of the educational differential on its own would have caused the wage differential between men and women to increase by 7 percent between 1955 and 1969.[14] Finally, the average labor market experience of women was roughly constant, as the growing experience of previous labor market entrants was offset by the low experience of the new entrants. Together, these human capital factors go a long way toward explaining the lack of convergence between male and female wages through the 1970s.

The rapid improvement in the gender-earnings gap in the 1980s can likewise be largely explained by human capital factors. During the 1980s the labor-force participation rates of college-educated women rose faster than those of less educated women. This compositional effect served to increase the average educational attainment of working women relative to that of working men. Furthermore, average labor market experience among working women started to increase as the positive impact of the experience gained by women who had previously entered the labor market began to outweigh the negative impact of the low experience of new entrants. With substantially larger increases in the average education and experience of working women, it is not surprising that the gender gap started to decline in the 1980s after holding steady for several decades.

The overall picture that emerges is that human capital factors have been important in reducing between-group inequality. Consistent with the massive literature on earnings functions, which uniformly show significant returns to education, the timing of changes in mean education and mean earnings strongly reinforces the view that leveling human capital investments is a viable way of narrowing inequalities among groups.

Impact of Training on Low-Income People
While it is true that increases in human capital have been important in reducing the earnings gap between blacks and whites and between women and men, similar broad statements cannot be made about the impact of training programs on economically disadvantaged minorities and women. The hope of the War on Poverty that "if children of poor families can be given skills and motivation, they will not become poor adults" has not been met.[15]

The evidence on the long-term impact of compensatory education shows modest short-term gains, which disappear as time passes.[16] Likewise the effectiveness of employment and training programs does not live up to the expectations of the 1960s. As Bassi and Ashenfelter's review of the literature concludes, "employment and training programs have been neither an overwhelming success nor a complete failure in terms of their ability to increase long-term employment and earnings of disadvantaged workers" (1986, 149).

The question is why success in raising wages for disadvantaged minorities and women has been so limited when compared to the large impact education has had on the average wage received by minorities and women. It is, of course, possible that programs are in fact effective, but that inadequate data or methods have failed to show a positive impact. There is broad consensus that the evaluations of the early 1970s were based on weak data and that the statistical methods used did not properly account for the selection into training programs. The largely negative results of these studies can, therefore, be partially discounted.

However, the 1970s and 1980s were marked by significant improvements in data and methodology that make it difficult to dismiss later findings of mixed effects. New statistical techniques were developed to control for selection in studies using nonexperimental data; carefully designed social experiments, in which individuals were randomly assigned to control and experimental groups, offered an alternative to statistical controls for selection.[17] As the results of the improved evaluations started coming in during the 1980s, the conventional wisdom of the 1970s that nothing worked shifted to the somewhat more optimistic view that some programs worked some of the time. While one could point to the Job Corps and Supported Work for AFDC mothers as success stories, studies of a large number of other programs showed no significant impact on earnings of participants, even when sound methods were applied to good data.[18] Clearly, training has not been as consistent in reducing within-group inequality as education was in reducing between-group differences.

One possible explanation for the limited success of government training programs is that, unlike formal education, training does not raise earnings even in the private sector. Until recently the evidence for the effects of on-the-job training was largely indirect. It was argued that the growth in wages over a person's lifetime reflected the payback on an increasingly large stock of human capital gained on the job and a decline in the proportion of earnings capacity devoted to human capital investments. Since human capital is inherently unobservable, at best this test was indirect.

The problem of measuring the impact of training on earnings was recently confronted by Lynch (1989). Her study used direct measures of training provided by private employers to their employees. Her results show large and significant effects of both specific and general training on earnings even after accounting for unobservable differences between trainees and the comparison group. In fact, private training has an even larger impact than schooling. Since private training seems to be effective, the question of why public training programs for the disadvantaged have not been more effective in raising earnings remains.

A useful way to explore the difference between public and private training is to break down the relationship between training and earnings into two steps. To be effective training must produce skills, and those skills must lead in turn to higher earnings.[19] We do not know whether public programs do not provide skills or whether the skills provided in public programs are not rewarded by higher wages.

Since evaluations of training programs focus almost exclusively on increases in earnings, there is very little direct information on their effectiveness in providing skills. The indirect evidence, however, suggests that useful skills are being taught, at least in some programs, and that even the most disadvantaged participants are capable of benefiting from skills training. In fact, Bassi and Ashenfelter's (1986) review of the literature concludes that the least advantaged benefited the most from CETA training. Likewise, Supported Work was successful in raising the earnings of long-term welfare recipients, a group that might be expected to benefit the least. This suggests that the problem is not just that training programs provide useless skills or try to serve people who are incapable of being helped.

The second link in the chain between training and earnings is between skills and earnings. While there is little direct evidence on employers' reactions to publicly trained workers, indirect evidence on employers' reactions to tax incentives for hiring disadvantaged workers suggests that they are skeptical of hiring people who have been identified as needing assistance.[20] The Targeted Jobs Tax Credit (TJTC) gave tax credits to firms hiring specific groups experiencing labor market disadvantages: youth from low-income households; Vietnam veterans; some disabled workers; and some welfare recipients.[21] A special TJTC was available in the summer of 1983 that made it possible for an employer to hire disadvantaged youths aged sixteen to seventeen for only fifty cents an hour.

Somewhat surprisingly, tax credits were claimed for only 3 percent of the newly hired youth who were eligible for the general TJTC program in 1980, indicating a general lack of interest on the part of employers. Similarly, a wage subsidy offered to employers hiring youth under the Youth Incentive Entitlement Pilot Project was taken up by only 20 percent of the firms contacted, in spite of the fact that the subsidy would pay 100 percent of the wage bill (Hahn and

Lerman 1985, 82). O'Neill (1982) speculates that the reason for the low "take-up rate" in the TJTC was that employers were reluctant to ask potential new employees for information that would identify them as being eligible, and job applicants were reluctant to volunteer the information for fear it would stigmatize them.

This view is supported by results from the Dayton Employment Opportunity Pilot Program (EOPP) site where able-bodied welfare recipients were divided into three groups. The first group was provided with tax-credit voucher information for prospective employers, the second group was provided with a comparable voucher for a cash payment rather than the tax credit, and the third group was given no information to provide to prospective employers. Burtless (1985) reports that 21 percent of the unvouchered group found jobs within an eight-week period, but only 13 percent of the vouchered groups found jobs within that same time frame. Likewise, Bishop (1989) cites evidence that WIN clients in Racine/Eau Claire who were instructed to tell potential employers that they were eligible for a tax credit were half as likely to receive an offer as clients who were told not to give out this information. The fact that unsubsidized workers were more likely to be hired strongly suggests that employers view subsidized workers as less able.

Bishop and Kang (1988) present direct evidence on the stigma effects of participating in government programs. They report that 28 percent of employers who had heard of TJTC believed that subsidized workers "make poorer new employees" than unsubsidized workers (7 percent thought they made better workers). The percentage was even higher for employers who chose not to participate, implying that the low esteem in which subsidized workers were held may have been a reason for employers not to participate.

While the evidence is only indirect, it does raise the question of whether the weak link in the chain is not the employer. Faced with imperfect information and a number of qualified candidates from which to choose, employers may very well use program participation as an indicator of unobservable differences in applicants. Inasmuch as training (or subsidy) programs are aimed at people with unusually low pre-program skills, the use of this screen may be reasonable from the employer's vantagepoint. Without sufficient experience to determine whether the training (or subsidy) compensates sufficiently for the prior disadvantage, employers may be willing to forgo useful training (or large subsidies) in order to avoid the uncertainty.

Increased employer involvement in designing and implementing training programs may help overcome some of these negative consequences of public programs. The fact that the Job Training Partnership Act (JTPA), which requires substantial private-sector input, has had some recent successes may, in fact, reflect the effects of employer involvement. However, this is likely to be only part of the solution. The number of firms involved in program design will almost certainly be small compared to the number of firms in which trainees will seek employment. Furthermore, even if one branch of a firm is involved in designing the program, this does not ensure that other employers in the firm will either know about the firm's involvement or be willing to undertake the perceived risk of hiring a program participant. Getting firms to "sign on" by involving them in the process can, however, only help overcome this difficult signaling problem.

The preceding discussion of the connections between training and skills and between skills and earnings makes it clear how little we know about these two vital links. We know from the success stories that skills are sometimes imparted and rewarded but we do not know where the process fails when training is not effective. At this time it is impossible to make any strong statements about whether unsuccessful training programs are not providing skills or whether employers are not rewarding those skills that are learned.

The distinction between lack of skills and lack of rewards for skills has important policy implications. If training is not improving skill levels, then we should continue to experiment with different training strategies, and we should pay more attention to enrollees' abilities to benefit from the training. The latter may require changing the target population from the most needy to those best able to benefit from the program. If, on the other hand, employers' reluctance to hire persons who have participated in government programs turns out to be key, then programs need to be redesigned to avoid the stigma generated by participation. This may require placing disadvantaged people in private programs open to the wider population, or making the public programs less targeted on disadvantaged people.

Trying to understand why employers are not hiring participants in public training programs will require more attention to institutional detail.[22] We need to know a lot more about employers' hiring decisions before proceeding to controlled experiments in which trainees divulge varying amounts of information to employers about their skill levels and their participation in public programs. Why are enrollees in some programs, such as the Job Corps and Supported Work, hired by firms, while similar firms do not seem willing to hire enrollees from other programs? Do these firms believe that the skills gained in some programs are different, or do they think their hiring strategy enables them to weed out applicants who probably did not overcome their initial labor market disadvantage? Is there a correspondence between what firms believe and outcomes of the program?

Conclusions

Data from the decennial census make it clear that there has been long-term convergence of earnings between blacks and whites and to a lesser extent between men and women. While the decrease in labor force participation rates among less skilled blacks has undoubtedly served to overstate blacks' gains relative to whites, the increase in labor force participation rates of women with low education and experience has probably tended to understate women's gains relative to those of men. In any event, conditioning on observables and correcting for selection biases does not reverse the favorable trends found in the unconditional data.

A less favorable picture emerges when we focus on persons in the lower tail of the earnings distribution. While mean earnings of minorities and women have risen faster than mean earnings for men and whites respectively, inequality of earnings has increased rapidly for all groups in the 1980s. The result is that those at the bottom of the earnings distribution have not experienced the average rate of growth.

A review of the effectiveness of past policies suggests that antidiscrimination and human capital programs have been largely successful in raising the average income of minorities and women but have had relatively little impact on the very disadvantaged. The reason for this anomaly is not known, but I offer the hypothesis that the problem lies in the way employers make hiring decisions. Exploration of this hypothesis will require research that goes behind employers' hiring decisions to ask why those decisions were made.

Notes

1. While average hourly earnings might have been a preferable measure of labor market position, the census data on hours per week are not consistent

over time. In the 1970 Census, the definition was changed from usual hours per week to hours last week. Because the week preceding the 1970 Census included Good Friday, hours worked per week is unrepresentative in that year.

2. Note that this is different from the issue usually raised in the selection literature, reviewed later, concerning what wage should be attributed to these nonworkers. See Heckman (1979) for a discussion of this latter issue.

3. The assumption of equal employment probabilities is included in order not to cloud the issue by introducing the question of how to attribute wages to nonworkers.

4. In practice it is probably impossible to distinguish between the effects of employer discrimination and voluntary withdrawal from the labor market. If, however, members of different races have different propensities to withdraw from the labor market, one must again address the question of whether this reflects race-specific tastes or other forms of discrimination.

5. See Gottschalk and Danziger (1985) for details on the relationship between changes in the proportion poor and changes in the mean and higher level moments of the income distribution.

6. Burtless (1989) and Moffitt (1989) also find increases in inequality during the 1980s, but their data show inequality increasing in the 1970s as well.

7. Separate log regressions were fit to the four columns in table 9.3. Sex-specific log unemployment rates and a time trend, which was allowed to change after 1979, were included as regressors. The yearly time trends were 0.001 higher after 1979 for all groups. All these changes are statistically significant at the 0.05 level.

8. See Burtless (1989) for a current presentation of the factual evidence, and Danziger and Gottschalk (1988) for a discussion of causes.

9. Dooley and Gottschalk (1984) develop links between cohort size and inequality within education and experience groups. They show that increases in cohort size were partially responsible for the increase in inequality during the 1970s. Murphy and Welch (1988) show that demand-side factors had to be at work during the 1980s.

10. Ideally one would like to have information on the proportion of persons with earnings below a fixed cutoff to see the net impact of changes in the level and changes in the shape of the earnings distribution. This is, however, only available for males of all races for 1967 to 1978 (Dooley and Gottschalk 1985). However, given what we know about the importance of changes in income inequality in accounting for changes in income poverty, the importance of changes in earnings inequality is likely to be large. Gottschalk and Danziger (1985) show that, between 1968 and 1983, increases in income inequality were more important than changes in mean income in explaining changes in poverty for blacks and whites broken down by sex of head of household.

11. Freeman (1981) also speculates that the tendency for more advantaged blacks to make more progress may have been caused by changes in discriminatory practices. He shows an increase in recruitment for college-educated blacks but does not show that this was larger than the increase in demand for less educated blacks.

12. See Anderson and Wallace (1975) for a review written in the 1970s.

13. This is consistent with evidence in Heckman and Payner (1989) that salaries and expenditure per pupil were rising faster in black Southern schools than in white Southern schools well before the desegregation cases of the 1950s.

14. Blau and Beller (1988) report that changes in mean education served to increase the gender gap for whites and to narrow the gender gap for blacks by small amounts between 1971 and 1981.

15. This quotation from the 1964 Economic Report of the President appears in Glazer (1986, 153).

16. Jencks (1986, 177) claims to know of no evidence that "compensatory education has long-term effects on students' cognitive skills."

17. While improvements were made in both nonexperimental and experimental evaluations, the debate over which is the more appropriate technique remains unresolved. See Ashenfelter and Card (1985), Burtless and Orr (1986), Hausman and Wise (1985), and Heckman and Robb (1985).

18. For overviews see Bassi and Ashenfelter (1986), and Gottschalk and Gottschalk (1988); Betsey et al. (1985) review programs aimed at youth, and Hollister et al. (1984) evaluate Supported Work.

19. These skills may be nothing more than job-readiness skills that enable participants to demonstrate that they have traits the employer seeks.

20. Employers' reactions to training and to tax credits may be similar since both lower the cost per effective hour of work. However, employers' reactions may differ if their employees must have a minimal level of skills.

21. The subsidy amounted to 50 percent of the first $5,600 of wages paid to an eligible worker in the first year and 25 percent in the second year. The subsidies were available to all employers, whether their total employment increased or not.

22. While Heckman's work has been largely econometric, he also argues for the "value of more disaggregated industrial and institutional analysis in assessing the contribution of federal activity to black status" (Heckman and Payner 1989).

References

Anderson, Bernard, and Wallace, Phyllis. 1975. "Public Policy and Black Economic Progress: A Review of the Evidence," *American Economic Review* 65 (May), 47–52.

Ashenfelter, Orley, and Card, David. 1985. "Using the Longitudinal Structure of Earnings to Estimate the Effect of Training Programs," *Review of Economics and Statistics* 67 (November), 648–660.

Ashenfelter, Orley, and Heckman, James. 1976. "Measuring the Effect of an Antidiscrimination Program," in Orley Ashenfelter and James Blum, eds., *Evaluating the Labor Market Effects of Social Programs*. Princeton: Princeton University Press, 46–84.

Bassi, Lauri, and Ashenfelter, Orley. 1986. "The Effect of Direct Job Creation and Training Programs on Low-Skilled Workers," in Sheldon Danziger and Daniel Weinberg, eds., *Fighting Poverty: What Works and What Doesn't*. Cambridge, Massachusetts: Harvard University Press, 133–151.

Becker, Gary. 1985. "Human Capital, Effort, and the Sexual Division of Labor," *Journal of Labor Economics* 3 (January), S33–S58.

Betsey, Charles L. et al., eds. 1985. *Youth Employment and Training Programs: The YEDPA Years*. Washington, D.C.: National Academy Press.

Bishop, John H. 1989. "Toward More Valid Evaluations of Training Programs Serving the Disadvantaged," *Journal of Policy Analysis and Management* 8 (Spring), 209–228.

Bishop, John H., and Kang, Suk. 1988. "Applying for Entitlements: Employers and the Targeted Jobs Tax Credit." Ithaca, New York: Cornell University, New York State School of Industrial and Labor Relations Working Paper No. 88-04.

Blau, Francine, and Beller, Andrea. 1988. "Trends in Earnings Differentials by Gender, 1971–1981," *Industrial and Labor Relations Review* 41 (July), 513–529.

Brown, Charles. 1984. "Black-White Earnings Ratios Since the Civil Rights Act of 1964: Importance of Labor Market Dropouts," *Quarterly Journal of Economics* 99 (February), 34–44.

Burtless, Gary. 1985. "Are Targeted Wage Subsidies Harmful? Evidence from a Wage Voucher Experiment," *Industrial and Labor Relations Review* 39 (October), 105–114.

Burtless, Gary. 1989. "Earnings Inequality over the Business and Demographic Cycles." Washington, D.C.: Brookings Institution Discussion Paper in Economics.

Burtless, Gary, and Orr, Larry. 1986. "Are Classical Experiments Needed for Manpower Policy?" *The Journal of Human Resources* 21 (Fall), 606–639.

Butler, Richard, and Heckman, James. 1977. "The Impact of Government on the Labor Market Status of Black Americans: A Critical Review of the Literature and Some New Evidence," in Leonard J. Hausman et al., eds., *Equal Rights and Industrial Relations*. Madison: Industrial Research Association, 235–281.

Danziger, Sheldon, and Gottschalk, Peter. 1987. "Earnings Inequality, the Spatial Concentration of Poverty, and the Underclass," *American Economic Review* 77 (May), 211–215.

Danziger, Sheldon, and Gottschalk, Peter. 1988. "Increasing Inequality in the United States: What We Know and What We Don't," *Journal of Post-Keynesian Economics* 11 (Winter), 174–195.

Dooley, Martin, and Gottschalk, Peter. 1984. "Earnings Inequality Among Males in the United States: Trends and the Effect of Labor Force Growth," *Journal of Political Economy* 92 (February), 59–89.

Dooley, Martin, and Gottschalk, Peter. 1985. "The Increasing Proportion of Men with Low Earnings in the United States," *Demography* 22 (February), 25–34.

Flanagan, Robert J., 1976. "Actual Versus Potential Impact of Government Antidiscrimination Programs," *Industrial and Labor Relations Review* 29 (July) 486–507.

Freeman, Richard B. 1973. "Changes in the Labor Market for Black Americans," *Brookings Paper on Economic Activity* (1), 67–120.

Freeman, Richard B. 1981. "Black Economic Progress after 1964: Who Has Gained and Why?" in Sherwin Rosen, ed., *Studies in Labor Markets*. Chicago: University of Chicago Press, 247–285.

Glazer, Nathan. 1986. "Education and Training Programs and Poverty," in Sheldon Danziger and Daniel Weinberg, eds., *Fighting Poverty: What Works and What Doesn't*. Cambridge, Massachusetts: Harvard University Press, 152–173.

Gottschalk, Peter, and Danziger, Sheldon. 1985. "A Framework for Evaluating the Effects of Economic Growth and Transfers on Poverty," *American Economic Review* 75 (March), 153–161.

Gottschalk, Peter, Danziger, Sheldon, and Engberg, John. 1989. "Decomposing Changes in the Black-White Earnings Gap: 1969–1979," *Research on Economic Inequality* 1, 311–326.

Gottschalk, Barbara, and Gottschalk, Peter. 1988. "Antipoverty Policy in the United States: What Works?" Boston: Boston College Department of Economics Working Paper.

Hahn, Andrew, and Lerman, Robert. 1985. *What Works in Youth Employment Policy? How to Help Young Workers from Poor Families*. Washington, D.C.: National Planning Association.

Hausman, J., and Wise, D., eds. 1985. *Social Experimentation*. Chicago: University of Chicago Press.

Heckman, James J. 1979. "Sample Selection Bias as a Specification Error," *Econometrica* 47 (January), 153–161.

Heckman, James J., and Payner, Brook S. 1989. "Determining the Impact of Federal Antidiscrimination Policy on the Economic Status of Blacks: A Study of South Carolina," *American Economic Review* 79 (March), 138–177.

Heckman, James J., and Robb, Richard, Jr. 1985. "Alternative Methods for Evaluating the Impact of Interventions," in James J. Heckman and Burton Singer, eds., *Longitudinal Analysis of Labor Market Data*. Cambridge, England: Cambridge University Press.

Hollister, Robinson G., Jr., et al. 1984. *The National Supported Work Demonstration*. Madison: University of Wisconsin Press.

Jencks, Christopher. 1986. "Comment on 'Education and Training Programs and Poverty,'" in Sheldon Danziger and Daniel Weinberg, eds., *Fighting Poverty: What Works and What Doesn't*. Cambridge, Massachusetts: Harvard University Press, 173–179.

Leonard, Jonathan. 1984a. "Employment and Occupational Advance Under Affirmative Action," *Review of Economics and Statistics*, 66 (August), 377–385.

Leonard, Jonathan. 1984b. "The Impact of Affirmative Action on Employment," *Journal of Labor Economics* 2 (October), 439–469.

Leonard, Jonathan. 1985. "Affirmative Action as Earnings Redistribution: The Targeting of Compliance Reviews," *Journal of Labor Economics* 3 (July), 363–384.

Leonard, Jonathan. 1986. "The Effectiveness of Equal Employment Opportunity Law and Affirmative Action Regulation," in Ronald Ehrenberg, ed., *Research in Labor Economics* Vol. 8, Part B. Greenwich: JAI Press, 319–350.

Lynch, Lisa M. 1989. "Private Sector Training and Its Impact on the Career Patterns of Young Workers." Cambridge, Massachusetts: NBER Working Paper No. 2872.

Murphy, Kevin, and Welch, Finis. 1988. "The Structure of Wages." Los Angeles: Unicon Discussion Paper.

Moffitt, Robert. 1989. "The Distribution of Earnings and the Welfare State." Washington, D.C.: Brookings Institution Discussion Paper in Economics.

O'Neill, David. 1982. "Employment Tax Credit Programs: The Effects of Socio-economic Targetting Provisions," *Journal of Human Resources* 17 (Summer), 449–459.

O'Neill, June. 1985. "The Trend in the Male-Female Wage Gap in the United States," *Journal of Labor Economics* 3 (January), S91-S116.

Sawhill, Isabel. 1988. "Poverty in the U.S.: Why is it so Persistent?" *Journal of Economic Literature* 26 (September), 1073–1119.

Smith, James, and Ward, Michael. 1984. *Women's Wages and Work in the Twentieth Century*. Santa Monica: The Rand Corporation.

Smith, James, and Welch, Finis. 1984. "Affirmative Action and Labor Markets," *Journal of Labor Economics* 2 (April), 269–301.

Smith, James, and Welch, Finis. 1986. *Closing the Gap*. Santa Monica: The Rand Corporation, Report R-330-DOL.

Comment by Jim Rebitzer

This paper documents two important facts about race and gender in American labor markets. First, the mean earnings of nonwhites relative to whites and women relative to men have moved closer together since the 1960s. Second, there has been an increase in earnings inequality within all race/gender groups.

The author argues that the convergence of mean earnings is due in large measure to affirmative action programs, antidiscrimination legislation, and increasing investments in human capital on the part of working nonwhites and women. In contrast, the author does not feel he can identify the causes of the increase in earnings inequality. He suggests, however, that an important part of the problem is the failure of the "disadvantaged" within each group to keep up with their counterparts in the upper parts of the earnings distribution.

The final section of the paper asks why government training programs directed to disadvantaged minorities and women have had such limited success in increasing earnings when increasing investments in human capital have been so important in reducing the difference in average wage levels between genders and races. One plausible explanation suggested by the author is that there is a stigma associated with participation in a government program directed at the "disadvantaged." Participation in such programs signals to employers that there is something "wrong" with the job seeker. Employers will therefore engage in a kind of statistical discrimination against program participants.

I found the empirical evidence presented in tables 9.1 to 9.3 to be very thought provoking. Unfortunately, it is not possible to get a clear idea about the underlying processes generating convergence in average wages across groups and increasing intra-group inequality without knowing more about how the distribution of earnings has been changing within each race and gender group.

In thinking through the ambiguities associated with tables 9.1 to 9.3, I found it helpful to construct two simple but contrasting numerical examples of a hypothetical economy composed of four men and four women, presented here in table 9.4. In each example the economy begins with an arbitrarily specified distribution of wages across men and women. In example 1, changes in the structure of jobs result in the disappearance of the middle of the wage distribution for both men and women. In example 2, the changes for men are the same as in example 1, but for women, changes in the structure of jobs result in an increase in the proportion of high-wage jobs and a reduction in the proportion of low-wage jobs. The important point is that, given the way the examples have been constructed, these very different processes each result in a narrowing of the gap between average wages across groups and an increase in inequality within each group.

The author's emphasis on the role played by investments in human capital also raises questions about the impact that changes in returns to education have had on average wages and on the distribution of wages within each race/gender group. Recent research by Katz and Revenga (1989) indicates that the wage gap between college and high school graduates has increased dramatically since 1979. How has this change influenced the mean and the variance of wages in each race and gender group? The answer to this question requires a more disaggregated look at the distribution of wages within race and gender groups.

In discussing public policy, the paper contrasts the poor results of government training programs with the large wage effects found by Lynch (1989) for private-sector training programs. Lynch found, for example, that a six-month on-the-job training program had a larger effect on wages than a year of additional schooling. Lynch also found, however, that the effects of on-the-job training were very firm-specific. Training received at one firm had no significant effect on wages at another firm. These findings suggest that government training programs are not a good substitute for participation in an on-the-job training program.

Lynch's study also reveals that both women and blacks are less likely to be included in either on-the-job training programs or apprenticeship programs. If inclusion in training programs corresponds to entrance into a firm's internal labor market, Lynch's results can be interpreted as indicating that firms discriminate in part by keeping women and minorities out of the primary jobs that constitute the firm's internal labor market. Evidence consistent with a pattern of racial exclusion from primary jobs was also found by Dickens and

Table 9.4
Comparative status of men and women in a hypothetical economy

Example 1: The disappearing middle

	Men before			Women before		
Wages	$5.00	$7.50	$10.00	$4.00	$6.00	$10.00
Number with Wage:	1	2	1	1	2	1
Mean Wage:	$7.50			$6.50		
Variance of Log of Earnings	0.081			0.141		

	Men after			Women after		
Wages	$5.00	$7.50	$10.00	$4.00	$6.00	$10.00
Number with Wage:	2	0	2	2	0	2
Mean Wage:	$7.50			$7.00		
Variance of Log of Earnings	0.161			0.280		

Example 2: Proportion of low-wage jobs for women falls and proportion of high-wage jobs for women increases

	Men before			Women before		
Wages	$5.00	$7.50	$10.00	$4.00	$6.00	$10.00
Number with Wage:	1	2	1	1	2	1
Mean Wage:	$7.50			$6.50		
Variance of Log of Earnings	0.081			0.141		

	Men after			Women after		
Wages	$5.00	$7.50	$10.00	$4.00	$6.00	$10.00
Number with Wage:	2	0	2	1	1	2
Mean Wage:	$7.50			$7.50		
Variance of Log of Earnings	0.161			0.197		

Lang (1985). Theoretical models of dual labor markets also suggest that firms will exclude women from primary jobs (see, for example, Bulow and Summers 1986). It seems to me that persistent discrimination in the context of dual labor markets may be important in explaining both the ineffectiveness of government training programs and the stubbornly persistent race- and gender-based wage gaps documented in this paper.

References for Rebitzer Comment

Bulow, Jeremy, and Summers, Lawrence H. 1986. "A Theory of Dual Labor Markets with Applications to Industrial Policy, Discrimination and Keynsian Unemployment," *Journal of Labor Economics* 4 (July), 376–414.

Dickens, William, and Lang, Kevin. 1985. "A Test of Dual Labor Market Theory," *American Economic Review* 75 (September), 792–805.

Katz, Lawrence F., and Ravenga, Ana L. 1989. "Changes in the Structure of Wages: The U.S. vs. Japan." Cambridge, Massachusetts: NBER Working Paper No. 3021.

Lynch, Lisa M. 1989. "Private Sector Training and Its Impact on the Earnings of Young Workers." Cambridge, Massachusetts: NBER Working Paper No. 2872.

10 Government and the Labor Market

Robert M. Solow

It is worth remembering from the very beginning that governments—among them the government of the United States—intervene in the operation of the labor market in many ways. The fairly direct interventions include occupational health and safely legislation; the regulation of wages and hours, including the statutory minimum wage and the Walsh-Healy and Davis-Bacon acts; the various acts governing union organization and labor relations; laws about job discrimination and equal employment opportunity; the operation of the U.S. Employment Service; unemployment insurance; various devices, formal and informal, for influencing or determining wages; and of course the whole conglomerate that we usually call manpower legislation. That is a haphazard and incomplete list, and I mean only to refer to the last item on it.

I called those interventions "direct" because they represent the government deliberately and consciously trying to make something happen or not happen in the labor market. There are plenty of other things governments do that are not so directly "labor market policies" but that nevertheless affect the labor market surely enough that no one has a right to be surprised at the fact, even if the explicit purpose is different. This list could be indefinitely long. I mention tariffs and quotas as one example and changes in the scope of public assistance as another, just to give the flavor. The variety is so great that there cannot be very much that is systematic to be said about the reasons why and the ways in which governments do more or less to influence outcomes in the labor market. Even if there were, I do not have the intellectual equipment to say it.

I am, let's face it, an economic theorist who has fallen among manpower specialists. (It is anthropologically interesting that in our culture the phrase "manpower policy" or "manpower specialist" tells you immediately that we are talking about the low end of the labor market: low skills, low wages, low status. An "auto mechanic" is not automatically someone who works on 1968 Plymouths with 350,000 miles on the odometer. Subsidization of medical education is not described as "manpower policy.") Anyway, that is what I am. Everybody has a comparative advantage in something, the textbook keeps telling me. Mine, I think, is to talk about two things. First I shall reflect on the manpower policy scene as observed by an economist who has been marginally engaged in it (how else?) for 25 years. And then I would like to spend a few minutes discussing the undiscussable. We all know that economists and manpower specialists are natural enemies. Economists think that manpower specialists are fuzzy-minded, incomprehending do-gooders, and probably knee-jerk liberals besides. Manpower specialists think that economists are narrow-minded, ignorant know-it-alls who profess to have the answer before they have heard the question. I want to think aloud about why this happens. I may be an appropriate person to do this because, although I come from the economists' side of the fence and intend to stay there, I have a certain amount of *analytical* sympathy for the manpower specialists' view of the matter. That will come out in due course.

My first exposure to this whole complicated business came in February 1961 when I arrived in Washington to join the staff of the Council of Economic Advisers at the beginning of the Kennedy administration. Manpower problems and manpower policy were the furthest thing from my mind. A minor recession had begun in the spring of 1960, the third in half-a-dozen years. Each had started from a slightly higher unemployment rate than the one before. In the month I arrived, the unemployment rate reached 6.8 percent, pretty high by the standard of the time. That is just about where it is now (June 1987); but then it was clearly a recession phenomenon. It seemed to us at the Council that there was slack everywhere in the economy, had been for quite a while, and that it would certainly respond to fiscal and monetary stimulus.

I think it came as a surprise to us to realize that the main serious opposition to this view argued that so many of the unemployed were unemployable that what appeared to be slack was an illusion. Youths, women, and uneducated and unskilled people were not really available resources. An expansion that started from the demand side would very soon run into *labor* bottlenecks and merely produce wage-driven inflation. I do not mean to suggest that this was the only tactical problem we faced; there was the standard fear of deficit finance (now dissolved into hypocrisy), but that was an old story. The "structural unemployment" argument needed to be understood. Walter Heller, James Tobin, and Kermit Gordon assigned me to look into it. All of a sudden I was in the manpower business.

It still leaves me open-mouthed that by March 6 we had produced our "mini-Economic Report" to serve as a basis for the Council's first appearance before the new Congress. It is even more astonishing that when I read it now it seems to me to have been dead right. Here is what we said about the subject at hand.

Some have attributed the growth of unemployment in recent years to changing characteristics of the labor force rather than to deficiencies in total demand. According to this view, the new unemployment is concentrated among workers who are intrinsically unemployable by reason of sex, age, location, occupation or skill. Expansion of overall demand, it is argued, will not meet this problem; it can only be met by educating, retraining, and relocating unsuccessful job-seekers.

The facts (which are examined in Supplement B) clearly refute this explanation of the rise of unemployment over the last eight years. Only an insignificant fraction of this rise can be traced to the shift in composition of the labor force. The growth of unemployment has been a pervasive one, hitting all segments of the labor force.

In the free economy as large as ours, a certain amount of frictional unemployment caused by changes in the structure of industry and manpower is unavoidable. In addition, a small fraction of the adult population is unemployable. Yet there is no evidence that hard-core unemployment has been growing as a percent of the labor force. Measures to improve the mobility of labor to jobs and of jobs to labor, to better our educational facilities, to match future supplies of different skills and occupations to the probable pattern of future demand, and to improve the health of our population— these are and should be high on the agenda of national policy. But they are no substitute for fiscal, monetary, and credit policies for national recovery. Adjustments that now seem difficult and unemployment pockets that now seem intractable will turn out to be manageable after all in an environment of full prosperity.[1]

"Supplement B," produced by the Council's instant manpower specialist and the late Edward Kalachek, consisted of five pages of text and ten tables[2] that cut the data every which way and concluded that only a minor fraction of the apparently chronic increase in unemployment since 1957, say, could be blamed on "manpower problems." The rest could be expected to dissolve in any general economic expansion. That is exactly what happened, almost five years later. In some ways it has been downhill ever since, both for the economy and for macroeconomics.

Just thinking about that episode brings back memories so intense that I cannot resist turning temporarily to my second theme, the them-and-us part of the story. Having become a manpower person in less than thirty days (and thirty nights, my wife reminds me) I discovered to my surprise that I had become an enemy of the real manpower people. Just the opposite of Groucho, I was trying to join a club that didn't want me for a member. Why? Some of the hostility was no doubt a matter of turf. Scholars who had devoted years to the study of the labor force and its pathologies must have regarded me—with some justice—as just another cocky economist who, having looked at a few numbers, not even knowing where they came from, was immediately ready to lay down dogma. Not content with talking about the demand for labor never having met a payroll, I was talking about the supply of labor never having met an AFDC mother. It was all true, of course. Still, that would have been an unworthy reason to attack our conclusions; and in fact I do not think that mere territoriality was an important factor.

The more important accusation was that we were *against* manpower policy; we were prepared to sell it down the river for a mere snippet of tax reduction for the middle classes. Not at all, we replied. It says right here that manpower policies "are and should be high on the agenda of national policy." We merely want to establish the simple and important truth that "structural unemployment" has not *worsened*, that we can have higher employment right now, and having it will make the true structural problems easier to solve. No soap. There is no point in telling a girl she is high on your agenda when she wants to be loved more than anyone else. (This sort of thing happens all the time. We discovered later that merely referring to the "wage-price spiral" could be regarded as an antilabor act. At the Council we were careful to alternate "wage-price spiral" with "price-wage spiral.")

There are two more observations I want to make on this subject, at least one of which will be with me to the end of this paper. The manpower specialists, partisans of the underclass, tended to regard themselves as the left in this story, and the narrow-minded, macro-oriented economists as the right. In context, however, it was the other way around. Objectively, as a good Marxist might say, the labor-market-policy orientation was conservative. It was the Republicans' last-ditch defense against macroeconomic policy activism—monetary and fiscal—that they appeared to fear more than spending some money on the underclass. Nowadays the political affinities are not so clear, perhaps because macroeconomic activism is not on the agenda, perhaps because the real right, having gained in strength, has shifted its tactics, perhaps because the objective situation has changed in the labor market itself.

The second point is more fundamental. It seemed to be implicit in conversations I had then that if one did not think that the cure for unemployment was primarily some change in the unemployed themselves or in the operation of the labor market, it must be that one thought the labor market to be perfect or efficient. There was not much excuse for that inference then; we pushers of macropolicy believed no such thing. The economic system is capable of having two sorts of market failure at the same time, maybe three. I was a little taken aback when I realized into which pigeonhole I had fallen. Today, of course, manpower specialists would be more nearly right on a statistical basis. A larger fraction of the macroeconomists they talk to take it as an everyday operational guide that the labor market clears efficiently, like any other market. That is a question I want to return to later on.

When the Kennedy-Heller Council of Economic Advisers came to write its first full Economic Report in early 1962, it stuck to its guns on the nature of the current unemployment, though it did not repeat the details. The first chapter included a section on labor market policies.[3] It endorsed improvement of the Employment Service and its separation from the administration of unemployment insurance. Then it proposed a package of three pilot programs in the training area: one for on-the-job training of unskilled but employed workers, one for public service employment combined with education and training, and one for a Youth Conservation Corps that would again emphasize preparation for the labor market. The report emphasized the importance of compensating workers engaged in training programs. Finally there was a suggestion for study of the pattern of future demands for labor, so that training programs could be realistic.

The second chapter of the 1962 Report focused on economic growth, meaning longer-term growth of capacity to produce. To that end, we cast as much as we could in investment terms: investment is what you do to promote growth. There was a section on investment in human resources; it emphasized that expenditures on education and health could be regarded as investments, current expenditures that expand future capacity. We pointed out carefully that policies to reduce racial discrimination, besides responding to an ethical imperative, could also be interpreted the same way. We believed everything we wrote, and indeed it was all true. Reading it now, however, all that talk about investment sounds as if we were packaging those policies for sale to reluctant consumers. If so, maybe they bought.

In any case, the Manpower Development and Training Act (MDTA) passed into law in 1962. It was not the first manpower program, of course, but it was the start of manpower policy as a systematic year-in, year-out intervention in the labor market. It had bipartisan support, for reasons I have just explained: Democrats favored it, and Republicans could hardly oppose it. MDTA reflected the intellectual environment in which it originated. It was primarily a training program, even a classroom training program. It was aimed almost entirely at retraining experienced workers, fathers of families, who had lost their jobs to technological progress. It was not a program for the least employable, at least not at the start. There was no public service employment option, for example. In short, MDTA was not an attempt to increase aggregate employment; that was a function of macroeconomic policy. It was an attempt to improve occupational mobility, and to correct one pathology of the labor market, the one that inflicted the capital loss of obsolescent skills on workers who had no way to defend themselves and no way to anticipate long-delayed changes in the demand for labor.[4]

In 1964 the manpower net was extended to cover some of the hardest-to-employ in the amendment of MDTA and the enactment of the Equal Opportunity Act. In particular the Job Corps (which is what survived of the notion of a Youth Conservation Corps) and the Neighborhood Youth Corps were aimed at hard cases among the young.

During the next few years there were no new initiatives of any moment, for the obvious reasons. The economy was prospering, overheating in fact, and unemployment continued to fall. That wonderful public service employment program for the disadvantaged that was the Vietnam War took care of the rest. The only noteworthy event was President Nixon's veto of a public-service employment initiative in 1970. That probably marked the dissolution of the *de facto* coalition for manpower policy that had formed almost a decade earlier. Even so, direct job creation got a foot in the door in 1971 through an Emergency Employment Act intended to provide jobs for returning veterans of the war.

The next evolutionary step was the Comprehensive Employment and Training Act (CETA), at the end of 1973. The history illustrates neatly the dual character of manpower policy that has led to so much confusion. The original Title I of CETA was a program of vocational education, training, and retraining for disadvantaged workers. On average the participants had very little education and job experience, and came mostly from families below the official poverty line. It was not until the onset of the pretty deep recession of 1974–1975 that Congress added Title VI providing for countercyclical job creation in high-unemployment areas. Participants here tended to be a cross-section of unemployed people. They were offered subsidized employment in the local public sector with no special emphasis on training. The total came to some 300,000 jobs. (There were important organizational and administrative changes between MDTA and CETA, but that is the business of real practitioners, not of amateurs like me.)

During the Carter administration CETA was expanded. The number of public-service employment slots was increased. The program focused more explicitly on the structurally unemployed, including some tax incentives (with the usual fatuous names) to draw the private sector into the act. An extensive Youth Act was passed that combined elements of income maintenance, incentives to remain in or return to school, and some direct job creation. I suspect that the Carter people were caught in a bind. The recovery from the 1975 recession was nothing to write home about; but the continuing inflation ruled out the standard macropolicy response. It was perhaps natural to think of direct job creation as a sanitized substitute. But of course I am leading up to the point that manpower policy is simply not a substitute for macropolicy. I imagine that both intellectual communities were beginning to realize that just as political practice was trying to fuzz up the distinction.

Up to that point a sensible division of labor appeared to be emerging. The job of fiscal and monetary policy—with or without some form of intervention in wage and price making, depending on your beliefs and goals—is to look after aggregate output and employment. When macropolicy fails, through inattention, incompetence, or incapacity (as with stagflation), temporary, countercyclical, direct job creation may make a contribution to economic stabilization. It is then really just a focused form of fiscal policy, descended more or less directly from the WPA. (I said "may make a contribution" because, when it takes the form of subsidized employment in the local public sector, the beneficiaries may simply displace regular employees.) The unique, specialized role for manpower policy is in education, training, retraining, and the creation of job-readiness, the transformation of hard cases into potential workers. Manpower policy is, if I may coin a phrase, a supply-side policy. It adds to the supply of effective labor by mobilizing the disadvantaged. Or so one hopes.

There has been a tendency on both sides to elide this important distinction. Manpower specialists tend to gloss it over because they like to think of themselves as creating jobs, not merely as creating potential competitors for a given number of jobs. Macroeconomists— I mean non-Panglossian macroeconomists who at least know trouble when they see it—tend to gloss it over because, in the modern stagflationary age, they need *something* to do. Naturally a profession that rewards itself for subtlety will find subtle arguments. Papers have been written[5]—I have written one myself—to consider seriously the possibility that manpower policy, precisely by increasing the effective supply of labor, may improve the Phillips curve and thus allow higher aggregate employment without faster inflation. Today this would be called "lowering the natural rate of unemployment." No doubt the possibility exists, just as it is true that spitting in the ocean raises the water level. Small interactions like that do not alter the basic truth. Manpower policy does not on any meaningful scale add to the number of lottery prizes. It just distributes more lottery tickets, and hopes to give some to people who would ordinarily have no shot at all at a prize.

This is a very important point, so I will push it a little further. There have been a number of calculations attempting to assess the effectiveness of manpower programs. One of the most recent and best is by David Card and Orley Ashenfelter (1985), and studies experiences under CETA. The details are interesting and useful but do not concern me here. What I want to put on record is the basic conclusion that "CETA participation increased the probability of employment in the three years after training by from 2 to 5 percentage points. Classroom training programs appear to have had significantly larger effects than on-the-job programs, although the estimated effects of both kinds of programs are consistently positive." These results are consistent with a broad survey of evaluations compiled by Michael Borus (1980), including his own, which suggests that CETA programs increased the post-program annual earnings of participants by something like $300 to $500 in current prices. It is the orders of magnitude that I am after; these are also consistent with the results obtained by the Manpower Demonstration Research Corporation (MDRC) in its studies of Supported Work[6] and again in its ongoing studies of the work/welfare demonstrations,[7] which I have not yet discussed. In every case the appropriate conclusion is that at least some classes of participants have experienced *definite* but *small* improvements in their employment prospects and in their wage prospects if they make out in the open market. (Some subgroups seem to gain nothing at all.)

The key point is that participation in training programs buys a small increase in the probability of labor-market success. Cost-benefit comparisons usually suggest that manpower programs are a net gain to society, though the margin is sufficiently narrow that one wonders if "society" is patient enough to be grateful for small favors. "Success in the labor market" is here defined as private success. It means that participants have, on average, done better than a randomly selected control group. It does *not* mean that the additional jobs achieved by participants represent net new jobs. Participants may simply be getting a larger fraction of a fixed number of jobs. For damned sure, the employment gains of participants, small in any case, are *in part* at the expense of nonparticipants, so the net gain is smaller still. This is known in the trade as the "displacement problem." We know almost nothing about its magnitude in quantitative terms, and it is very unlikely we will ever find out very much. I do not want to play games about the burden of proof: a reasonable person's conclusion would certainly be that manpower policies do not create net jobs on any significant scale, except to the extent that net expenditures are large enough to constitute fiscal policy in their own right.

There is no implication that manpower policies are not a good idea. As I have mentioned, even in the program phase itself participants may partially displace other workers, as when local governments substitute subsidized public service employees for regular employees. Monitoring of level-of-effort may limit this effect but can hardly eliminate it. So even the pure fiscal policy effects may be muted. This problem is not special to manpower policies; Cary Brown's classic study (1956) of fiscal policy in the 1930s concluded that much of the stimulus from New Deal deficit spending was simply offset by contractionary actions of state and local government. The tendency within the manpower community is more or less to ignore displacement effects in calculating benefit-cost numbers. I do not regard that as sinful: the effects cannot be measured, and there are no doubt unmeasurable favorable effects that go unmentioned too.

The most recent major step in the evolution of manpower policy has been the work/welfare movement set off by the response of various states to the flexibility offered in the Omnibus Budget Reconciliation Act of 1981. Obviously this change cannot be understood in narrowly economic terms. It was a political and social-psychological event. It is, nevertheless, an event in the manpower-policy arena, too. Here we have the advantage that carefully thought through and analytically sophisticated evaluations by MDRC have been built into many state programs from the very beginning. There are only two things I want to say about workfare, one of them directly relevant to my main argument and the other just in hope of stimulating a discussion that will help me make up my own mind. I take that point first.

What opinion should a decent, not especially ideological person have about workfare? It seems to me that it should depend on a balance between two things. Ours really is a culture in which people get a lot of their identity and self-respect from their jobs. (In the light of eternity this may be a good thing or a bad thing about the culture, but we might as well take it for granted.) Other things equal, therefore, it probably does more good than harm to push indigent people into employment, unless that is obviously inappropriate to individual circumstances. Work *is* better than welfare. The economist's reaction is to say that it would be enough to offer the opportunity of employment and allow choice. I do not know how much truth there is to "culture of poverty" notions. Unless the correct answer is "nothing," at least a nudge in the direction of employment would seem to be reasonable. I think one can say this without attaching any credibility at all to the Reaganesque notion that the AFDC rolls are made up of welfare queens and vodka guzzlers.

The main source of doubt about this conclusion is, as usual, the *ceteris paribus* clause. Especially given the source of the workfare impulse, one should legitimately worry that programs might be administered in a punitive or demeaning way. The "employment" might turn out to be obviously "mickey mouse," with the result that participants might suffer the worst of both worlds: silly or uncomfortable work plus the welfare stigma. There is a strain in the American ideology that wants to believe that unemployment and poverty are always the fault of the unemployed and poor; this might operate here. The MDRC studies seem to show that participants in state work/welfare programs are glad to participate, feel that they are earning their way, and regard themselves as competent workers (see Heroz and Hanson 1986). This is all to the good. I suppose there is some possibility that they tell the interviewer what they think the interviewer wants to hear. The main qualification to this testimony, however, is that we are still dealing with demonstration programs run by skilled professionals. This is creaming of a different kind, and may not tell us what a full-scale, national, saturation program would be like. Presumably the proper attitude is a watchful, open mind.

This is all digression. What I really need to say about workfare programs is that evaluation results confirm the quantitative conclusion already stated as the general outcome of CETA evaluations. Post-program experience suggests that workfare participation—whether job search or work experience—has small but statistically significant favorable effects on the probability of subsequent employment as against control or comparison groups. Early MDRC estimates suggest 3 to 7 percentage point gains (see Gueron 1987). Even if that increment represented only net new jobs, we would be talking small numbers, not a serious dent in unemployment. In fact they cannot all be net new jobs, so the true effect is even smaller. Workfare, like other manpower policies, should be judged in terms of its effects on the lives of participants, not as a form of macroeconomic stabilization policy.

From this point of view most manpower programs, especially training and work-experience schemes, should be regarded as government interventions in the labor market with several combined purposes. The main purposes are redistribution of economic opportunity, pure income transfer, and improvement of "occupational" mobility within the labor force. (Many of these programs also perform a socialization function, teaching skills that are interpersonal or that mediate between the individual and institutions. This may be very important, but it is outside my scope.) Even within the framework of orthodox economics these are legitimate objects of economic policy. This is to say, even if the labor market functioned like a classical market there would be no good reason to suppose that it could not benefit from some tinkering along the lines just mentioned. There would be no valid cause here for hostilities between economists and manpower specialists.

The more important and more interesting issue is the degree to which the labor market really does function like a classical market. I suspect that is the main source of the mutual incomprehension I mentioned at the beginning. Our instinct—I reveal my true colors—is to abstract as much as possible from the concrete institutional detail of each market and treat them all as machines that equate supply and demand by varying price. A manpower specialist's instinct is to revel in the institutional detail, and to regard the labor market as all warts. I regret to say that I want to propose a compromise between those two positions, wishy-washy as that may be.

Abstraction is a necessary part of understanding. I like to quote the English philosopher John Austin, who said that one would be inclined to call oversimplification the occupational disease of philosophers, were it not their occupation. But of course that goes for theorists of all kinds. Suppose that specialists in the fishing industry insisted on all the institutional detail of the fisheries, and students of housing insisted that you couldn't talk about housing unless you paid full attention to the ins and outs of the trade, and similarly for bank stocks, breakfast cereals, and programmable robots. We would know a lot about labor, fish, houses, bank stocks, corn flakes, and robots, but we would know precious little about the economy. We would be in the situation that a noncom of my acquaintance once ascribed to a second lieutenant: He knows a lot, but he don't realize nothing. That is the economist's case.

The manpower specialist's case is that some abstractions are dead wrong, and it matters. There are probably nonclassical elements in the market for fish, too; the difference is that the deviations are bigger in the labor market, and, since the labor market pervades the economy as the fish market does not, it is more serious an error to ignore them. The labor market does not behave more or less like a machine for equating supply and demand by varying price. If you treat the labor market as if it did, you will misunderstand a lot about economic fluctuations and economic policy.

The good news is that more and more macroeconomists, even theoretically oriented macroeconomists, are coming to view the labor market more realistically, to pay more attention to its idiosyncrasies. They are looking for the right way to capture, at *their* level of abstraction, the sources of unemployment and its differential incidence from group to group. Students of the nitty-gritty of the labor market, manpower specialists, and industrial relations experts all could do the profession and the world a favor by helping out. To do that, they have to be willing to understand the theorist's questions, to play the theorist's game, to try to understand what it is that gives the labor market its fundamental character and determines the shape of its large-scale behavior. If they don't, we ignorant theorists will go on in our infuriating way. On the other hand, if manpower specialists provide the right kind of assistance they are entitled to demand what Henry Stubbe demanded in his *The Lord Bacon's Relation of the Sweating Sickness Examined* in 1671: "In an historian we are not to be critical for every punctilio not relating to his main design; yet I think 'tis but just to demand that what he doth write be true."

Notes

1. This has been republished in Tobin and Weidenbaum (1988, 30).

2. Tobin and Weidenbaum (1988, 60–72).

3. See U.S. Council of Economic Advisors (1961, 93–95).

4. For historical and other comment on manpower policy in the United States, see Ginzberg (1980).

5. See Baily and Tobin (1977).

6. See Manpower Demonstration Research Corporation (1980).

7. See Heroz and Hanson (1986, 28–35).

References

Baily, Martin, and Tobin, James. 1977. "Macroeconomic Effects of Selective Public Employment and Wage Subsidies," *Brookings Papers on Economic Activity* (2), 511–541.

Brown, E.C. 1956. "Fiscal Policy in the Thirties: A Reappraisal," *American Economic Review* 46, 859–879.

Borus, Michael. 1980. "Assessing the Impact of Training Programs," in Eli Ginzberg, ed., *Employing the Unemployed.* New York: Basic Books, 25–40.

Card, David, and Ashenfelter, Orley. 1985. "Using Longitudinal Structure of Earnings to Estimate the Effect of Training Programs," *Review of Economics and Statistics* 67 (November), 648–660.

Ginzberg, Eli. 1980. "Overview: The $64 Billion Innovation," in Eli Ginzberg, ed., *Employing the Unemployed.* New York: Basic Books, 3–24.

Gueron, Judith M. 1987. "Reforming Welfare with Work." New York: Ford Foundation Report.

Heroz, Gregory, and Hanson, Karla, eds. 1986. "A Survey of Participants and Worksite Supervisors in the New York City Work Experience Program." New York: Manpower Demonstration Research Corporation Report (September), 28–35.

Tobin, James, and Weidenbaum, Murray, eds. 1988. *Two Revolutions in Economic Policy*, Cambridge, Massachusetts: MIT Press.

Manpower Demonstration Research Corporation, 1980. *Summary and Findings of the National Supported Work Demonstration*. Cambridge, Massachusetts: Ballinger.

U.S. Council of Economic Advisors. 1961. *The Economic Report of the President, 1961*. Washington, D.C.: Government Printing Office.

Comment by Albert Rees

It is always a great pleasure to read or listen to a paper by Bob Solow, and it is a privilege to be asked to discuss one. Unfortunately, I am probably the wrong discussant. I have somewhat greater claim than Bob does to be called a manpower specialist, having taught labor economics for thirty years until I became a philanthropoid. Nevertheless, I was on his side in the controversies of the early 1960s, and find that I still am.

The basic question raised by the paper is whether a case can be made for manpower policies even if their net job-creating effects are small or even zero. Bob answers affirmatively, and so would I. Let me elaborate a bit on my reasons for this view.

National economic policy has two important sets of objectives. The first is to raise output and employment subject to the constraint of not causing an unacceptable rate of inflation. That is the job of macroeconomic policy. Programs that reduce frictions in the economy may ease this task, but they play a secondary role. The job of maintaining high employment without inflation has gotten much more difficult recently, and we are much less sure than we used to be that we know how to do it; but nevertheless it remains the job of macroeconomic policy. The second set of objectives of economic policy is to increase equality, both the equality of opportunities and the equality of outcomes. If manpower policies or welfare reform programs can obtain for unemployed black or Hispanic youth, or for mothers with children growing up in poverty, jobs which otherwise would have gone to middle-class youth whose parents must support them a few months more, I regard this as a desirable outcome. Of course, it is robbing Peter to pay Paul, but the whole tax and transfer system explicitly robs Peter to pay Paul in the first place, even after the recent cuts in marginal tax rates. One would want to spend much more on manpower policies if they were also an efficient way of creating new jobs, but I think that present expenditures can be justified on distributional grounds.

Economic theory teaches us that cash transfers are the efficient way to redistribute income, and we have no lack of examples of grossly inefficient noncash transfer schemes, such as agricultural price supports. But this theory neglects the question of how long transfers will be necessary. A less efficient transfer scheme may be better than cash if it reduces the length of the period for which transfers are needed.

One can even argue that manpower programs have benefits for the rest of society as well as for the program participants. None of us wants to feel that the existence of a jobless underclass in the United States is an intractable problem, doomed to persist or even to grow worse no matter what we do. In an optimistic society like ours, it is much better to try with only modest success than never to have tried at all.

It may also be interesting to speculate on why the success of manpower programs has been so limited. My guess is that they start too late in the life of the program participant. One can play catch-up successfully in some cases, but it would be better yet to teach basic skills and healthy attitudes toward work very early in life. This is a task for families and schools, in which the role of the federal government is and should remain limited.

Discussion

Michael Piore (MIT) took issue with the paper's characterization of the difference between mainstream macroeconomists and manpower economists, arguing that it is unfair to suggest that manpower economists are uncomfortable with theoretical abstractions. Rather, Piore continued, the important difference between the two groups is that they have very different ideas about what ought to be central and what ought to be peripheral in a theory of the economy. Whereas standard theory abstracts to focus on the price system, manpower economists' theories abstract to focus on class conflict, power relations, and so on. In Piore's view, a fundamental failure of standard theory is that it has so little to say about problems of distribution and race. Sar Levitan (George Washington University) commented that the 1962 Economic Report of the President might not have looked so prescient in its statements concerning unemployment had it not been for the Vietnam War. More importantly, he continued, the report completely missed the country's emerging race problems.

Much of the discussion focused on the question of why the success of manpower programs has been so limited. Lester Thurow (MIT) commented that manpower programs have had marginal effects because they have been designed as marginal programs. Expensive programs such as the Job Corps have been shown to work well, Thurow continued, but we have been unwilling to support this sort of investment on any wide scale. Ann Witte (Wellesley) noted that Head Start programs also have had demonstrated successes, but that these programs, too, are relatively expensive. Paul Osterman (MIT) expressed the view that manpower policy oriented toward helping disadvantaged workers will always be marginal in its impact. A more promising strategy, he continued, would be to design mechanisms for encouraging training more widely within the economy and then to use these mechanisms, rather than a set of separate programs, to help poor people.

Maryellen Kelley (University of Massachusetts) commented that a key belief underlying manpower programs is that moving disadvantaged workers into "core" jobs will provide them with income and employment security. In fact, primary-sector jobs may do this less well today than they did in the past.

Name Index

Subject Index